Red Rocks Select

RED ROCKS
S E L E C T

Compiled by
Todd Swain

Chockstone Press
Evergreen, Colorado

RED ROCKS SELECT

Printed in the United States of America.

Front cover photo of Mount Wilson by Chuck Ward, Bureau of Land Management.
Front cover photo of Dan McQuade on Choad Warrior, 5.12–, by Randy Marsh.
Back cover photo of Mike Ward and Nick Nordblom on **Sergeant Slaughter,** Rainbow Wall by Kurt Mauer.
All uncredited photos by Todd Swain.

ISBN: 0-934641-45-5

PUBLISHED AND DISTRIBUTED BY:
CHOCKSTONE PRESS, INC.
Post Office Box 3505
Evergreen, Colorado 80439

WARNING: CLIMBING IS A SPORT WHERE YOU MAY BE SERIOUSLY INJURED OR DIE.

READ THIS BEFORE YOU USE THIS BOOK.

This guidebook is a compilation of unverified information gathered from many different climbers. The author cannot assure the accuracy of any of the information in this book, including the topos and route descriptions, the difficulty ratings, and the protection ratings. These may be incorrect or misleading and it is impossible for any one author to climb all the routes to confirm the information about each route. Also, ratings of climbing difficulty and danger are always subjective and depend on the physical characteristics (for example, height), experience, technical ability, confidence and physical fitness of the climber who supplied the rating. Additionally, climbers who achieve first ascents sometimes underrate the difficulty or danger of the climbing route out of fear of being ridiculed if a climb is later down-rated by subsequent ascents. Therefore, be warned that you must exercise your own judgment on where a climbing route goes, its difficulty and your ability to safely protect yourself from the risks of rock climbing. Examples of some of these risks are: falling due to technical difficulty or due to natural hazards such as holds breaking, falling rock, climbing equipment dropped by other climbers, hazards of weather and lightning, your own equipment failure, and failure of fixed protection.

You should not depend on any information gleaned from this book for your personal safety; your safety depends on your own good judgment, based on experience and a realistic assessment of your climbing ability. If you have any doubt as to your ability to safely climb a route described in this book, do not attempt it.

The following are some ways to make your use of this book safer:

1. **CONSULTATION:** You should consult with other climbers about the difficulty and danger of a particular climb prior to attempting it. Most local climbers are glad to give advice on routes in their area and we suggest that you contact locals to confirm ratings and safety of particular routes and to obtain first-hand information about a route chosen from this book.
2. **INSTRUCTION:** Most climbing areas have local climbing instructors and guides available. We recommend that you engage an instructor or guide to learn safety techniques and to become familiar with the routes and hazards of the areas described in this book. Even after you are proficient in climbing safely, occasional use of a guide is a safe way to raise your climbing standard and learn advanced techniques.
3. **FIXED PROTECTION:** Many of the routes in this book use bolts and pitons which are permanently placed in the rock. Because of variances in the manner of placement, weathering, metal fatique, the quality of the metal used, and many other factors, these fixed protection pieces should always be considered suspect and should always be backed up by equipment that you place yourself. Never depend for your safety on a single piece of fixed protection because you never can tell whether it will hold weight.

Be aware of the following specific potential hazards which could arise in using this book:

1. **MISDESCRIPTIONS OF ROUTES:** If you climb a route and you have a doubt as to where the route may go, you should not go on unless you are sure that you can go that way safely. Route descriptions and topos in this book may be inaccurate or misleading.
2. **INCORRECT DIFFICULTY RATING:** A route may, in fact be more difficult than the rating indicates. Do not be lulled into a false sense of security by the difficulty rating.
3. **INCORRECT PROTECTION RATING:** If you climb a route and you are unable to arrange adequate protection from the risk of falling through the use of fixed pitons or bolts and by placing your own protection devices, do not assume that there is adequate protection available higher just because the route protection rating indicates the route is not an "X" or an "R" rating. Every route is potentially an "X" (a fall may be deadly), due to the inherent hazards of climbing, including, for example, failure of fixed protection, your own equipment's failure, or improper use of climbing equipment.

THERE ARE NO WARRANTIES, WHETHER EXPRESS OR IMPLIED, THAT THIS GUIDEBOOK IS ACCURATE OR THAT THE INFORMATION CONTAINED IN IT IS RELIABLE. THERE ARE NO WARRANTIES OF FITNESS FOR A PARTICULAR PURPOSE OR THAT THIS GUIDE IS MERCHANTABLE. YOUR USE OF THIS BOOK INDICATES YOUR ASSUMPTION OF THE RISK THAT IT MAY CONTAIN ERRORS AND IS AN ACKNOWLEDGEMENT OF YOUR OWN SOLE RESPONSIBILITY FOR YOUR CLIMBING SAFETY.

To my climbing partners,
past, present and future -
Thanks for putting up with me!

AUTHOR'S NOTE:

Not being a Red Rocks local (I live in Joshua Tree), I've felt a bit funny about this project from the start. When I agreed to write this guide, I'd only done about 75 climbs in the area, and hadn't even visited major canyons such as Oak Creek. My bold plan was to climb all the routes in the guide rated 5.11+ and below, to ensure consistent ratings and obtain accurate information. About six months into the project, reality finally reared its ugly head. I was way behind schedule, and the list of routes to be included continued to grow! By press time, I'd done more than 200 of the climbs listed in this book, but still needed a vast amount of information. This was given to me by local climbers, land managers and friends. They have been essential to producing what you see here.

First, I need to thank my regular climbing partners. They repeatedly endured my hellish disposition, and, in the case of our ascent of the Rainbow Wall, 105-degree Fahrenheit heat. Debbie Brenchley, Mike Dimitri, Mark Hoffman and Jeff Rickerl should be in the Climbing Hall of Fame.

Also of incredible importance was the team at Chockstone Press. After publishing *The Gunks Guide,* I can't believe they put up with me again!

Mike and Tim Ward at Desert Rock Sports in Las Vegas were invaluable sources. Not only did they have a wealth of information, they allowed me to use their shop as a meeting ground for sessions with other knowledgeable locals.

Harris Fogel of Palm Springs, California and Dave Saball of Henniker, New Hampshire helped me greatly with the cliff photos.

Thanks to Amy Filerman and Bobby Knight for helping me proof the draft of this guide. You'll definitely find some mistakes in the book, but hopefully not as many as we did!

The extremely helpful and knowledgeable locals who helped me compile information included: Nick Nordblom, Brad Stewart, Paul Van Betten, Greg and "Chucky" Mayer, Wendell Broussard, Richard Harrison, Sal Mamusia, Mike Tupper, Randy Faulk, Randy Marsh, Randy Grandstaff, Robert Finlay, Danny Meyers, Alan Busby, Bob Conz . . .

I also got a wealth of information from the Bureau of Land Management, particularly from Chris Miller and Chuck Ward.

To all who helped out, thanks VERY much!

ABOUT THIS BOOK

If you want a complete climbing guide to Red Rocks, you're out of luck. Joanne and Jorge Urioste wrote the first (and only) comprehensive climbing guide to the area in 1984, and it contained 221 routes. This book contains nearly 500 climbs, but is not meant to be comprehensive, or even a true "best of" guide. The climbs described here are meant to be representative of the Red Rocks climbing experience. My original plan was to include about 200 climbs, but much to my publisher's dismay, the book grew and grew, taking more than a year to complete (we originally thought I could pound it out in a couple months!). Deciding which climbs belong in a book like this was a bit like fishing with dynamite – you don't get 'em all, but a lot of stuff surfaces that's a bit too good to throw back. I think I've included most of the best routes (marked by a 👍), but for the sake of clarity, I had to include neighboring routes of lesser quality (these are marked by a 👎), and routes of average quality (unmarked). If I left out your favorite route or area, I'm sorry. Let me know about new and/or overlooked routes, and perhaps they'll make it into the second edition of this guide.

TABLE OF CONTENTS

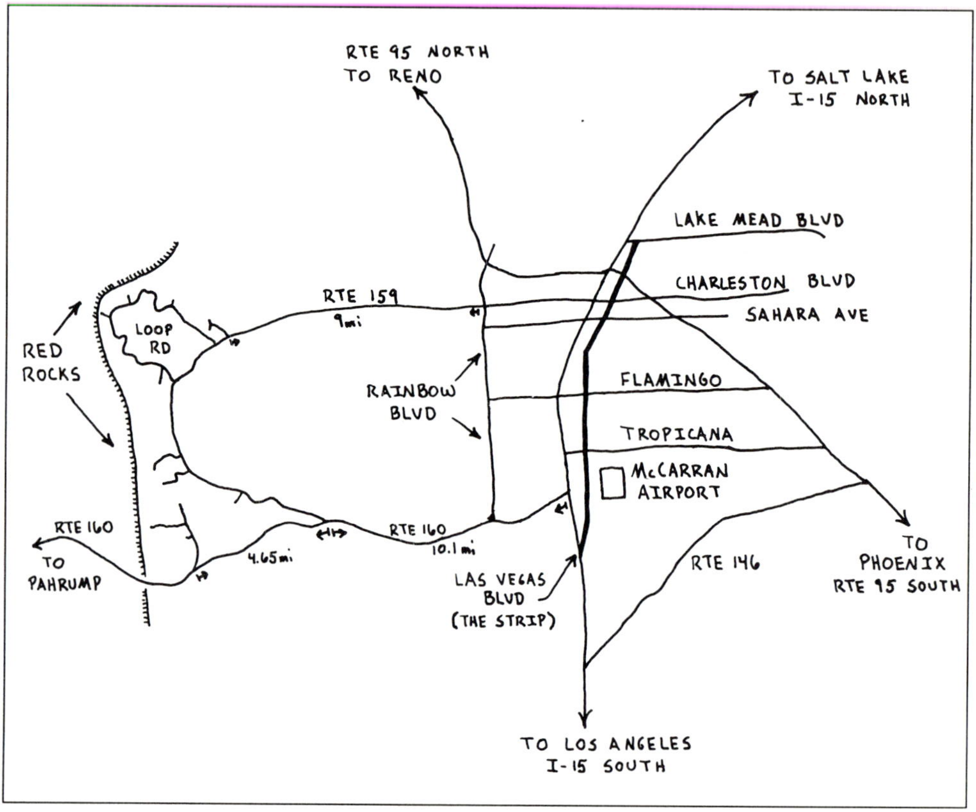

Map of Greater Las Vegas area

INTRODUCTION

Most climbers have heard of "Red Rocks," and know that it lies just outside of Las Vegas, Nevada. While this guidebook contains nearly 500 selected climbs, Red Rocks currently offers more than 1,000 different routes of all grades and lengths. From the popular sport climbs of the Calico Hills to the multi-day routes in Juniper Canyon, the area hosts numerous climbs of world-class stature. Officially, the area is known as the Red Rock Canyon National Conservation Area (RRCNCA), and is administered by the Bureau of Land Management (BLM), a federal agency within the United States Department of the Interior.

Getting There

Once you arrive in Las Vegas, you'll find that it's pretty simple to get around. McCarran Airport is right off the Strip; Interstate 15 and State Highway 95 divide the city roughly into quarters. The Red Rock escarpment is about 15 miles west of Las Vegas, and is typically approached via West Charleston Boulevard (State Route 159). With the exception of Black Velvet Canyon, all climbing at Red Rocks is accessed by Route 159 and a one-way scenic loop road. This loop road is within the National Conservation area, is gated, and is closed at night. Typically, the road is open from early morning until just after dark. Check with the BLM Visitor Center or local climbing shops for current opening and closing times. Black Velvet Canyon is accessed via State Route 160. Maps scattered throughout the book should help you navigate around Las Vegas and Red Rocks.

The introductions to each chapter of this guide describe how to get to the trailhead for that certain area. The individual route descriptions then tell you how to get from your car to the base of the climb. Hiking approach times at Red Rocks range from a few minutes to four hours, and are noted in the chapter and route introductions.

The Land

Like all climbing areas, Red Rock Canyon National Conservation Area should be treated with the utmost respect. The area was first recognized as the Red Rock Canyon Recreation Lands in 1967. The scenic loop road was completed in 1978. The current designation as a National Conservation Area (NCA) was given in 1990, and is defined as: "An area of the public lands managed by the Bureau of Land Management (BLM) which has been established by Congress for the purpose of protecting and conserving identified resource values of national interest. A Conservation Area is managed for multiple use and sustained yield in conformance with the Resource Management Plan, and in accordance with a general management plan which reflects the dominant and compatible uses for specific tracts."

Red Rock Canyon NCA currently encompasses 83,100 acres, and hosts nearly 800,000 visitors each year. There is a very nice visitor center located just off the scenic loop road, that has interpretive displays, books, postcards and a helpful staff. The visitor center is typically open from 9 a.m. to 4 p.m.

As visitation by climbers increases, land managers at Red Rocks and other desert parks are becoming more concerned about a number of climber impacts. Please abide by posted regulations and closure times, and be courteous to other user groups. The following climbing-related regulations currently are in effect at Red Rock Canyon National Conservation Area:

• It is prohibited to chip, chisel, glue or scar the rock.

• Climbing is not allowed within 20 feet of any Native American rock art site (petroglyphs and/or pictographs).

• Digging, or in any way disturbing archaeological sites is prohibited.

Note: These first three regulations are extremely important. Violations will most likely lead to the closure of climbing areas.

• Camping is allowed only in designated roadside areas, or in backpacking areas above 5,000 feet in elevation. When backpacking, you must camp more than 200 feet from archaeological sites and water sources.

Note: As of press time, roadside camping was allowed at Oak Creek Campground. Plans call for a new campground to be built on the spur road just inside the exit to the loop road.

• Vehicles must be outside the gated sections of the loop road BEFORE closing time. (If there's one thing that annoys the rangers at Red Rocks, it's waiting for tardy visitors to get back to the car and get off the loop road.)

• Permits are required for backpacking and bivouacs. Contact the NCA Visitor Center for more details.

• Fires are only allowed within furnished fire grates.

• Gathering of native vegetation is prohibited. Bring your own firewood.

In addition, a number of very important low-impact policies should be followed:

• Do not climb on wet sandstone! The rock becomes very brittle and typically needs at least 24 hours to dry after a rain or thunderstorm.

• Pack out all trash, whether it's yours or not.

• **Pack out all toilet paper and human waste,** or bury the human waste six inches deep, and carry out the toilet paper.

• Stay on maintained trails as much as possible, and try to minimize impacts to plants and soil through erosion and trampling.

• New routes should be established away from the view of the general public.

• All bolts and anchors should be painted to match the color of the rock. If webbing is used, it should also match the color of the rock.

• Remove all retreat or "bail" slings you encounter, to help keep the visual impacts of climbing to a minimum.

• Do not use chalk on areas visible to the general public. This especially applies to the boulders at Willow Spring Picnic Area and Sandstone Quarry.

The BLM has a number of handouts useful for planning your visit to Red Rocks. These include a park brochure and the following titles: *Climbing and Camping, Hiking, Mammals, Birds, Geology, Plants,* and *Archeology of Southern Nevada.* For more information, brochures, or a list of other publications available, contact the Bureau of Land Management, Las Vegas District Office; P.O. Box 26569, Las Vegas, NV 89126. The telephone number is (702) 647-5000. The NCA Visitor Center telephone number is (702) 363-1921.

Photo: Randy Marsh

Dan McQuade climbs Stratocaster Direct, 5.12a, Sandstone Quarry area.

The Rules of the Game

Not being a local, perhaps I can offer an objective view of the long-standing ethical conflicts at Red Rocks. Apparently, there have been many confrontations between the so-called "Trads" and "Rads," some of which have gone beyond reasonable "debates." These incidents have included vandalism to opposing climbers' cars, pouring dung off the tops of cliffs onto climbers below, and chopping routes. Personally, I find all of this juvenile, and extremely dangerous in light of the bigger issue of climbing access. The Vulgarians got away with this sort of behavior at the Gunks in the sixties, but this isn't the sixties, it's the nineties. No modern-day land manager is going to respect or trust a bunch of knuckleheads who continually fight amongst themselves, and go so far as to destroy property belonging to others. How a route is established (whether from the ground up, or on rappel) will never be as important as having the opportunity to climb. These factions of disagreeing climbers need to realize that land managers have the ability and authority to prohibit climbing, and will do so if they perceive the resource is being destroyed or abused. Wake up and smell the coffee, people! Climb to have fun, not to aggravate others or upset land managers.

These are the ethics currently accepted by the majority of climbers at Red Rocks:

• Routes may be established from the ground up, or on rappel. In terms of boldness and historical perspective, ground up is more desirable. Hooks are typically used on ground up ascents.

• Bolts should be at least three-eighths-inch diameter, but preferably half-inch by four inches, using grade 5 material.

• All bolts and anchors should be painted to match the color of the rock.

• New routes should not be established within view of the general public.

• Climbs that are still in progress will have a red ribbon tied to the first bolt. Please do not attempt these routes until they have been completed or abandoned by the party that installed the bolts.

• A new route is complete when the leader starts at the bottom of the cliff and climbs to the top without falling, grabbing slings, hanging on the rope, or using a toprope. At Red Rocks, Flash, Red Point, Pink Point, or Yo-Yo are all acceptable methods of completing a new route.

Ratings

The Yosemite Decimal System (YDS) is used throughout this book to rate climbs. Currently, technical rock climbs at Red Rocks range from 5.0 to 5.13. The higher the number, the more difficult the climb. To differentiate between true sport climbs (quickdraws only) and routes where gear is needed, I have used two different types of sub-grading methods. True sport climbs have ratings subdivided by letter grades (a-d), as was introduced by Jim Bridwell of Yosemite fame. Routes that require some amount of traditional gear have the subdivisions of – and +. These "gear subdivisions" apply only to climbs 5.10 or harder, with a rating of 5.10– being equal in difficulty to 5.10a. Routes easier than 5.10 may have a + or –, and this applies only to difficulty.

As with any rating system, the ratings are not meant to be definitive, but are intended to give you a rough idea of the difficulty that may be encountered. Height, reach, finger size, and flexibility vary for each climber, thus making the rating system somewhat inaccurate. Just because a route is rated 5.9 doesn't mean it's 5.9 for you. Remember, I haven't done all of the routes in this guide, thus the information may be suspect.

I also have used the protection rating system first introduced by Jim Erickson in his climbing guide to Boulder, Colorado. This system is based on the movie rating system (G, PG, R, X), with X-rated routes being VERY dangerous. I have dropped the G ("safe") rating and used only the other three grades. These ratings assume the leader is competent at the grade and has both the proper equipment for the route and an attentive belayer. Roughly, the ratings mean the following:

PG Protection is generally considered adequate, although the leader may fall up to 15 feet. The leader probably will not get injured in the fall. These routes might seem a little bit sporty.

R Protection is usually considered inadequate, and the leader will probably get injured if he/she falls. These routes are potentially dangerous and runout.

X Protection is nonexistent. A falling leader will probably suffer severe injuries, and/or death. These are death routes or solos.

Again, there may be very dangerous climbs listed in this book that don't have an R or X rating. Use caution and good judgement when leading!

Terms

The President's term is four years, not to exceed two consecutive terms, or three... OOPS!!! Wrong book.

The following climbing terms are used throughout this guide: FA- First Ascent; FFA- First Free Ascent; FRA- First Recorded Ascent; FRFA- First Recorded Free Ascent. Generally, the person whose name appears first led the crux of the route.

Directions (left, right) assume the reader is facing the cliff. Variations to the normal route are shown as V1, V2, etc., and are listed at the end of the route description. Pitches are listed as P1, P2, etc.

Symbols used on topo maps of routes are shown at right.

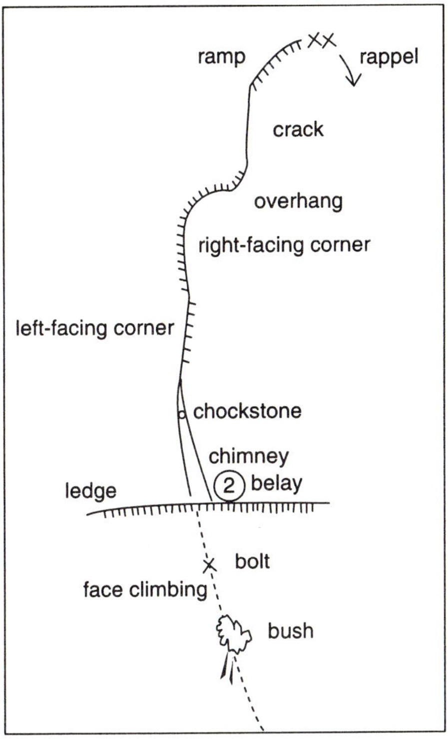

Gear

The joy of sport routes is that you need only a rope, quickdraws and strong fingers to climb. For the traditional routes, you want to carry a good selection of wires, TCUs, Friends and slings. Any "specialty" gear needed is noted in the description of the climb. For the longer canyon routes, you'll usually need two ropes to descend. Again, this will be noted in the climb description.

Weather

You can climb at Red Rocks all year, but the majority of people visit the area in the spring and fall. For the latest weather forecast, call (702) 736-3854 or (702) 734-2010. The "typical" weather for each season is detailed below:

Spring: While the weather can be good in early season, it's likely there will be windy and wet conditions in March. By May, the temperatures could reach 100° F. Shade, combined with down-canyon winds, can make places like Black Velvet feel much colder than the sunny cliffs of the Calico Hills.

Summer: It is common for temperatures to reach 106° F or higher. Thunderstorms are the norm in late July and all of August, and these rains frequently cause flash floods. Climb in the early morning and evening hours, and avoid the sun. Drink LOTS of water!

Fall: This is probably the best time to visit the area, although the days get shorter. As November rolls around, expect it to get cold in the shady canyons. Places like the Gallery often are warm enough for climbing in shorts and t-shirts.

Winter: Sunny cliffs such as The Gallery and The Trophy are extremely popular. Snow is common at the higher elevations, and forces closure of the loop road on occasion. Shady canyon climbs usually are out of the question. Shaded descents (such as on **Solar Slab**) may remain icy for long periods of time.

Emergencies

The BLM and Las Vegas Metropolitan Police Department (Metro) provide emergency services at Red Rocks. Between 9 a.m. and 4 p.m., report any accident to the NCA Visitor Center, if possible. After hours, call 911 from pay phones at the town of Blue Diamond, Old Nevada (Bonnie Springs Ranch), outside the NCA Visitor Center, or Las Vegas.

EMERGENCY TELEPHONE NUMBERS:
Red Rock Canyon NCA Visitor Center: (702) 363-1921

Las Vegas Metropolitan Police: 911

BLM Las Vegas Dispatch: (702) 647-5090

If you need medical attention, these are the closest facilities to the crags:

University Medical Center (UMC)
1800 West Charleston
Las Vegas, NV
(702) 383-2000

UMC Quick Care - Lakes
2760 Lake Sahara Drive
Las Vegas, NV
(702) 254-4900

Where To Stay

Las Vegas has more than 77,000 rooms available for its visitors, ranging in cost from astonishingly cheap to astronomically expensive. Many of the huge casinos on the Strip offer great deals and are only minutes away from the crags. As a general rule, prices are quite a bit higher on weekends and in the summer. At least one hotel offers discounts to climbers – check with the climbing shops for details.

For those who want to camp, the choices are a bit more limited. Historically, the BLM has allowed climbers and other users to camp at Oak Creek and at the mouth of Black Velvet Canyon. As of November 1992, Oak Creek Campground was still open, but will most likely be closed in the near future. A new camping area is planned near the end of the scenic loop, on a spur road. Due to the huge increase in use, I foresee camping will be more limited and restricted than it has in the past. Check with the BLM or local climbing shops for the latest information. There also are commercial campgrounds in Las Vegas, some of which provide showers to those staying elsewhere.

Supplies and Other Important Stuff

At the intersection of West Charleston (Route 159) and Rainbow, you'll find grocery stores and numerous restaurants. A favorite eatery in the area is the Soup Exchange, an all-you-can-eat salad-bar-type place.

Numerous movie theaters also are found in the local area. The Red Rock Cinema (870-1423) is about one mile east of Rainbow at 5201 West Charleston. The Torrey Pines Theater (876-4334; 6344 West Sahara at Torrey Pines) offers cheaper, second-run movies.

Showers are available at some commercial campgrounds and fitness centers. Check with the local climbing shops for the latest information. DO NOT use the NCA Visitor Center bathrooms to bathe in.

The preferred telephone number for local weather reports is: (702) 736-3854. You also can call (702) 734-2010.

A new public library is being built on West Charleston, between Jones and Torrey Pines. There is also a branch library in Blue Diamond.

Water is available at the NCA Visitor Center, and at various places in town.

Las Vegas

If you haven't been to Vegas yet, you're missing out! Before your trip, rent the following films at your local video store to get a feel for the area:

Viva Las Vegas, starring Elvis; *Bugsy,* starring Warren Beatty; and *Honeymoon in Vegas,* starring Nicholas Cage.

Here's a list of my favorite attractions to show first-time visitors to Las Vegas:

Caesar's Palace: The most opulent of the casinos, you'll find a higher-class clientele here than you will in Circus, Circus. Take in a movie at the large-screen Omnimax Theater, and don't miss The Forum, an amazing shopping area features talking statues, and a "sky" that changes as the day progresses.

Circus, Circus: A bit tacky, but a brilliant idea for sucking families into a casino. Check out the free circus acts (running from about noon til midnight), the midway and "The World's Largest Buffet."

Excaliber: This was the biggest (and gaudiest) hotel in the world when it was built. It sports a medieval motif, and was built by Circus, Circus. Don't miss the Magic Motion Machine on the lowest level of the casino. For those with money, the dinner theater features jousting and other knightly derring-do.

"Glitter Gulch:" This is the downtown part of Vegas. The buildings aren't as tall as those on the Strip, but their closeness makes the neon that much more impressive.

The Mirage: Quite spiffy, with a bunch of different things to experience. Don't miss the exploding "volcano" in front of the casino. It erupts on a regular basis all evening. Inside, you'll find rare white tigers (usually sleeping), a tropical jungle, a huge tropical aquarium (behind the check-in desk), and dolphin shows (behind the casino).

Coming Attractions: Circus, Circus is building a huge water park called Grand Slam Canyon behind the Circus, Circus casino. It's supposed to include a rollercoaster, a Magic Motion-type ride, and lots of exciting water park stuff.

In addition to Grand Slam Canyon, Circus, Circus is building a new casino near the Excaliber. It will be shaped like a pyramid, have an Egyptian theme, and be called **Luxor.** MGM also is building a new casino near the Excaliber. It will include a family theme park touted to be comparable to Disneyland. Another new casino is being built by the Mirage. This one will have a pirate theme and be called **Treasure Island.**

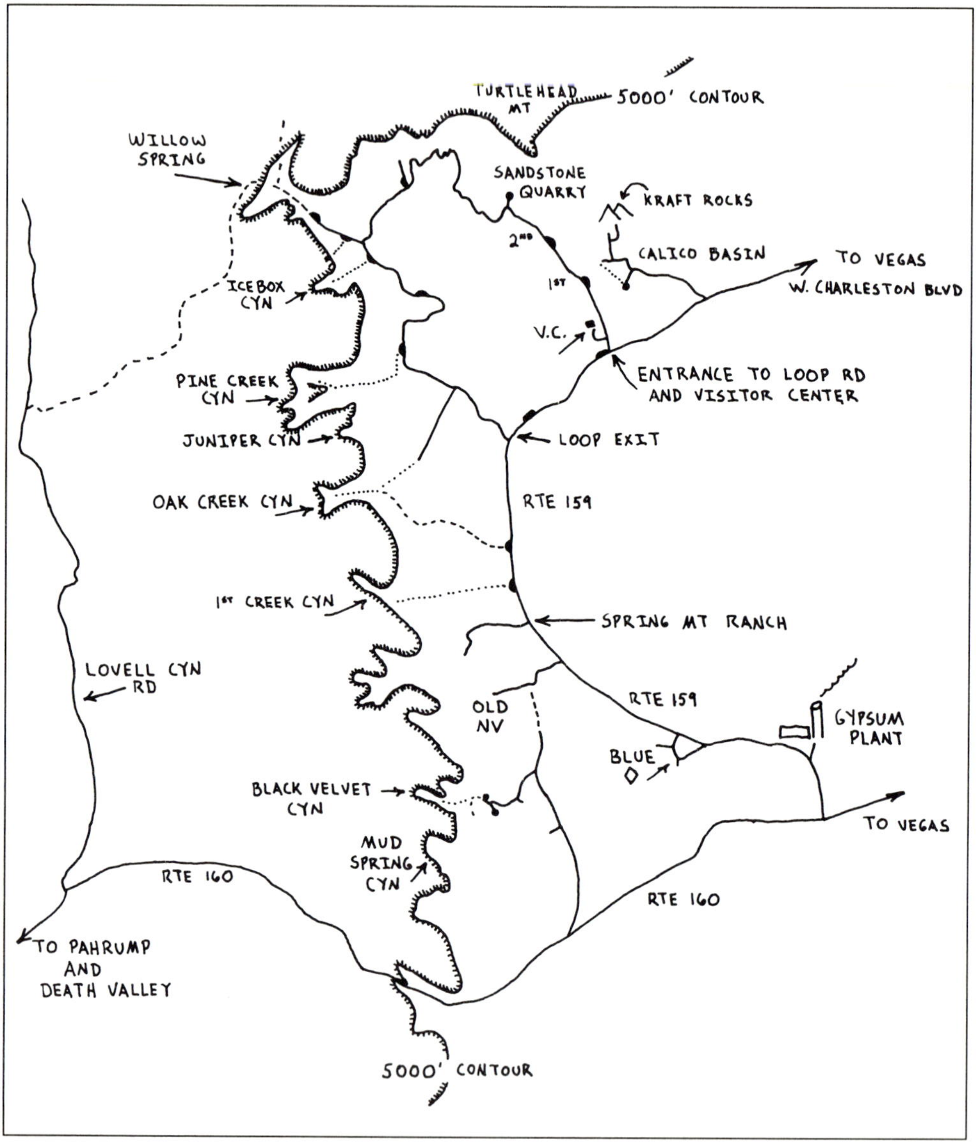

Map of Red Rocks

Local Climbing Shops

Desert Rock Sports
West Charleston Boulevard (west of Rainbow)
Las Vegas, NV 89117
(702) 254-1143

Adventure Outfitters
2550 South Rainbow
Las Vegas, NV
(702) 252-7114

Gary's Backpacking and Mountaineering
4251 West Sahara, Suite B
Las Vegas, NV 89102
(702) 368-2225

Local Guide Services

Sky's The Limit
Randy Grandstaff
HCR 33 Box 1
Calico Basin
Red Rock, NV 89124
(702) 363-4533

Mountain Skills
Jim Munson
(702) 256-7078 or (914) 687-9643

High and Wild Mountain Guides
Jay Smith
Box 11905
Tahoe Paradise, CA 96155
(916) 577-2370

Further Reading About Climbing at Red Rocks

At least three other guidebooks have been written about climbing at Red Rocks, as well as numerous articles. This is not meant to be a complete list of published material, but will get you started in your quest for more routes (once you've done all of the routes listed in this book, of course!):

The Red Rocks of Southern Nevada by Joanne Urioste. Published by the American Alpine Club, 1984

Climber's Guide to North American Rock Climbs; West Coast Rock Climbs, by John Harlin III. Published by Chockstone Press, 1987

A Climber's Guide to the Red Rocks of Nevada by Randy Faulk. Published by RT Publications, 1992.

Rock and Ice Magazine, issues 18, 36, 50

Climbing Magazine, issues 128, 131

Sport Climbing, Vol. 1, #3 and Vol. 2, #4

Mountain Magazine, issue 140

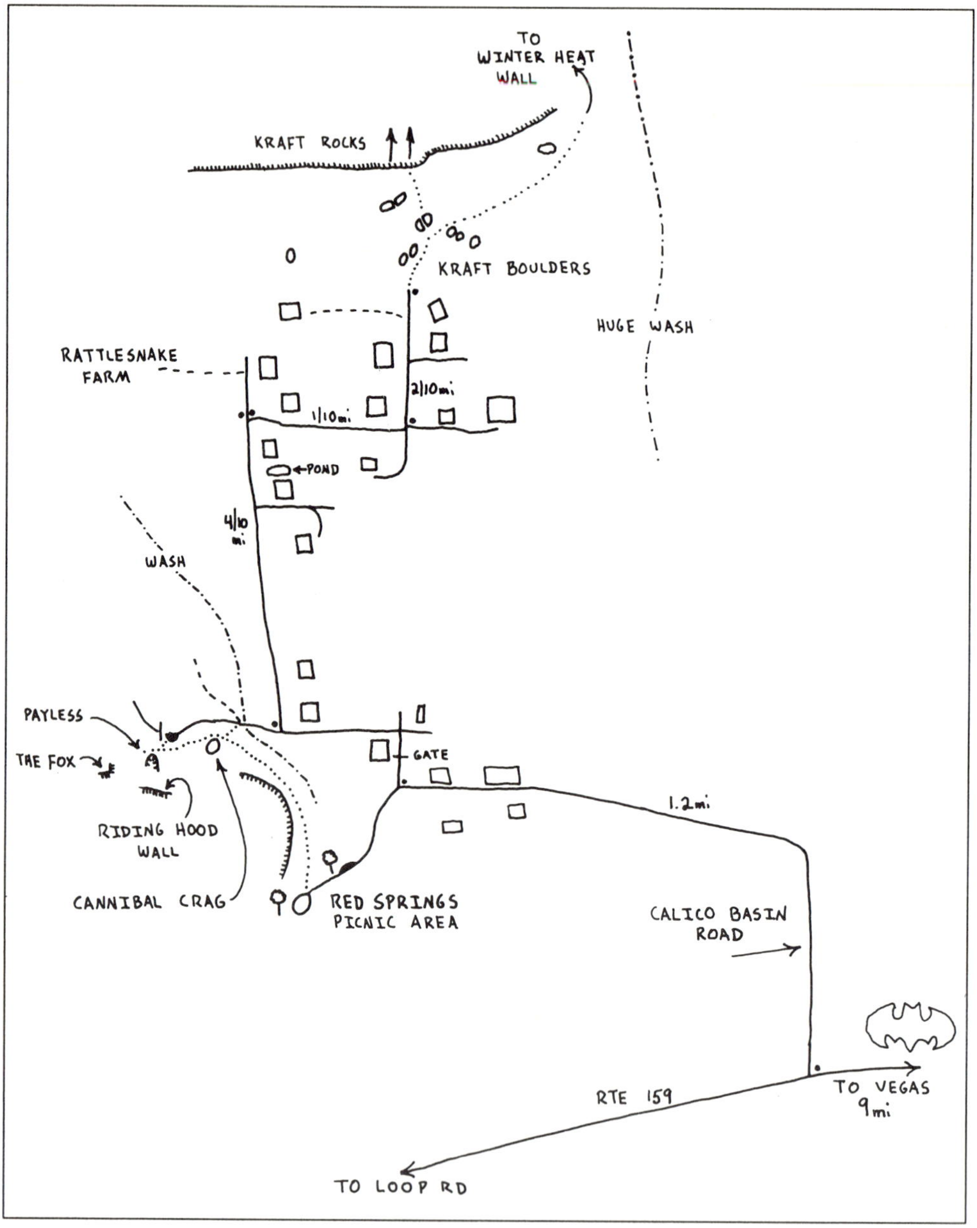

Map of Calico Basin area

CALICO BASIN

ROCK SPRINGS AREA

This area has been mostly ignored by visiting climbers in the past, but a recent new route boom will undoubtedly bring a few curious souls into the basin. Most of the routes included in this guidebook are on a series of primarily north facing formations to the northwest of Red Springs Picnic Area.

To access the first climbs described, turn off West Charleston (Route 159) onto Calico Basin Road and follow it 1.2 miles to a "T" intersection. Turn right (the Red Springs Picnic Area will be to the left) and go through a gate marked "private property." Turn left about 40 yards inside the gate, and follow the street about 200 yards. At the next curve, go left on a less-traveled road that crosses a wash. Follow this road up a short hill to a locked gate. Park on the left, making sure not to block the gate. From the "T" intersection to the parking area is 4/10 of a mile.

The following routes are all on the north-facing hillside to the left and left center (west) of the gate. They are described from left to right as viewed from the parking area. Please do not block the road or gate, and be respectful of the private landowners in this area!

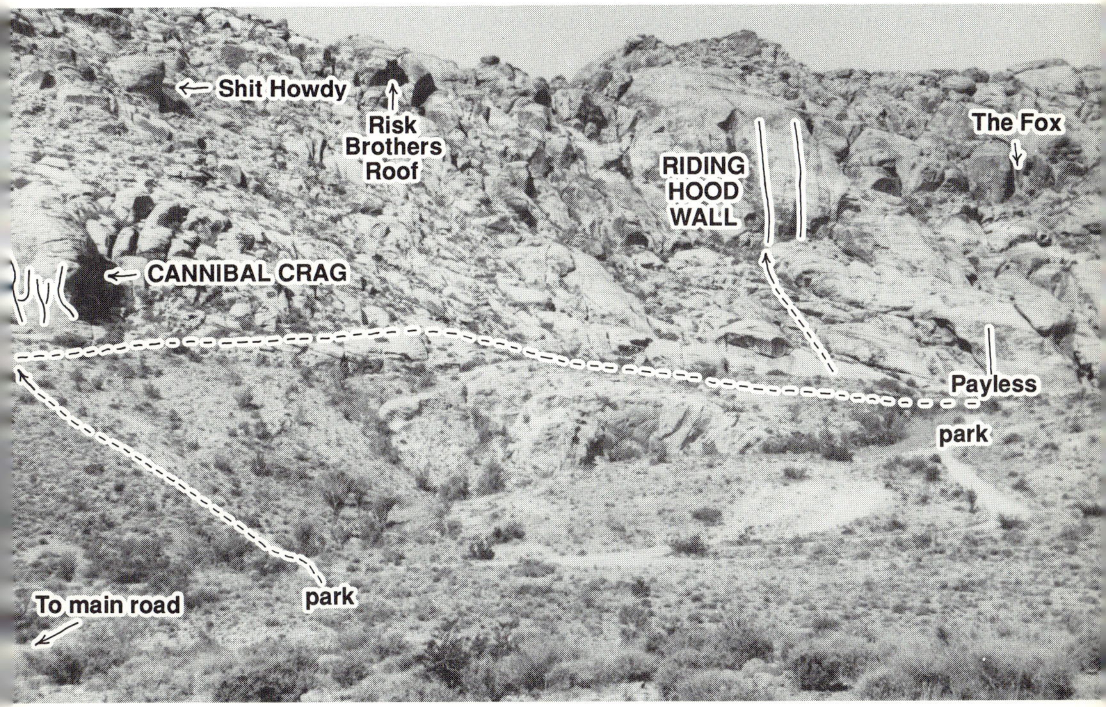

Calico Basin, south side overview.

Cannibal Crag

This is a huge boulder that is best approached by parking on the right side of the road just after you cross the wash, but before you go up the steep hill to the gate at the end of the road. Follow a faint trail uphill from your vehicle for 250 yards, crossing a well-defined trail that contours along the hillside just below the cliff. The boulder is seen easily from the road, and harbors some excellent climbs. Most routes are in the sun for a good part of the day. Climbs are described from right to left, starting on the varnished west face. As you approach the cliff, you will arrive on the east face, near **Pickled C.**

1 **Ma & Pa In Kettle 5.7-**
FA: Todd Swain, Randy & Andy Schenkel – June, 1992
Start at a varnished left-facing corner that is at the very right edge of the west face and 20 feet right of a white boulder leaning against the cliff. Three bolts provide protection on the face above the corner, and TCUs make up the belay. Walk off right (southwest).

2 **Mac & Ronnie In Cheese 5.10- PG/R**
FA: Todd Swain, Debbie Brenchley – June, 1992
Begin on the right edge of a white boulder leaning against the west face of the cliff. Angle up and right to a bolt, then straight up past another bolt to the top. You may want to bring a few TCUs for the climb and the belay. Walk off right (southwest).

3 **A Man In Every Pot 5.8+**
FA: Debbie Brenchley, Todd Swain – June, 1992
Begin seven feet left of the last route, at the left edge of the white boulder leaning against the crag. Scamper up the face past three bolts to the top. Bring a couple TCUs for pro and the anchor.

4 **What's Eating You? 5.9+**
FA: Todd Swain, Randy & Andy Schenkel – June, 1992
Start 10 feet left of **A Man In Every Pot** at a left-facing flake leading to a bulge. Saunter past three bolts to the top, where you'll need TCUs or Friends for the anchor.

5 **Elbows of Mac & Ronnie 5.11a**
FA: Todd Swain – June, 1992
Begin 10 feet left of the previous route at a right-leaning flake/ramp. Climb up and right pasta four bolts to da cold shut anchor.

A new route recently was completed between **Elbows of Mac & Ronnie** and **Have A Beer With Fear.** Three bolts lead to two cold shuts at the top. No name or grade was available at press time.

6 **Have A Beer With Fear 5.11a**
FA: Richard Harrison , Paul Van Betten – August, 1992
Start 15 feet left of **Elbows of Mac & Ronnie,** at the left edge of the wall. Climb past four bolts, either lowering off the last bolt, or going to the summit. The crux is by the first bolt, and is perhaps height-related.

7 **Pickled C 5.11a**
FA: Paul Van Betten, Dan Krulevski, Shelby Shelton, Richard Harrison, Sal Mamusia – 1991
This route climbs the arête separating the east and west faces, and is directly above the well-worn trail that contours along the hillside. Start to the right of the arête and climb easy rock out left onto the edge. Most people lower off at the fourth bolt.

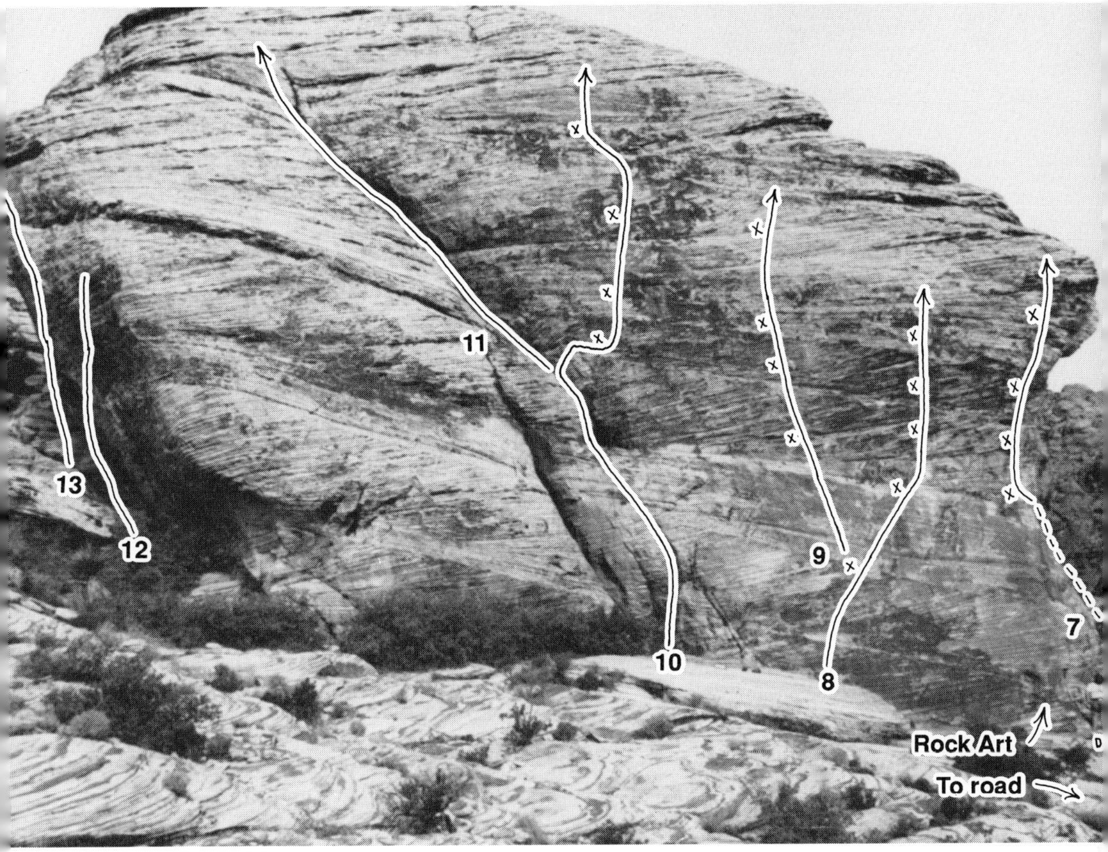

Cannibal Crag

13 New Wave Hookers 5.12c
12 F This Sport 5.12a/b
11 You Are What You Eat 5.3
10 Suck Upon My Baseboy 5.10d
9 Save The Heart To Eat Later 5.12a
8 Caustic C 5.11c
7 Pickled C 5.11a

8 Caustic C 5.11c

FA: Paul Van Betten, Sal Mamusia, Richard Harrison – August, 1991

Begin 40 feet left of **Pickled C,** and just left of some Native American petroglyphs shown in photo above (do not touch!). Shoot up a slabby face to a bolt, then angle up right past four bolts. It's common to lower off the last bolt.

9 Save The Heart To Eat Later 5.12a

FA: Sal Mamusia, Paul Van Betten, Shelby Shelton, Richard Harrison – August, 1991

Begin as for **Caustic C,** but angle up left past three bolts before lowering off.

10 Suck Upon My Baseboy 5.10d PG

FA: Paul Van Betten, Richard Harrison, Sal Mamusia – August, 1991

Rope up 15 feet left of the previous two routes, at the base of a left-leaning crack. Jam up the crack 20 feet, clip two bolts, then move right and up past one more. Lower off the fourth bolt, or go to the top.

11 **You Are What You Eat 5.3**
FA: Unknown – early 1990s
Climb the left-leaning crack mentioned above.

The next four climbs are on the overhanging southeast face, 75 feet left of the last route.

12 **F This Sport 5.12a/b**
FA: Paul Van Betten, Richard Harrison, Sal Mamusia – July, 1991
Angle out right toward the arête, passing five bolts.

13 **New Wave Hookers 5.12c**
FA: Paul Van Betten, Richard Harrison, Sal Mamusia – July, 1991
Begin 12 feet up and left, just above a pit, and power past six bolts heading right, then up.

14 **Wonderstuff 5.12c**
FA: Paul Van Betten, Richard Harrison, Sal Mamusia – July, 1991
Rope up as for the last route, but follow the left line of six bolts.

15 **Man-eater 5.12a**
FA: Dan McQuade – Spring 1992
You'll find another four bolts that lead to a cold shut anchor eight feet left of **Wonderstuff.**

16 **Shit Howdy 5.10+**
FA: Paul Van Betten, Sal Mamusia – 1986
This unique climb lies above and right of Cannibal Crag. It is best approached from the gate at the end of the road, and faces to the west. From the gate, walk up and left (south) about 350 yards to an obvious, large boulder/cliff. On the right (west) face, climb a crack that arches right, paralleling the slope of the hillside. Bring pro to three inches.

The next two routes are near the top of the hillside, midway between **Shit Howdy** and Riding Hood Wall. From the gate, head straight uphill (southwest) to an east-facing crag with a large streaked roof.

17 **Risk Brothers Roof 5.11-**
FA: Paul Van Betten, Sal Mamusia, Richard Harrison – Winter 1985/86
Climb a crack up and left through the roof.

18 **Zona Rosa 5.9**
FA: Robert Finlay (solo) – circa 1986
Named for the "Pink Zone" in Panama City, where some American servicemen were killed. About 60 feet right and around the corner from **Risk Brothers Roof,** you'll find a fingers to offwidth crack.

Riding Hood Wall

From the gate at the end of the road, walk about 50 yards southwest to a wash. Go straight up the rocky hillside 150 yards, to the biggest section of rock visible. This cliff is in the shade in the afternoon. Descend down the gully to the right (west) of the routes.

19 **Physical Graffiti 5.7**
FA: Jon Martinet, Randy Grandstaff, Scott Gordon – 1973
Not too many rolling stones on this one. Start at the northeast corner of the formation at a varnished dihedral with a crack running up and slightly right.

P1 Follow the crack up about 130 feet, then move right into the main crack system of **Over the Hill . . .** Belay above at rope's end. 150 ft, 5.7.

P2 Continue up the easy crack and face to the top. 110 ft, 5.5.

20 **Over The Hill To Grandmother's House 5.9+**

FA: Bob Logerquist, John Williamson – September, 1970

Difficult to start, no matter which way you go. Begin this journey 50 feet right of **Physical Graffiti,** atop boulders and below a vertical crack running through a roof.

P1 & 2 Climb a short, smooth face to a roof, then over the roof at an obvious crack (crux, V1). Follow the crack to a stance 40 feet up. Rappel off jammed slings, or continue up the easy but awkward crack for about 200 feet to the top of the buttress.

V1 Climb the right-leaning crack 15 feet left of the normal start until it intersects with the main crack about 40 feet up. 5.9+.

Ranch Hands Crag

To reach this crag from the gate at the end of the road, walk 200 yards west to a low, overhanging buttress. The cliff has two tiers - the lower tier faces east, the upper tier to the north. The next five routes are on the lower tier, and are in the shade in the afternoon. For all routes on this buttress, walk off left (southeast), and bring gear for an anchor on top.

21 **Payless Cashways 5.11a**

FA: Richard Harrison, Sal Mamusia, Paul Van Betten, Shelby Shelton – June, 1991

Shelby dropped Sal's Bosch, and they had to go to Payless to buy another! Start at the left (south) edge of the lower tier, at the base of a left-leaning crack that leads to a cave. Move up and right past a hueco to the first bolt (half-inch with a blue hanger), then straight up the face past four more bolts. Bring #3.5 and 4 Friends for the belay.

22 **Spanky 5.11-**

FA: Richard Harrison, Sal Mamusia, Paul Van Betten, Shelby Shelton – June, 1991

Begin atop a boulder slightly downhill and 10 feet right of **Payless Cashways.** A difficult boulder problem to a pocket leads to face climbing past four bolts. Finish up a short crack. Bring #3.5 and 4 Friends for the belay.

23 **Mexican Secret Agent Man 5.11b**

FA: Paul Van Betten, Richard Harrison – July, 1991

Start eight feet right of **Spanky** off the same boulder. Climb past four bolts, trending slightly right. Many people lower off the last bolt, or bring #3.5 and 4 Friends for the belay.

24 **Swilderness Experience 5.11b/c**

FA: Paul Van Betten, Richard Harrison, Shelby Shelton – July, 1991

Rope up 10 feet right of **Mexican Secret Agent Man,** near the bottom of the boulder mentioned in the previous two routes. Traverse out right along flakes, passing one bolt, then go up past four more bolts to the top.

25 **Swilderness Permit 5.12b/c**

FA: Sal Mamusia, Paul Van Betten, Richard Harrison – July, 1991

Begin 20 feet downhill of **Swilderness Experience,** below very overhanging, brown rock. Power past a bunch of moonscoops to lower-angled rock. There are seven bolts enroute; most folks lower off the last one.

The next three routes are on the upper tier, which is best approached by climbing up the easy north face (5.4) to the base of the overhanging wall. These routes are in the shade all day.

26 **Jack Officers 5.12b/c**

FA: Paul Van Betten, Richard Harrison, Sal Mamusia – April, 1991

Angle up left from the center of the wall past three bolts.

27 **Ranch Hands 5.12b/c**
FA: Richard Harrison, Paul Van Betten, Bob Conz, Sal Mamusia – January, 1991
Angle slightly up right from the center of the wall past four bolts to a two-bolt rap station.

28 **Blood Stains 5.10 R/X**
FA: Richard Harrison, Sal Mamusia, Paul Van Betten – September, 1990
Dangerously loose. If the block at midheight comes off, there could be blood stains! Start on the ledge as for the previous two routes. Traverse out right to a loose crack, and go up the crack to an overhang formed by a loose block. Pull the ceiling, then up the steep face past one bolt to another ceiling. Swing over this, then go left to the **Ranch Hands** rappel anchor.

To approach the next route, walk 300 yards west from the gate (about 100 yards right of the previous routes). A striking crack in a right-facing corner is about 250 yards up the hillside. This climb is in the shade all day.

29 **The Fox 5.10+**
FA: Unknown – early 70s FFA: Unknown – mid 70s
One of the finest pitches at Red Rocks. Bring a full set of camming devices, with extra of the biggest sizes. Climb the widening crack in a right-facing corner for 150 feet. Descend to the left (east) down the rocky slope.

Dickies Cliff

These formations are both about 100 yards right (west) of **The Fox,** and 200 yards right (west) of Ranch Hands Crag. The cliffs face roughly north, and are near the level of the desert floor. Routes will be described from left to right, starting on Dickies Cliff.

30 **Gigantor 5.10**
FA: Richard Harrison, Paul Van Betten, Wendell Broussard, Mike Forkash – July, 1991
Follow three bolts up and right, then continue straight up, using gear for pro. Walk off right (west).

31 **Boobytrap 5.12b/c PG**
FA: Sal Mamusia, Paul Van Betten – July, 1991
The FA party says no stick clipping the first bolt! After a very hard start, climb past five bolts to the summit. Walk (or crawl) off right.

32 **Stukas Over Disneyland 5.12-**
FA: Paul Van Betten, Richard Harrison – July, 1991
Follow two bolts to a roof, then climb a 5.10 crack above. Bring wires and TCUs.

33 **Monster Island 5.10+**
FA: Paul Van Betten, Sal Mamusia – July, 1991
This route climbs along a seam near the right edge of the cliff, and uses bolts and gear (up to #2.5 Friend) for protection.

Gnat Man Crag

The next three routes are on a terrace slightly up and right (west) of the Dickies Cliff. The routes also are described from left to right.

34 **P-Coat Sleeve 5.10-**
FA: Paul Van Betten, Sal Mamusia – November, 1991
Jam up the obvious hand crack, then walk off right (west).

35 **Gnat Man On Ranch Hands 5.11c**
FA: Paul Van Betten, Sal Mamusia – November, 1991
Climb the bolted face right of the crack, using scoops at the start.

36 **Knock The Bottom Out Of It 5.10a**
FA: Paul Van Betten, Sal Mamusia – November, 1991
Five bolts lead up the right side of the face. Walk off right.

Kraft Crags and Kraft Boulders

Named for local landowner Ozzie Kraft, this large hill (some might call it a mountain) forms the north wall of Calico Basin. The south face of the massif has numerous cliffs, and lots of broken sections. Only a few routes will be described on the south face, and they are roughly above the Kraft Rocks bouldering area, which is considered by many to be the finest in the area.

To access these climbs, turn off West Charleston (Route 159) onto Calico Basin Road and follow it 1.2 miles to a "T" intersection. Turn right (the Rock Springs Picnic Area is to the left) and go through a gate marked "private property." Turn left about 40 yards inside the gate, and follow the street for about 200 yards. At the next curve, go right, following the larger road for 4/10 of a mile. Turn right just after a house on the right with a pond and very green lawn, and about 100 yards before this road ends. Drive 1/10 of a mile, turn left (the obvious way to go), and drive another 2/10 of a mile to the end of this road.

When viewed from the parking area, the bouldering is spread out just right of center, and the climbs described are almost directly in front of you, about 200 yards uphill on a pinkish cliff. Remember, all of the climbing here is surrounded by private land - be considerate and unobtrusive!

37 **High Roller 5.11+/12– PG/R**
FA: Paul Van Betten, Jay Smith – 1986
Start about 50 feet left of the **Shark Vegas** overhang/cave in the center of the cliff.

P1 Climb a shallow left-facing dihedral over a roof (scary; thin pro). Belay at the base of an offwidth crack. 80 ft, 5.11+/12-

P2 Swim up the awfulwidth above. 80 ft, 5.10+

38 **Shark Vegas 5.11– PG**
FA: Paul Van Betten, Nick Nordblom – 1986
Start in the center of the cliff, below a large overhang/cave midway up the cliff, and to the right of two big boulders at the cliff's base. Wander up lower-angled rock along vertical fissures to a short, varnished slab 50 feet up (bolt). Climb the striking, left-facing flake/crack up and left to the top.

39 **Viva Las Vegas 5.11– PG/R**
FA: Robert Finlay, Paul Van Betten, Mike Ward, Randy Grandstaff – 1986
Begin just right of **Shark Vegas** and climb the face to an obvious vertical crack, which is followed to the top. The small wires at the start of the route might be a bit questionable, hence the protection rating.

40 **Vegas Girls 5.11 PG/R**
FA: Paul Crawford, Paul Van Betten, Paul Obenheim, Nick Nordblom – 1986
Start just right of **Viva Las Vegas** and climb huecos and a shallow arête past three bolts to the top. There is an important natural thread in the ceiling.

Kraft Crags

38 **Shark Vegas** 5.11– PG
39 **Viva Las Vegas** 5.11– PG/R
41 **Porch Pirate** 5.11 R

41 **Porch Pirate 5.11 R**
FA: Paul Van Betten, Paul Crawford, Sal Mamusia – October, 1991
This scary but good-looking route begins about 150 yards right and uphill from **Vegas Girls,** near a large, prickly bush. Scramble up and left about 40 feet on a ramp to a ledge, where you should find a "fixed" Hot Wheels car in a crack. Follow faint cracks up and left to a very shallow dihedral. Climb this, clipping a few bolts, then run it out up the face above to the top.

Winter Heat Wall

This cliff looks very similar to Ragged Edges Cliff, and is in the shade most of the day. Approach by walking right (east) from the Kraft Boulders, then heading up the obvious drainage/canyon that comes down from the back (north) side of the Kraft Rocks. As you hike up this drainage, the cliff is on the left (south) side. Approach time is about 20 minutes. Routes are described from left to right, and the descent is down a gully to the left of the face.

42 **Couldn't Be Schmooter 5.8+**
FA: Wendell Broussard, Richard Harrison, Paul Crawford – Spring 1983
Climb the line of heucos on the left side of the wall.

43 **Winter Heat 5.11+**
FA: Paul Crawford, Jay Smith, Richard Harrison, Paul Van Betten – Spring 1983
A great face climb in the center of the cliff that was a popular toprope before being led.

44 **High Class Hoe 5.10–**
FA: Richard Harrison, Wendell Broussard, Nick Nordblom, Paul Van Betten – Spring 1983
Climb a finger-to-hands crack to a ledge, then past a bulge to a sloping dihedral/ramp and the top.

Photo: Mike Ward Collection

Mike Ward on belay in the shadow of Rainbow Wall.

FIRST PULLOUT

Seven crags are described in this chapter, probably the best of which are Universal City and the Fixx Cliff. The Fixx Cliff was one of the first small, modern cliffs to be developed at Red Rocks, and this subsequently led to establishing popular cliffs like The Gallery. All of these routes have very short approaches, and are in the sun most of the day. To reach the First Pullout, drive the scenic loop road for 1.1 miles, and park in the area on the right.

First Pullout Area as seen from parking lot

34 Cactus Massacre 5.11
35 Cactus Root 5.11+
36 Prime Ticket 5.11b/c
39 Star Search 5.11c

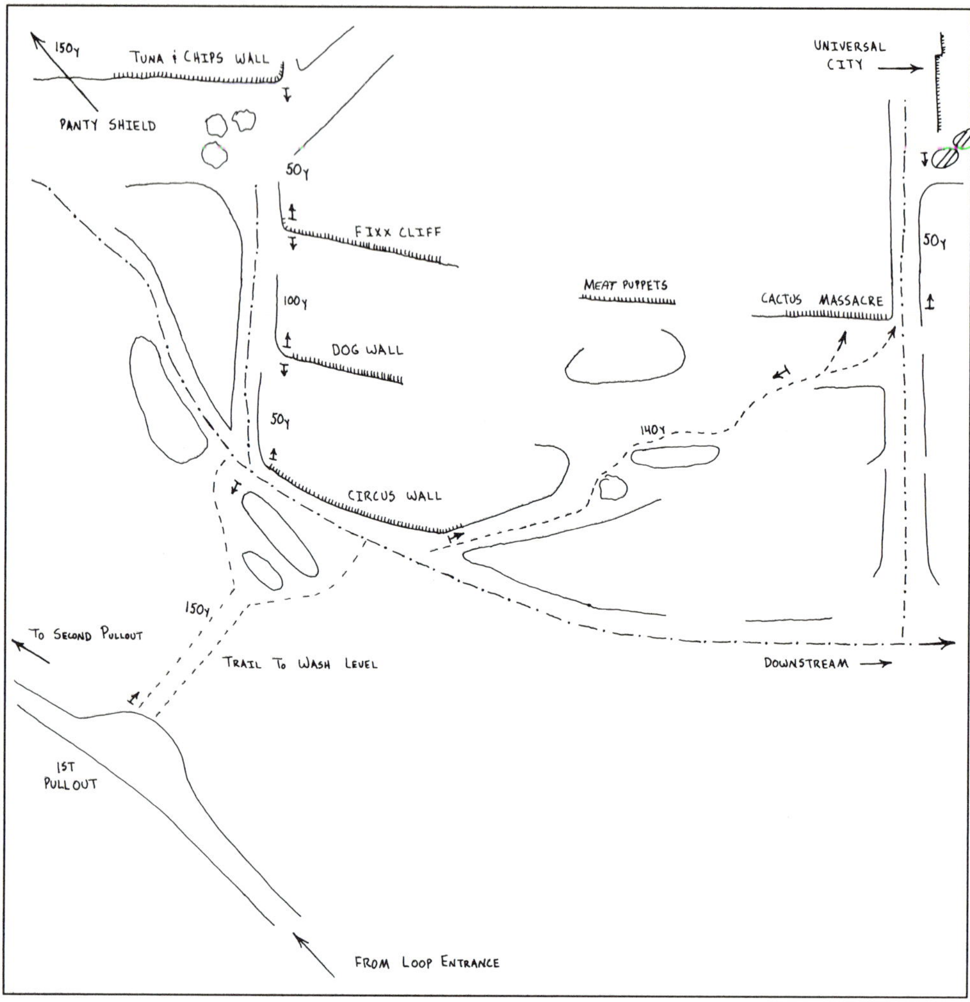

Map of First Pullout Area

Circus Wall

This somewhat rotten cliff is right at the level of the wash, and is characterized by a large arch/ceiling in its middle. It is not quite visible from the parking lot, but as you walk straight down the trail toward the wash, it becomes obvious. Numerous routes have been done on the Circus Wall, but only four routes are described here, and all go out the arch/roof. Climbs are listed from left to right on this sunny cliff.

1 **Circus Boy 5.11+**
FA: Paul Van Betten, Sal Mamusia – December, 1987
This route climbs out the left side of the arch, using two bolts.

2 **Main Attraction 5.12+**
FA: Paul Van Betten, Sal Mamusia – December, 1987
Climb out the center of the roof, using one bolt. There are chains to rap from.

3 **Midway** 5.12
FA: Paul Van Betten, Nick Nordblom – December, 1987
Power out the right side of the arch, using four bolts (missing hanger on one at press time). Descend from the chain anchor.

4 **Crowd Pleaser** 5.11+/12-
FA: Paul Van Betten, Sal Mamusia – December, 1987
Starting just right of the arch, climb the left-leaning crack past four bolts.

Dog Wall

A popular sport cliff with a quick approach. Walk straight down the trail from the parking lot to the wash, then go left 150 feet to the edge of the Circus Wall. The Dog Wall is about 200 feet up a gully to the right, on the next level above the Circus Wall. This cliff is the lowest worthwhile face plainly visible from the trailhead. Routes are described from left to right. To access the top, continue up the gully about 50 feet, then go right. From the top of the cliff, walk off left.

5 **Wok The Dog** 5.7
FA: Todd Swain – January, 1992
Bring your pooper scooper. Begin near the left edge of the crag and above the approach gully. Climb a low-angled, right-leaning ramp to the top of the wall.

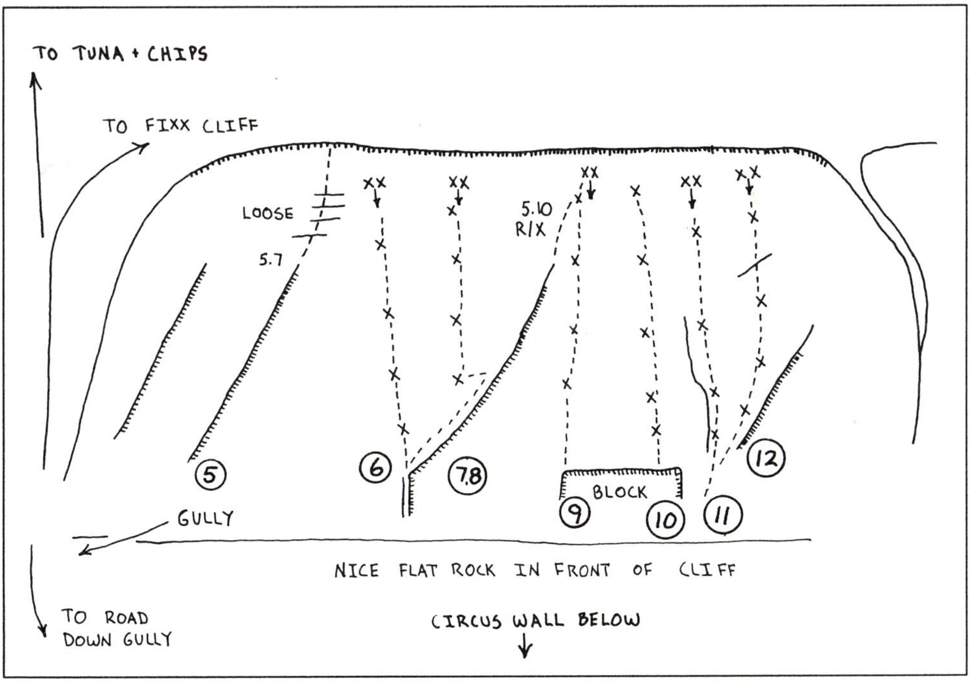

Dog Wall

5 **Wok The Dog** 5.7
6 **Cat Walk** 5.10a/b
7 **It's A Bitch** 5.10b/c
8 **Man's Best Friend** 5.10 R/X
9 **Here Kitty, Kitty** 5.11c/d
10 **K-9** 5.12b
11 **Cujo** 5.11d/12a
12 **Poodle Chainsaw Massacre** 5.11c/d

6 **Cat Walk 5.10a/b** 👍
FA: Don Burroughs, Alan Busby – January, 1992
Begin 40 feet right, at the left end of a right-leaning ramp/flake, about 75 feet up from the drainage. Climb past four bolts to a chain anchor.

7 **It's A Bitch 5.10b/c** 👍
FA: California Dudes – circa 1987
Start five feet right of the last route, and crank past four bolts to a cold shut anchor. Rebolted by Randy Faulk and Leo Henson in 1991 after going many years with chopped bolts.

8 **Man's Best Friend 5.10 R/X** 👎
FA: Todd Swain – January, 1992
Not exactly. Climb the right-leaning ramp/flake mentioned in the last two routes, finishing up the unprotected face.

9 **Here Kitty, Kitty 5.11c/d**
FA: Geoff Weigand – circa 1987
Begin 30 feet right of the ramp/flake atop a block. Power past four bolts to a cold shut anchor. Rebolted in 1991 after having been chopped long ago.

10 **K-9 5.12b**
FA: Geoff Weigand – circa 1987
Gear up eight feet right of **Here Kitty, Kitty,** at the right end of a block at the base of the cliff. Climb past five bolts to the bolt anchor on top. Rebolted in 1991.

11 **Cujo 5.11d/12a**
FA: Geoff Weigand – circa 1987
Rope up five feet right of **K-9** at a white streak just left of a large flake. Clip five bolts enroute to a cold shut anchor. Rebolted in 1991.

12 **Poodle Chainsaw Massacre 5.11c/d**
FA: Randy Faulk, Karin Olson – October, 1991
Climb past four bolts to a cold shut anchor, starting at a right-leaning flake five feet right of **Cujo.**

Fixx Cliff

This is the first semi-sport cliff to be developed in the area. Bring traditional gear for the routes here. Follow the trail from the parking lot straight down to the wash, then turn left (northwest) and follow the drainage about 200 feet until it turns uphill. About 250 feet up from the bottom of the wash (and 100 feet above the turnoff for the Dog Wall) the drainage is split by a rock shaped like the prow of a ship. Take the right fork (straight ahead) and scramble up about 300 feet. The cliff is on your right. Like the Dog Wall, it is plainly visible from the trailhead, being level with the road and just left of center as you view the cliff bands. Routes are described from left to right. Descend off the right side.

13 **The Whiff 5.10-**
FA: Jay Smith, Mike Ward – March, 1987
The finger-and-hand crack near the left edge of the cliff.

14 **Snow Blind 5.11 R**
FA: Paul Crawford – March, 1987
Start 10 feet right of **The Whiff** and climb steep huecos past one bolt to a vague arête.

15 **Stand Or Fall 5.11-**
FA: Paul Van Betten, Jim "Frodo" Lybarger – March, 1987
Begin five feet right of **Snow Blind,** and climb steep huecos past one bolt to a crack.

16 **Crack 5.11**
FA: Paul Crawford, Jay Smith – March, 1987
Crank up the obvious finger crack eight feet right of **Stand or Fall.**

17 **Free Base 5.11+**
FA: Paul Crawford, Paul Van Betten, Jay Smith, Nick Nordblom – March, 1987
Rope up 10 feet right of **Crack,** and climb a vertical crack to three bolts along an overhanging seam.

18 **Saved By Zero 5.11**
FA: Nick Nordblom, Danny Meyers – May 1986
Climb the steep finger-and-hand crack 10 feet right of **Free Base.**

19 **Red Skies 5.11+**
FA: Paul Van Betten, Paul Crawford – March, 1987
Follow a seam and three bolts five feet right of **Saved By Zero.**

20 **The Geezer 5.11**
FA: Jay Smith, Paul Crawford – March, 1987
Start 10 feet right of **Red Skies.** Climb the pink face past a drilled angle.

21 **Cocaine Hotline 5.11**
FA: Paul Crawford, John Rosholt, Jay Smith – March, 1987
Begin eight feet right of **The Geezer** and climb a thin seam up varnished rock past one bolt.

22 **Reach The Beach 5.11**
FA: Nick Nordblom, Jenni Stone, Paul Crawford, Jay Smith – March, 1987
Rope up six feet right of **Cocaine Hotline** at the left edge of a low boulder and bushes. Climb a thin varnished seam past one bolt.

23 **Eight Ball 5.11**
FA: Paul Crawford, Jay Smith, Nick Nordblom, Jenni Stone – March, 1987
Start 10 feet right of **Reach The Beach** and face climb to a thin seam and a bolt.

24 **One Thing Leads To Another 5.11**
FA: Nick Nordblom, Jenni Stone, Paul Crawford, Jay Smith – March, 1987
Climb the thin seam eight feet right of **Eight Ball.**

25 **The Skagg 5.11**
FA: Mike Ward, Paul Van Betten, Paul Crawford, Jay Smith – March, 1987
Power up the 30-foot long seam that rises 10 feet right of **One Thing . . .**

26 **Running 5.11-**
FA: Nick Nordblom, Jenni Stone – March, 1987
Climb the next seam 10 feet to the right of **The Skagg.** This is also about 30 feet long.

27 **Outside the Envelope 5.11**
FA: Nick Nordblom (solo) – March, 1987
Crank up the seam eight feet right of **Running.** The seam is about 20 feet long.

28 **The Bindle 5.11**
FA: Unknown – 1987 or later
Shoot up the very short seam 10 feet right of **Outside the Envelope.** The seam is near the very right edge of the crag.

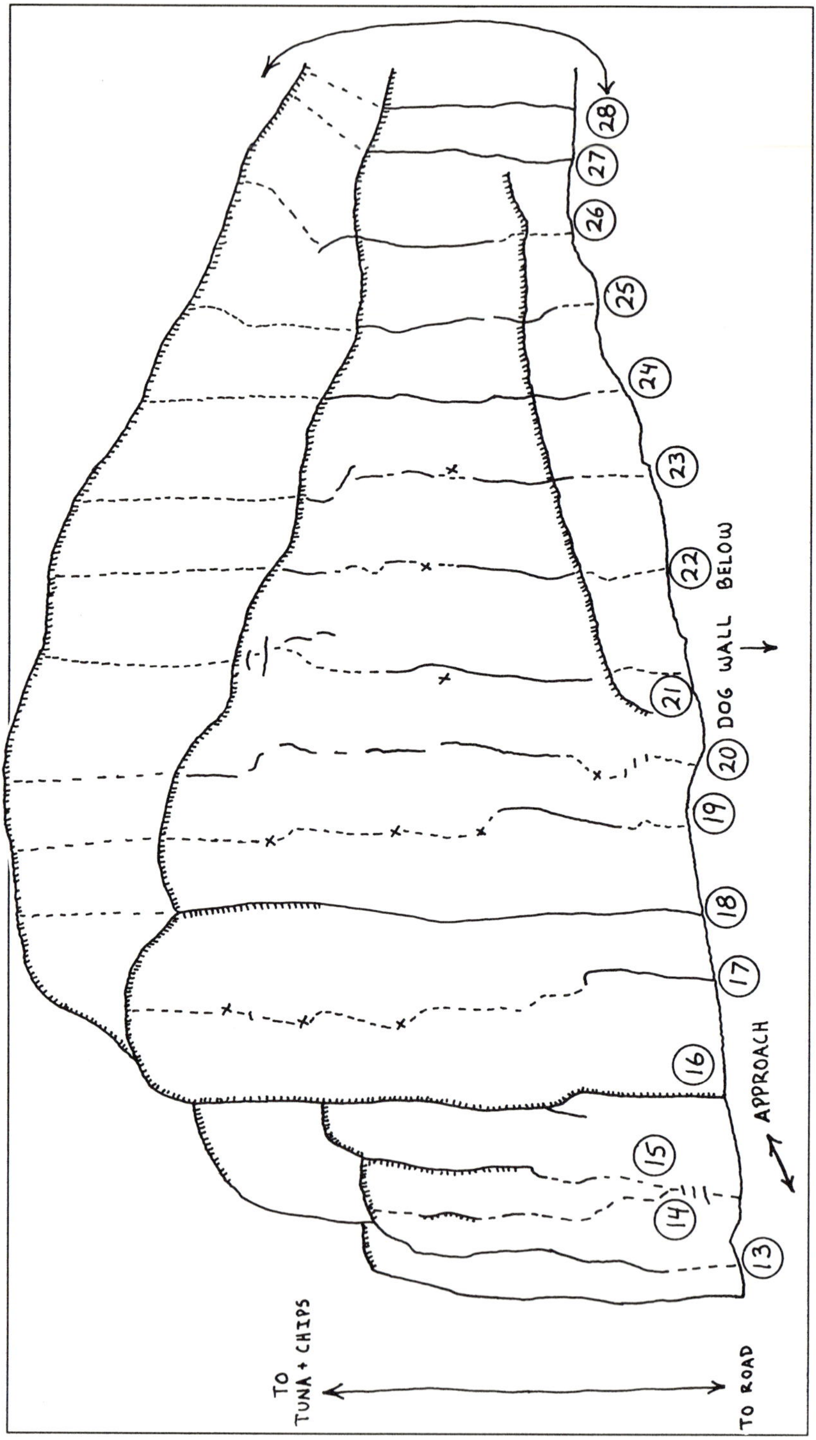
TO TUNA + CHIPS
TO ROAD
13
14
15
16
17
18
19
20
21
22
23
24
25
26
27
28
APPROACH
DOG WALL BELOW

Fixx Cliff

13 The Whiff 5.10-
14 Snow Blind 5.11 R
15 Stand Or Fall 5.11-
16 Crack 5.11
17 Free Base 5.11+ 👍
18 Saved By Zero 5.11 👍
19 Red Skies 5.11+
20 The Geezer 5.11

21 Cocaine Hotline 5.11
22 Reach The Beach 5.11
23 Eight Ball 5.11
24 One Thing Leads To Another 5.11
25 The Skagg 5.11
26 Running 5.11-
27 Outside the Envelope 5.11
28 The Bindle 5.11

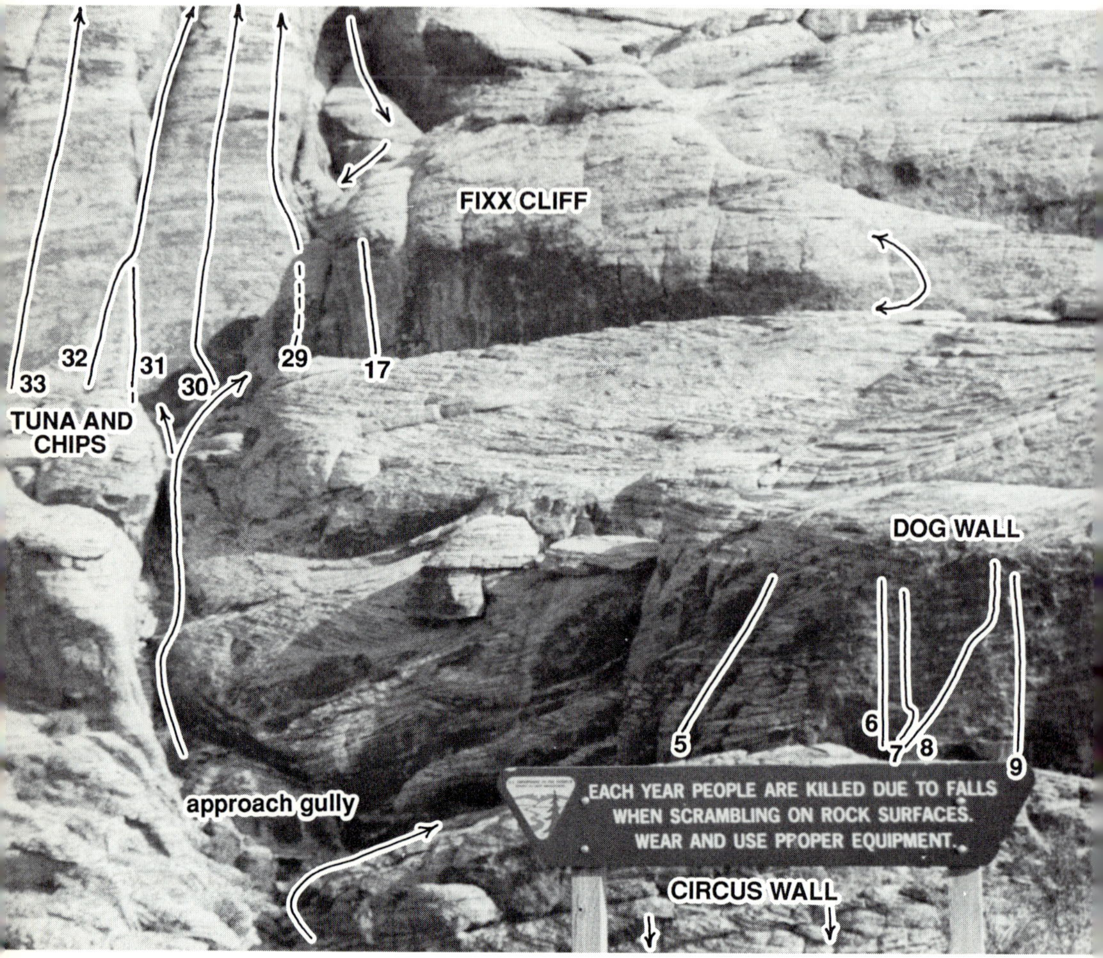

Tuna And Chips Wall, Fixx Cliff and Dog Wall

Tuna And Chips Wall

33 Tuna And Chips 5.8 R
32 Chips and Salsa 5.3
31 Waterstreak 5.8 or 5.10 PG
30 Tuna Cookies 5.7 R
29 Chips Ahoy! 5.9 R

Fixx Cliff

17 Free Base 5.11+

Dog Wall

5 Wok The Dog 5.7
6 Cat Walk 5.10a/b
7 It's A Bitch 5.10b/c
8 Man's Best Friend 5.10 R/X
9 Here Kitty, Kitty 5.11c/d

Tuna And Chips Wall

Follow the trail from the parking lot straight down to the wash, then turn left (northwest) and follow the drainage about 200 feet until it turns uphill. About 250 feet up from the bottom of the wash (and 100 feet above the turnoff for the Dog Wall), the drainage is split by a rock shaped like the prow of a ship. Take the right fork (straight ahead) and scramble up about 300 feet. The Fixx Cliff is on your right. Continue up the drainage past the Fixx Cliff about 150 feet to a big, plated cliff blocking the drainage. You should arrive at the center of the cliff, just right of a low-angled crack, and directly below a water streak. Routes on this sunny cliff are described from right to left. Walk off to the right (east), then follow a gully back to the base of the cliff.

29 **Chips Ahoy! 5.9 R**

FA: Mike Ward, Paul Van Betten – 1986

Start 50 feet right of the crack/gully in the center of the cliff, and atop boulders that lie below left-slanting seams.

P1 Climb steep varnished rock above the left slanting seams and continue up the plated face above passing two bolts. Power through the roof above (bolt, crux) to easier ground and a belay ledge. 150 ft, 5.9

P2 Scramble to the top of the formation. 100 ft, 5.2

30 **Tuna Cookies 5.7 R**

FA: National Outdoor Leadership School (NOLS) staff – circa 1987

If you've seen the movie *Traxx,* this route name will make sense. Begin just left of the previous route at several left-arching seams. Bring wires and gear to a #3 Friend.

P1 Climb up left to a bolt 30 feet up, then continue up the center of the long face past one more bolt to the ceiling. Climb past the left edge to a big ledge. 150 ft., 5.7.

P2 Scramble to the top. 100 ft., 5.2.

31 **Waterstreak 5.8 or 5.10 PG**

FA: Jim Kessler – 1987

The difficulty is dependant on exactly where you climb. Gear up 30 feet left of **Tuna Cookies,** at the base of an obvious water streak, and 20 feet right of a low-angled crack. Climb past three bolts to join the main crack/chimney system. A bolt and drilled piton are in the alcove. Rappel, or continue up the crack to the top.

32 **Chips and Salsa 5.3**

FA: Unknown – 1980s

Rope up at the base of the central crack/chimney system, and directly behind a block. Follow the crack for about 200 feet to the top.

33 **Tuna And Chips 5.8 R**

FA: Bob Conz and "Frodo" Lybarger – January, 1987

Start 20 feet left of the central crack at the left edge of a block. Climb a low angled face, keeping right of a black, left-facing flake to a bolt about 50 feet up. Continue up to a crack, and follow this through a bulge. Belay in the crack, then continue up the crack and face to the top (5.5, loose).

Note: The dark, varnished cliff about 150 yards up and left from the Tuna And Chips Wall is the Panty Wall. The cliff is visible from the road, and is characterized by a large pine tree growing next to the wall. Numerous traditional routes have been done on this wall, as well as a couple of bolted lines.

Cactus Massacre

This crag has two steep, and somewhat loose routes on it. The cliff is about 200 yards right (east) of the Dog Wall, at about the same level on the hillside. It is slightly below and right of the parking lot; both climbs are in the shade in the morning. Walk straight down the trail from the parking lot to the wash (150 yards), then go up right (southeast) on a ramp that is just right of the Circus Wall (the somewhat-rotten cliff that is at the level of the wash) for 50 yards to a small saddle (graffiti on the left side of this saddle says "T SOL"). Continue in the same direction (southeast), dropping down into a hole, then scrambling back up to the same elevation (40 yards). The gray-colored Cactus Massacre wall is 50 yards toward the hillside (left, east), and is characterized by a right-leaning crack crossing the cliff at one-third height.

34 **Cactus Massacre 5.11**

FA: Paul Van Betten, Sal Mamusia, Mike Ward – December, 1987

The leftmost route. Begin in the center of the cliff, just right of obvious, parallel, varnished, vertical seams. Scamper 15 feet up to a ledge, then climb past a bolt (either left, right, or center), continuing past three more bolts to a ledge. Either continue to the top, or downclimb and lower off the last bolt. Bring a #2.5 Friend and some TCUs.

35 **Cactus Root 5.11+**

FA: Paul Van Betten, Sal Mamusia, Jim Olsen – December, 1987

Bring a smattering of gear, including a #2.5 Friend. Start 30 feet right of the previous route at a left-slanting crack/corner that leads to a vertical crack. Follow the crack system past three bolts to the top.

Universal City

This crag is fairly new, and is located near the top of the hillside, to the right (east) of the parking area. It's about 50 yards above the Cactus Massacre, and just left of two boulders with right-leaning stripes on them. To approach this shady cliff, walk straight down the trail from the parking lot to the wash (150 yards), then go up and right (southeast) 50 yards on a ramp that is just right of the Circus Wall (the somewhat rotten cliff at the level of the wash, characterized by a large arch/ceiling). Go through a small saddle (graffiti on the left side of this saddle says "T SOL"). Continue in the same southeasterly direction, dropping down into a hole, then scrambling back up to the same elevation (another 40 yards). The gray-colored Cactus Massacre wall is 50 yards toward the hillside (left, east), and is characterized by a right-leaning crack crossing the cliff at one-third height. Walk 30 yards right from the Cactus Massacre to a gully; go up this about 50 yards, passing an arch formed by boulders leaning across the gully. Universal City is up on the right, and faces west. Routes are described from right to left.

36 **Prime Ticket 5.11b/c**

FA: Randy Faulk – November, 1991

Start atop a boulder just left of a crack/alcove. Seven bolts to cold shuts.

37 **Cameo Appearance 5.11c/d**

FA: Randy Faulk – November, 1991

Begin 15 feet left of **Prime Ticket,** between two bushes. Climb up right to a horizontal (bolt), then cruise along a vertical seam past three bolts. Continue up the steep face past two more bolts to a shared cold shut anchor.

38 **Celebrity Roast 5.12b**
FA: Leo Henson, Randy Faulk, Dan McQuade – November, 1991
Start as for the previous route, then move left at the horizontal and power past seven bolts and one cold shut to the anchor on **Cameo Appearance.**

39 **Star Search 5.11c**
FA: Randy Faulk, Doug Henze – November, 1991
Rope up five feet left of **Celebrity Roast**, near a block on the ground. Six bolts along a vertical seam lead to the anchor.

40 **Quiet On The Set 5.8 or 5.10c**
FA: Louie Anderson, Bart Groendycke – December, 1991
Begin five feet left of the last route and climb the arête just right of a corner. There are five bolts with black hangers on this somewhat contrived route.

41 **Ed MacMayonnaise 5.7**
FA: Todd Swain – July, 1992
Climb the obvious, left-facing corner on the left (north) side of the face.

Climb Bomb Cliff and Velvet Elvis Crag

These crags are right of Universal City, and about 50 yards right of the two boulders with right-leaning stripes on them. The Climb Bomb is characterized by two thin cracks that run up a steep wall; the Velvet Elvis Crag is about 30 feet to its right. Routes are described from left to right as you approach from Universal City.

42 **Climb Warp 5.11-**
FA: Paul Van Betten, Robert Finlay – December, 1988
Climb a thin crack up and over a ceiling, clipping one bolt above the ceiling.

43 **Climb Bomb 5.11+ R**
FA: Paul Van Betten, Robert Finlay – December, 1988
Climb a crack to a ceiling, passing one bolt underneath the ceiling.

Note: At least three routes have been done between **Climb Bomb** and **Velvet Elvis,** but no more is known.

44 **Velvet Elvis 5.12-**
FA: Paul Van Betten, Don Welsh – November, 1988
This route climbs a thin seam up an overhanging wall that faces the road. There are three bolts on the route.

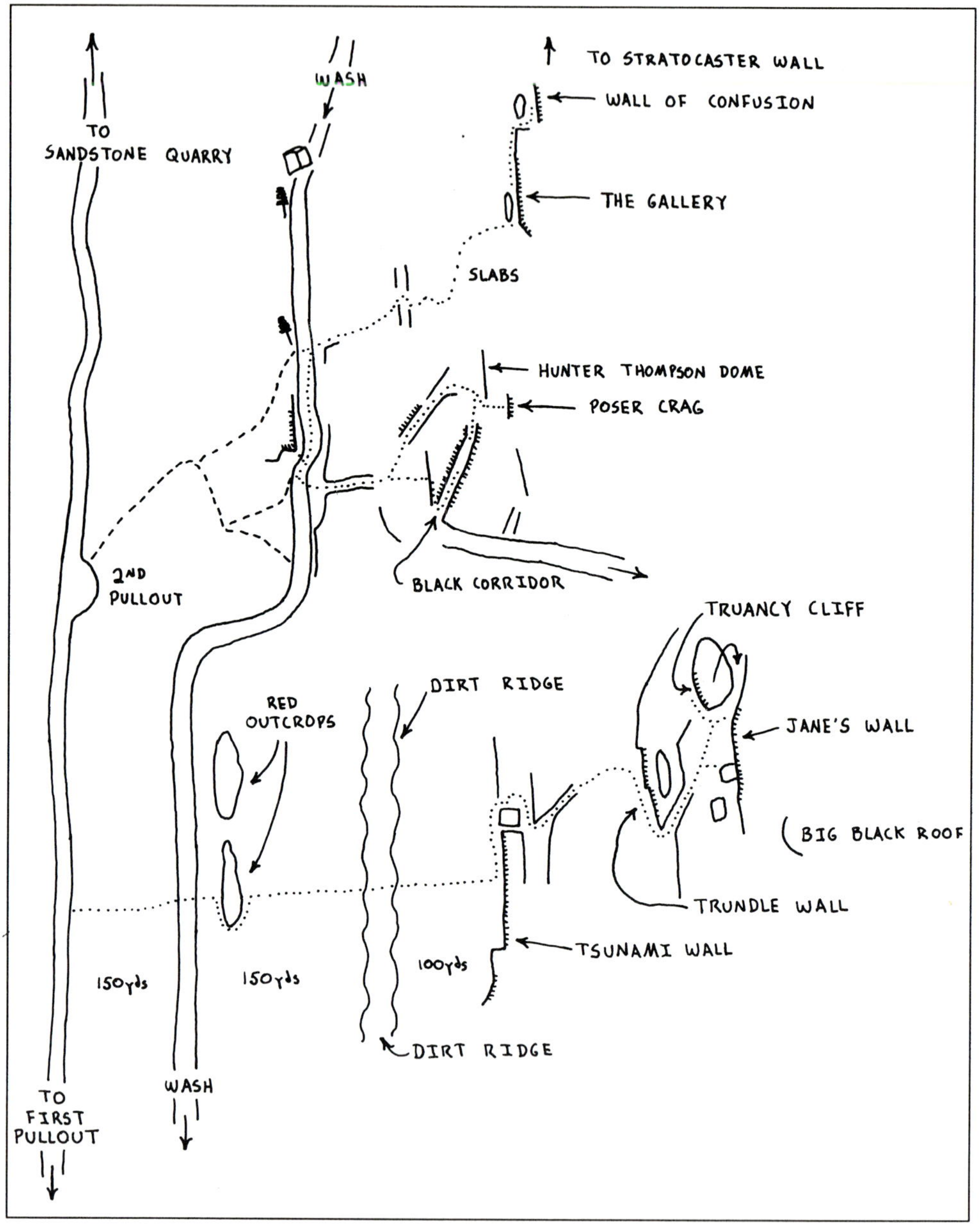

Map of the crags at the Second Pullout.

SECOND PULLOUT

This area has some of the best sport climbing cliffs at Red Rocks. Both The Gallery and the Wall of Confusion are of excellent quality, and extremely popular. Park at the Second Pullout, 1.7 miles from the start of the scenic loop road, to approach any of these crags.

The Gallery

From the parking area, walk down the main trail, then take the first trail branching off to the left (about 120 yards from the lot). Follow this lesser-used trail about 400 yards up over a red outcrop (the top of the **Meister's Edge** and **Jonny Rotten** formation), then down to a wash and pine tree. Cross the wash immediately (well before another pine and a large, red cube of rock) and follow a well-used path up broken slabs 100 yards to a small corridor running parallel to the hillside. Scramble up the far wall of the corridor (about 30 feet), then angle up left across slabs for 75 yards to the base of the wall. You should arrive at the right (east) end of the crag, under the most overhanging section of rock. This approach takes about 15 minutes, and involves some scrambling. The cliff is visible from the road (although it looks very small and insignificant) and is in the sun most of the day. Routes are described from right to left. All routes have anchors to grab, lower, rappel, or toprope from.

1 **Witch's Honor 5.8**
FA: Danny Meyers – circa 1988
This route is on the red slab to the right (east) of The Gallery, directly above the approach slabs. Start at a large hueco and climb a vertical crack until it heads right. Follow the crack right, then pull a bulge to a two-bolt belay. Rappel with two ropes.

2 **Glitch 5.12c/d**
FA: Mike Tupper – Winter 1990
Start 10 feet left of an alcove on the right side of the wall. Follow a right-leaning flake past four bolts, then continue up right past a hueco and two more bolts to the anchor.

3 **Nothing Shocking 5.13a/b**
FA: Don Welsh – Winter 1989/90
Climb **Glitch** to the third bolt, then power straight up past three more bolts to the end of **The Sissy Traverse.**

4 **Who Made Who 5.12c/d**
FA: Mike Tupper – Winter 1989/90
Climb **Glitch** to the second bolt, then continue up past three more.

5 **Where The Down Boys Go 5.12d**
FA: Mike Tupper – Winter 1989/90
Start at the bottom of the flake ascended in the previous three routes, and go up and slightly left past five bolts.

6 **The Gift 5.12d**
FA: Boone Speed – Winter 1989/90
Start at the base of **Yaak Crack** and climb up very steep rock past six bolts.

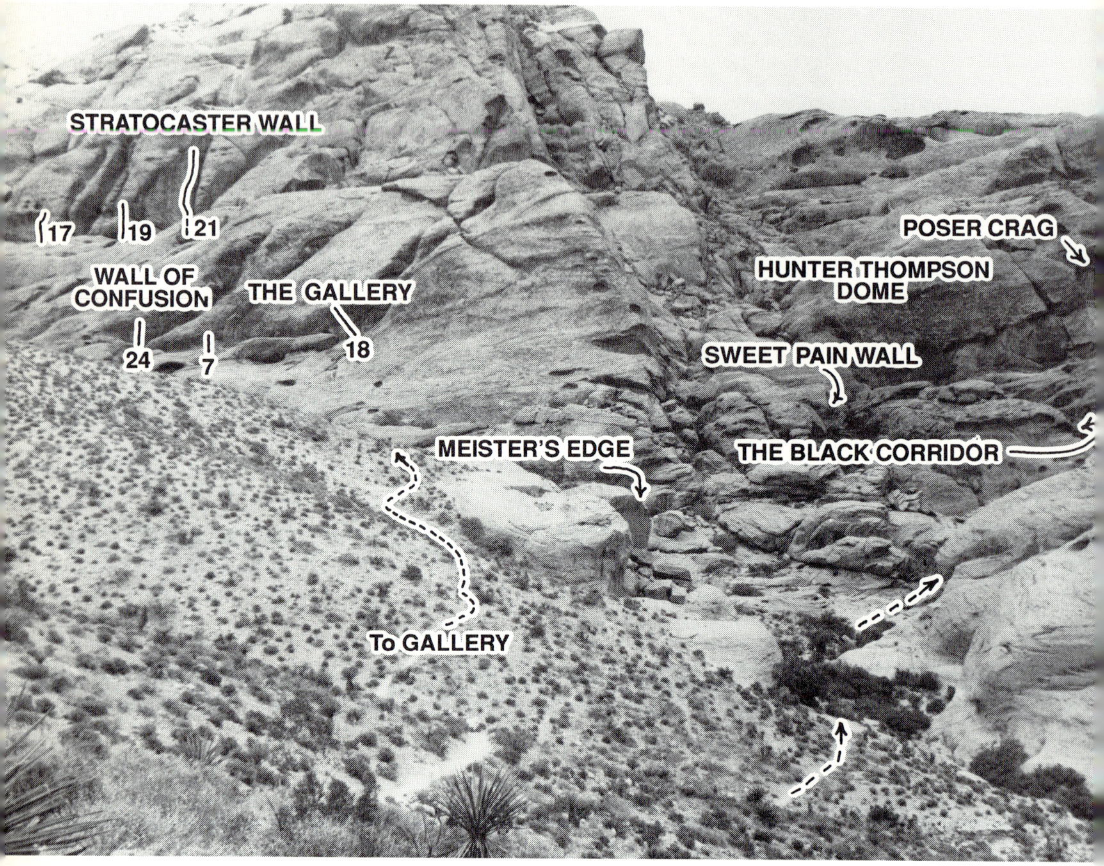

Second Pullout as seen from the parking area

Stratocaster Wall (*described in Sandstone Quarry Chapter*)
17 **Cut Loose 5.11–** 👍
19 **The Choad Warrior 5.12c** 👍
21 **Stratocaster 5.11+** 👍

Wall of Confusion
24 **Desert Pickle 5.11b/c**

The Gallery
7 **Yaak Crack 5.11c/d** 👍
18 **Range Of Motion 5.11a/b**

7 **Yaak Crack 5.11c/d** 👍
FA: Bill Boyle – Winter 1989/90
Begin eight feet left of the last four routes, and below the obvious, left-leaning crack. Climb the crack past six bolts.

8 **The Sissy Traverse 5.13b** 👍
FA: Don Welsh – Fall 1991
Start in the corridor behind the right edge of the huge boulder 15 feet left of **Yaak Crack.** The bolts on this route have been painted black, so you know you're on the right route! Climb up to the first bolt (V1), then angle right and up past eight more black bolts.

V1 Start at the base of **Yaak Crack** and climb past the first three bolts on **The Gift** before going up right past five more bolts. This seems to be the more logical line.

9 **Minstrel In The Gallery 5.12b/c**
FA: Mike Tupper – Winter 1989/90
The first route developed on the cliff. Start as for **The Sissy Traverse** and climb the face just left of **Yaak Crack** past five bolts.

10 **A Day In The Life 5.11b/c**
FA: Bill Boyle – Winter 1989/90
Begin 10 feet left of **Minstrel,** behind the huge boulder and on the left side of a cat's claw bush. Cruise out the right side of the pod past five bolts.

11 **Social Disorder 5.11d**
FA: Scott (aka Jimmy Dean), Bucky, and Jonathan Knight – 1991
Rope up as for **A Day In The Life,** then climb straight up from the pod past five bolts.

12 **Gridlock 5.11c/d**
FA: Greg Mayer – Spring 1990
Start as for the past two routes, but exit out the left side of the pod, passing four bolts with homemade hangers. It's a little easier to go left then back right between the second and third bolts.

13 **Running Amuck 5.10c**
FA: Greg Mayer – Spring 1990
Rope up 10 feet left of **Gridlock,** below a short, left-facing flake and up on a ledge. Run past four bolts to the same anchor as **Gridlock.**

14 **Pump First, Pay Later 5.10b/c**
FA: Greg Mayer – Spring 1990
Don't run out of gas before you get to the anchor! Start six feet left of **Running Amuck,** and clip four bolts.

15 **Gelatin Pooch 5.10a**
FA: Greg Mayer – Spring 1990
Begin six feet left of **Pump First, Pay Later,** and climb past four bolts (three have homemade hangers) to chains.

16 **Buck's Muscle World 5.9-**
FA: Greg Mayer – Spring 1990
You'll find this three-bolt route, with homemade hangers, eight feet left of **Gelatin Pooch.**

17 **Sport Climbing Is Neither 5.8**
FA: Unknown – Winter 1991
Start 10 feet left of **Buck's Muscle World** at a short, curving crack. Three bolts to an anchor. This was named after a bumper sticker on John Sherman's van.

18 **Range Of Motion 5.11a/b**
FA: Todd Swain, Dick Peterson, Peggy Buckey – May, 1990
Start about 75 feet left of **Buck's Muscle World,** and 20 feet left of a right-facing corner that doesn't reach the ground. Climb up through a pod, passing four bolts.

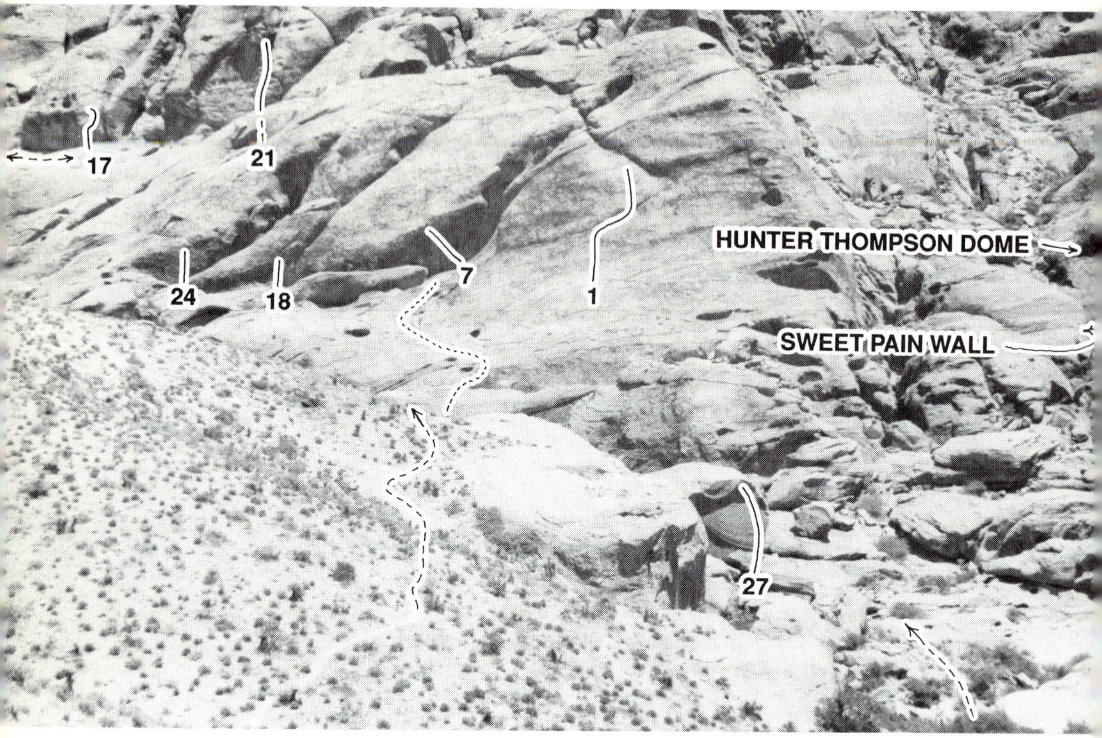

Overview of the Second Pullout area

Stratocaster Wall (described in Sandstone Quarry Chapter)
17 **Cut Loose 5.11–**
21 **Stratocaster 5.11+**
Wall of Confusion
24 **Desert Pickle 5.11b/c**

The Gallery
18 **Range Of Motion 5.11a/b**
7 **Yaak Crack 5.11c/d**
1 **Witch's Honor 5.8**
Meister's Edge
27 **Meister's Edge 5.11a**

Wall Of Confusion

This cliff is about 150 feet left of The Gallery, on the same level. Routes are described from right to left, as the normal approach is from The Gallery. All routes have anchors. Believe it or not, these routes were done before The Gallery was developed.

19 **Body English 5.12c**
FA: Mike Tupper – Winter 1988
Start 30 feet up and right of **Fear And Loathing** at the very right end of the cliff. Climb the steep corner past four bolts to chains (or go left to the **Fear...** anchor).

20 **Fear And Loathing 5.12a**
FA: Bill Boyle, Boone Speed – Winter 1988
One of the steepest routes you'll see - until you go to The Trophy. Start atop a boulder in an alcove and power past several roofs on an overhanging wall. Nine bolts provide convenient places to hang and rest.

21 **Promises In The Dark** **5.12b**
FA: Mike Tupper – Winter 1988
Begin 12 feet left of **Fear And Loathing** at a short dihedral capped by a ceiling. Zip past seven bolts to the anchor.

22 **Big Damage** **5.12b**
FA: Boone Speed – Winter 1988
Start six feet left of **Promises in the Dark** at a right-curving crack, and climb up and slightly left past seven bolts.

23 **Sudden Impact** **5.11c**
FA: Boone Speed, Bill Boyle – Winter 1988
Climb the face eight feet left of **Big Damage**, passing five bolts.

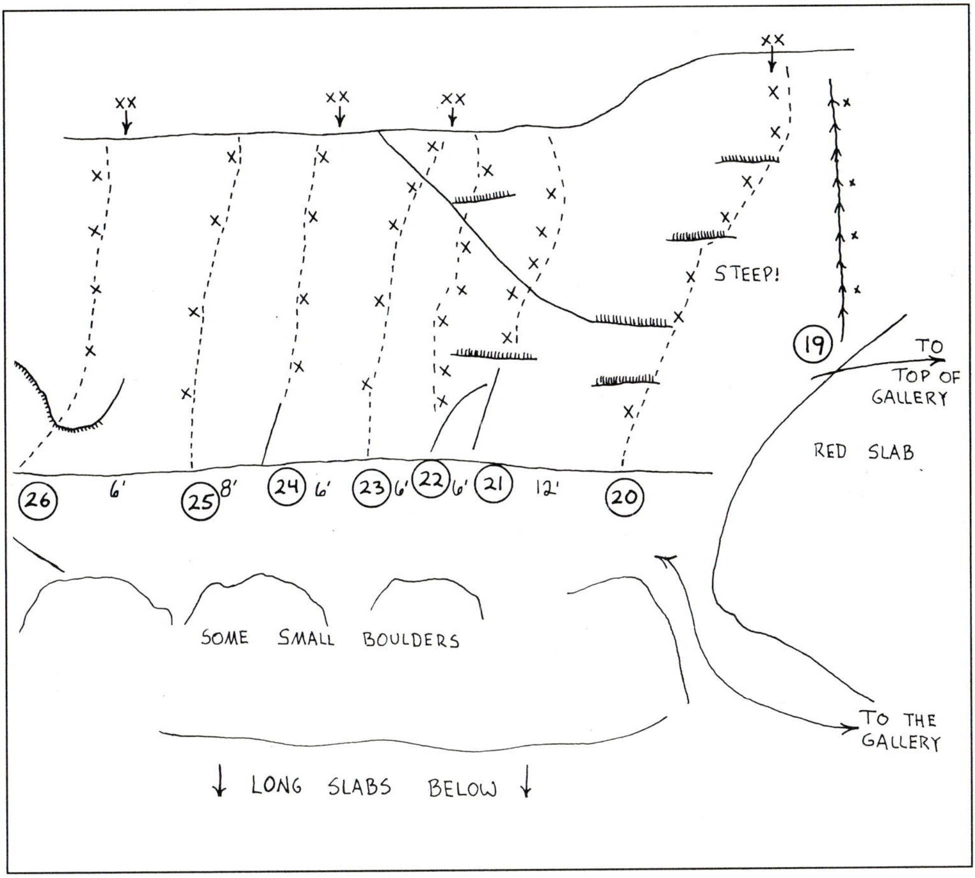

Wall of Confusion

26 **The Runaway** **5.10b** **PG**
25 **American Sportsman** **5.10c**
24 **Desert Pickle** **5.11b/c**
23 **Sudden Impact** **5.11c**
22 **Big Damage** **5.12b**
21 **Promises In The Dark** **5.12b**
20 **Fear And Loathing** **5.12a**
19 **Body English** **5.12c**

24 **Desert Pickle 5.11b/c**
FA: Bill Boyle, Boone Speed – Winter 1988
Power up the wall six feet left of **Sudden Impact**, using four bolts.

25 **American Sportsman 5.10c**
FA: Boone Speed, Bill Boyle – Winter 1988
Another four-bolt route six feet left of **American Sportsman.**

26 **The Runaway 5.10b PG**
FA: Greg Mayer – Spring 1989
The leftmost route on the cliff, this starts up on a ledge. Four bolts with homemade hangers provide the pro.

MEISTER'S EDGE AREA

27 **Meister's Edge 5.11a**
FA: Joe Herbst (TR) – early 1970s
This short but striking arête is located just above the wash as you approach the Black Corridor, or Sweet Pain Wall. It was bolted in 1988, after being soloed by at least a couple of brave locals. Follow the trail down from the second pullout and take the second left-branching trail (the first goes to The Gallery/Wall of Confusion). Follow this red, sandy trail for 50 yards along the base of a red, crumbly cliff, then turn slightly left and look up. The route starts off giant angular blocks, has three bolts on it, and no anchor.

28 **Jonny Rotten 5.11–**
FA: Sal Mamusia, Paul Van Betten – 1987
A typical Navajo sandstone crack climb. Not as good as **The Fox,** but maybe you'll like it . . . Climb the steep, loose, right-leaning crack 50 feet right of **Meister's Edge,** and right above the streambed. It's in the shade most of the day.

29 **Jonny Jamcrack 5.8**
FA: Sal Mamusia, Paul Van Betten – 1987
Climb the crack 15 feet right of **Jonny Rotten.**

Sweet Pain Wall

The approach is fairly straightforward, although this small crag can't be seen from the parking lot. Follow the trail down from the second pullout and take the second left (the first goes to The Gallery/Wall of Confusion). Follow this trail across a red sandy area, then turn slightly right into a drainage (the main wash curves left [west] toward The Gallery). Scramble 100 yards over rocks (you may have to avoid water) to an open area. Slightly left of center is an obvious gully with a steep wall on the left that faces northeast. This is the Sweet Pain Wall; it is about 80 yards up the gully from the open area. Routes are described from left to right as you approach the cliff. If you continue up the gully for another 150 feet, you'll come to a large, plated face. This is Hunter S. Thompson Dome (named for the author of *Fear and Loathing in Las Vegas*), and has numerous routes on it that aren't described in this guide. From here, you can access the Black Corridor's top entrance by simply walking down and right about 50 feet.

30 **Sweet Pain 5.12a**
FA: Leo Henson, Randy Faulk – 1991
Start in the center of the cliff at the bottom of a rotten, right leaning crack with blocky ceilings above. Five bolts lead up and left through angular ceilings to a chain anchor.

31 **Glitter Gulch 5.10b**
FA: Guys from Colorado – 1991
Begin 40 feet right of **Sweet Pain** on a ledge 15 feet off the ground. Angle up and left past six bolts to chains.

32 **Slave To The Grind 5.11b**
FA: Guys from Colorado – 1991
Start as for **Glitter Gulch,** but climb straight up, passing a right-leaning gash with a bush at midheight. Seven bolts with a cold shut anchor.

Note: On the back of the Sweet Pain formation is another wall with at least three routes:

33 **Stone Hammer 5.10**
FA: Mike Ward – 1986
This climbs a corner to a steep bolted face, then to a two-bolt belay. The next route is about 100 feet left and follows bolts up a brown varnished face over a bulge (5.10). It was done in August 1992 by Daryl Ellis. The face just left of this was toproped in the summer of 1992 by Brad Stewart.

THE BLACK CORRIDOR

This generally east - west running corridor hosts a total of about 25 routes on both walls. The climbs are generally of a moderate nature, making this a popular destination. For an added challenge, try to do all of the routes in a day! This is also a good place to experience the true meaning of "generic" sport climbs. Hopefully, this sort of "development" won't be repeated in too many other places . . .

The approach is quite simple, although neither the corridor or its entrance can be seen from the parking lot. Follow the trail down from the second pullout and take the second left (the first goes to The Gallery/Wall of Confusion). Follow this trail across a red sandy area, then turn slightly right into a drainage (the main wash curves left [west] toward The Gallery). Scramble 100 yards over rocks (you may have to avoid water) to an open area. Continue straight north 50 yards until progress is blocked by a bush-filled corridor. Traverse 75 feet right (east) on a ledge system just above the bushes, then curve left toward trees at the entrance of the corridor. This sounds complicated, but once you've done it, the approach takes less than ten minutes. These climbs are in the shade most of the time, and are described from the lower entrance up the corridor. All have anchors on top.

Left (south) Wall, Lower Level

34 **Bonaire 5.9**
FA: Jim Steagall, Kevin Sandefur, Chris Werner, Dave Sobocan
(all from Phoenix, AZ) – Fall 1990
Start 75 feet from the lower corridor entrance. Climb past six bolts with homemade hangers to a three-bolt anchor.

35 **Bon Ez 5.9+**
FA: Steagall, Sandefur, Werner, Sobocan – Fall 1990
Begin 20 feet right of **Bonaire** and climb past seven cold shuts to a three cold shut anchor.

36 **Crude Boys 5.10d PG**
FA: Steagall, Sandefur, Werner, Sobocan – Fall 1990
Rope up 15 feet right of **Bon Ez,** then clip six cold shuts enroute to a two-bolt anchor on top. There is an overhang in the middle of the route.

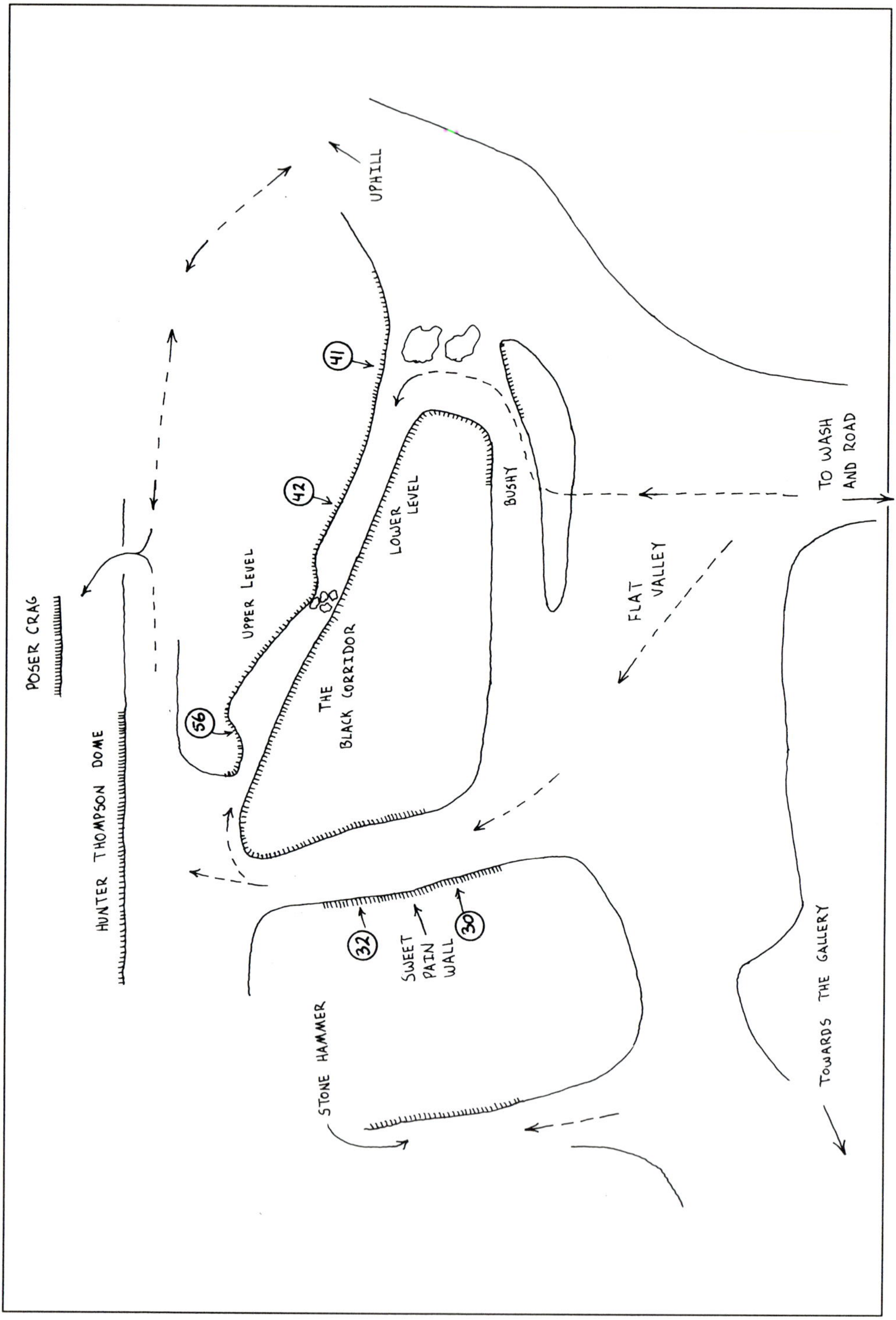
UPHILL
TO WASH
AND ROAD
BUSHY
LOWER
LEVEL
UPPER LEVEL
41
42
56
POSER CRAG
THE
BLACK CORRIDOR
FLAT
VALLEY
HUNTER THOMPSON DOME
32
SWEET
PAIN
WALL
30
STONE HAMMER
TOWARDS THE GALLERY

Black Corridor Area map (on pg. 40)

Sweet Pain Wall
30 **Sweet Pain** 5.12a
32 **Slave To The Grind** 5.11b

The Black Corridor
56 **Rebel Without A Pause** 5.11a/b
42 **Nightmare On Crude Street** 5.10d
41 **Adoption** 5.11b

37 **Black Corridor Route 4 Left** 5.11a/b
FA: who knows? – 1991 or later
This route has now been led at least up to the horizontal break, but still shares the anchor with **Crude Boys.** Deceptively difficult. Start eight feet right of **Crude Boys** and climb the slippery rock past two bolts to a horizontal crack. Move left and finish on **Crude Boys.**

38 **BCR 5L** 5.10+
FA: Steagall, Sandefur, Werner, Sobocan – Fall 1990
Begin 10 feet right of the **Black Corridor Route 4 Left** and 20 feet left of the boulders that divide the corridor into two levels. Climb past one bolt to a thin vertical crack, which is followed to the top.

39 **Vagabonds** 5.10a
FA: Steagall, Sandefur, Werner, Sobocan – Fall 1990
Climb the groove and face six feet right of the previous route, clipping eight cold shuts on your way to the anchor.

40 **Crude Control** 5.12a
FA: Steagall, Sandefur, Werner, Sobocan – Fall 1990
Contrived and difficult at the start. Begin 12 feet right of **Vagabonds,** and just left of the boulders that divide the corridor into two levels. Six cold shuts lead to the anchor.

Right (north) Wall, Basement

41 **Adoption** 5.11b
FA: Leo Henson, Karin Olson – November, 1991
Climb the plated face at the entrance to the corridor, passing six bolts.

42 **Nightmare On Crude Street** 5.10d
FA: Jim Steagall, Kevin Sandefur, Chris Werner, Dave Sobocan – Fall 1990
A little loose, but that gives it some character. This route is directly across from **Bonaire** (the route with homemade hangers), and climbs overhanging, red rock past four cold shuts and one bolt to a two shut anchor. Climbing directly between each bolt makes the climb about 5.11b and contrived.

Left Wall, Upper Level

43 **Thermal Breakdown** 5.9+
FA: Steagall, Sandefur, Werner, Sobocan – Fall 1990
Begin atop the dividing boulders and cruise past some big ledges and six cold shuts.

44 **Crude Street Blues** 5.9+
FA: Steagall, Sandefur, Werner, Sobocan – Fall 1990
Start 15 feet right of **Thermal Breakdown** at a cold shut. Climb past ledges and four more shuts to the anchor.

45 ***Crude Behavior 5.9+/10a***
FA: Steagall, Sandefur, Werner, Sobocan – Fall 1990
Rope up eight feet right of **Crude Street Blues** at a ramp. Scamper past four cold shuts to a two-shut anchor.

46 ***Dancin' With A God 5.10a***
FA: Steagall, Sandefur, Werner, Sobocan – Fall 1990
One of the better routes in its grade. Start 12 feet right of the last route and 35 feet right of the dividing boulders. Follow six cold shuts to a two-shut station.

47 ***Live Fast, Die Young 5.10d***
FA: Steagall, Sandefur, Werner, Sobocan – Fall 1990
This one may be harder for tall folks. It is eight feet right of **Dancin' With a God.** Five shuts lead to the anchor - if you can do the mantel at the start.

48 ***Black Gold 5.10b***
FA: Dudes From Phoenix – Fall 1990
Begin six feet to the right of **Live Fast, Die Young** at a small flake. Five bolts with hangers lead to chains.

49 ***Texas Tea 5.10a/b***
FA: Guys from Phoenix – Fall 1990
Start eight feet right of **Black Gold** at the left edge of a large flake. Climb the smooth face to a small ceiling (shut), then up past four more to a two cold shut anchor. The crux is at the bottom, and is contrived.

50 ***Fool's Gold 5.9+***
FA: Steagall, Sandefur, Werner, Sobocan – Fall 1990
Begin in the same place as **Texas Tea,** but walk up right on a ramp. Face climb past numerous huecos and five shuts to a two-shut anchor.

Right Wall, Second Story

51 ***Oils Well That Ends Well 5.11a***
FA: Steagall, Sandefur, Werner, Sobocan – Fall 1990
Start about 10 feet left of the dividing boulders and just left of a right leaning crack system. Climb past five cold shuts (if you get past the second, you should be home free) to the anchor.

52 ***Sandstone Enema 5.11b/c***
FA: Steagall, Sandefur, Werner, Sobocan – Fall 1990
Begin 10 feet left of **Oils Well . . .** below a short, right-leaning ramp, and 10 feet right of a sentry box. Tricky moves past the first two cold shuts lead to easier climbing past four more on the "slabby" face above. If you start on the left and climb by the hangerless, quarter-inch bolt, the route is 5.10d/11a.

53 ***Lude, Crude, And Misconstrued 5.9+ PG***
FA: Steagall, Sandefur, Werner, Sobocan – Fall 1990
One of the longer routes in the corridor. Start at a sentry box/left-facing corner 10 feet left of **Sandstone Enema,** and just left of a boulder in the corridor. Power up the corner and arête past six cold shuts to the anchor.

54 ***Texas Lite Sweet 5.11b PG***
FA: Rad Men From Phoenix – Fall 1990
Rope up six feet left of **Lude, Crude and Misconstrued,** and climb past three bolts with hangers to a chain anchor under a ceiling.

55 **Livin' On Borrowed Time 5.11c/d**
FA: Steagall, Sandefur, Werner, Sobocan – Fall 1990
Begin three feet left of the last route at smooth, varnished rock with a crescent-shaped hold by the first bolt. Four cold shuts lead to the anchor.

56 **Rebel Without A Pause 5.11a/b**
FA: Steagall, Sandefur, Werner, Sobocan – Fall 1990
Probably the best route here. Climb the overhanging huecos 50 feet left of the previous route, and just right of the upper entrance to the Black Corridor. Four bolts lead to a chain anchor.

Poser Crag

Two routes have been done on this wall, which is technically part of Hunter S. Thompson Dome. The Poser Crag is right, and slightly behind the main face on Hunter S. Thompson Dome, and directly above and behind the Black Corridor. To approach this southeast-facing cliff, follow the trail down from the second pullout and take the second left (the first goes to The Gallery/Wall of Confusion). Follow this trail across a red sandy area, then turn slightly right into a drainage (the main wash curves left [west] toward The Gallery). Scramble 100 yards over rocks (you may have to avoid water) to an open area. Slightly left of center is an obvious gully with a steep wall on the left that faces northeast. This is the Sweet Pain Wall; it is about 80 yards up the gully from the open area. If you continue up the gully 150 feet, you'll come to the large, plated face of the Hunter S. Thompson Dome. Walk right (east) along the base of this wall until you can scramble back up left to The Poser Crag. It is characterized by a large, dark patch of varnish near its right edge.

57 **Special Guest Posers 5.11a**
FA: Randy Marsh, Pier Locatelli – Fall 1990
This is the left route, and climbs past four bolts to chains.

58 **Tin Horn Posers 5.11c/d**
FA: Randy Marsh, Randy Faulk, Dimitri Barton (of Yosemite fame) – Fall 1990
The right route, with five bolts. This route climbs near the right arête of the formation.

TSUNAMI WALL, TRUNDLE WALL, JANE'S WALL AND TRUANCY CLIFF APPROACH

These four crags are all within 150 yards of each other, and are located about 500 yards northeast of the second pullout. All face the road and sit fairly high up on the hillside. The approach described here is not the most direct way to reach the cliffs, but once you've made it to the climbs, you can figure out a better way back to the parking lot.

Walk down the road from the second pullout toward the first pullout about 300 yards, to the end of the red rock outcrops within the drainage on your left. Looking at the larger hillside behind these outcrops, you now can see all of the aforementioned cliffs lined up in a row. The Tsunami Wall is the lowest crag, and is easily recognized by its rectangular boxcar shape, with a huge, detached block on its left side. The other three cliffs are about 100 yards directly above. From this point on the loop road, walk down into the drainage, then up the other side to the top of the dirt ridge above the outcrops (about 300 yards total). The Tsunami Wall is now about 100 yards in front of you.

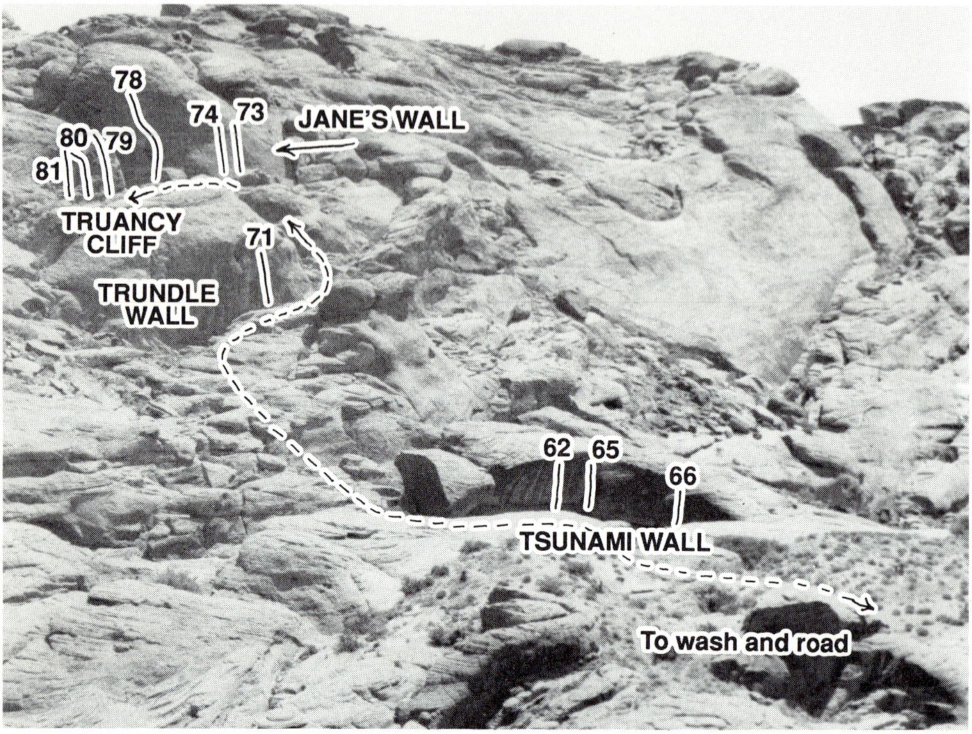

Tsunami Wall et al. as seen from the road

Truancy Cliff
81 **Doctor's Orders 5.10b**
80 **Playing Hooky 5.10a**
79 **Ditch Day 5.7**
Jane's Wall
78 **Every Mother's Nightmare 5.12b** 👍
74 **Idiots Rule 5.11b/c**
73 **See Dick Fly 5.10d**

Trundle Wall
71 **Life Out Of Balance 5.11c/d**
Tsunami Wall
62 **SOS 5.13a**
65 **Abandon Ship 5.12a**
66 **Tremor 5.10a/b**

Tsunami Wall

Routes on this wildly overhanging wave of rock are about 40 feet long, face the road and are in the shade in the morning. The righthand part of the wall is less steep, and smaller. Climbs are described from left to right. All have anchors on top.

59 **Land Shark 5.12b**
FA: Leo Henson – January, 1992
Rope up 40 feet right of a huge detached block, at a boulder under the low roof running along the base of the cliff. Three routes start here, and share the same first two bolts. Climb up and left past a total of six bolts to the anchor.

60 **Angler 5.12c**
FA: Leo Henson – January, 1992
Start as for **Land Shark,** but continue straight up after the third bolt to an anchor.

61 **Threadfin 5.12c**
FA: Leo Henson – January, 1992
Begin as for **Land Shark** and follow the line of bolts straight up to chains.

62 **SOS 5.13a**
FA: Leo Henson – January, 1992
You may need help on this one! Start 10 feet right of **Land Shark** on the left edge of a block under the low roof. Move left to a horn, then up the seam past five bolts.

63 **Man Overboard! 5.12d**
FA: Leo Henson – January, 1992
Begin five feet right of **SOS** in the center of the block under the low roof. Six bolts lead to chains.

64 **Aftershock 5.12b**
FA: Randy Faulk, Leo Henson – January, 1992
Rope up four feet right of **Man Overboard!**, at the right end of the block under the low roof. Five bolts and strong fingers will get you to the cold shut anchor.

65 **Abandon Ship 5.12a**
FA: Randy Faulk, Leo Henson – January, 1992
Start 10 feet right of **Aftershock** at a dihedral that marks the right edge of the "wave." Climb up and left past five bolts.

66 **Tremor 5.10a/b**
FA: Leo & Karin Henson – February, 1992
Begin 25 feet right of the **Abandon Ship** dihedral on a smaller, broken section of cliff. Four bolts and chains mark the route.

67 **Low Tide 5.10a/b**
FA: Leo & Karin Henson – February, 1992
Start 30 feet right of the last route on the right side of a low ceiling, and climb up along a varnished seam past four bolts.

Trundle Wall

As of press time, there were still some projects in the works here. To reach this crag, walk down the road from the second pullout toward the first pullout about 300 yards, to the end of the red rock outcrops within the drainage on your left. Looking at the larger hillside behind these outcrops in the drainage, you now can see all of the area cliffs lined up in a row. The Tsunami Wall is the lowest crag, and is easily recognized by its rectangular boxcar shape, with a huge, detached block on its left side. The Trundle Wall is about 100 yards directly above. From this point along the loop road, walk down into the drainage, then up the other side to the top of the dirt ridge right above the outcrops (about 300 yards total). The Tsunami Wall is about 100 yards in front of you. Walk past the left (west) edge of the Tsunami, and continue about 100 yards up the hillside to the next obvious cliff (Trundle Wall). These sunny routes are described from left to right as you approach the cliff.

68 **Standing In The Shadows 5.12a**
FA: Greg Mayer – Winter 1990
Begin 10 feet right of a big, rotten, right-facing corner. Climb up and left past two bolts to a left-facing flake/corner, then straight up past four more bolts to the chain anchor.

69 **Project At Press Time 5.12c/d?**
FA: ? – after November, 1992
Rope up five feet right of **Standing in the Shadows** and zip past five bolts with homemade hangers to chains.

70 **Pocket Rocket 5.11d**
FA: Mike Tupper – Winter 1990
Start 15 feet right of the last route. Power past two bolts with homemade, tan colored hangers, then go up and slightly left to the chains.

71 **Life Out Of Balance 5.11c/d**
FA: Mike Tupper, Greg Mayer – Winter 1990
Begin six feet right of **Pocket Rocket,** and just left of an obvious, right-facing flake/corner that leads to a huge hole. Finger traverse left, then up past four bolts to an anchor just left of the huge hole.

72 **Stop The Presses! 5.11a/b?**
FA: ? – after November, 1992
A line has been conceived to the right of the right facing flake/corner. At press time only the chain anchor had been installed.

Jane's Wall

Jane's Wall is a large, dark, rounded formation near the top of the ridge, with a huge, black roof just up and to its right. To reach this crag, walk down the road from the second pullout toward the first pullout about 300 yards, to the end of the red rock outcrops within the drainage on your left. Looking at the larger hillside behind these outcrops in the drainage, you can now see all the area cliffs lined up in a row. The Tsunami Wall is the lowest crag, and is easily recognized by its rectangular boxcar shape and the huge, detached block on its left side. Jane's Wall is the second obvious cliff about 150 yards directly above. From this point along the loop road, walk down into the drainage, then up the other side to the top of the dirt ridge right above the outcrops (about 300 yards total). The Tsunami Wall is about 100 yards in front of you. Walk past the left (west) edge of the Tsunami, and continue about 100 yards up the hillside to the next obvious cliff (the Trundle Wall). Go to the right (east) end of the wall, then scramble 150 feet up a gully to the base of Jane's Wall, which is characterized by a smooth black face capped by an overhang on its left side. The cliff faces the road, and is in the sun the majority of the day. All routes have anchors, and are described from right to left.

73 **See Dick Fly 5.10d**
FA: Greg Mayer – Spring 1991
Begin atop a block near the right edge of the crag. Climb a slab to steeper rock and the belay. The route has five bolts with homemade hangers.

74 **Idiots Rule 5.11b/c**
FA: Don Welsh – Fall 1990
Rope up 15 feet left of **See Dick Fly.** Scramble up a slab, step right, then up and slightly left past six bolts to a hook and chain.

75 **Pigs In Zen 5.12b**
FA: Don Welsh – Fall 1990
Start as for **Idiots Rule,** and scamper 40 feet up the slab to a cave. Exit left out of the cave, clipping a total of six bolts.

76 **Naked And Disfigured 5.12b/c**
FA: Don Welsh – Fall 1990

Begin 25 feet left of **Pigs In Zen,** at the mouth of a small corridor. Go up a low-angled, right-leaning ramp to the lowest point of the overhang; pull this, then power up the steep face to the anchor.

77 **Stealin' 5.12b**
FA: Don Welsh – Winter 1991
Done after **Every Mother's Nightmare,** this route is really a variation. Start at the mouth of the small corridor and zip up to a left-leaning crack under a sculptured arête. Follow bolts up the arête, then "escape" right and clip one more bolt before reaching the anchor.

78 **Every Mother's Nightmare 5.12b** 👍
FA: Greg Mayer – Fall 1990
Climb the overhanging, sculptured arête as for **Stealin',** then continue up left through roofs to the anchor. A total of six bolts are on the route.

Truancy Cliff

The three routes on this small cliff aren't too inspiring, but since they're within 50 feet of Jane's Wall, you can conveniently "tick" them off. To reach this crag, walk down the road from the second pullout toward the first pullout about 300 yards, to the end of the red rock outcrops within the drainage on your left. Looking at the larger hillside behind these outcrops in the drainage, you can now see all of the area cliffs lined up in a row. The Tsunami Wall is the lowest crag, and is easily recognized by its rectangular boxcar shape-and the huge, detached block on its left side. Jane's Wall is the second obvious cliff, about 150 yards directly above. From this point on the loop road, walk down into the drainage, then up the other side to the top of the dirt ridge above the outcrops (about 300 yards total). The Tsunami Wall is about 100 yards in front of you. Walk past the left (west) edge of the Tsunami, and continue about 100 yards up the hillside to the next obvious cliff (Trundle Wall). Go to the right (east) end of the wall, then scramble 150 feet up a gully to the base of Jane's Wall, which is characterized by a smooth black face capped by an overhang on its left side. Truancy Cliff is 50 feet to the left (west) of Jane's Wall. It faces the road, and is in the sun the majority of the day. Routes are described from right to left.

79 **Ditch Day 5.7**
FA: Todd Swain (solo) – July, 1991
Start near the right edge of the cliff below some very varnished huecos and horizontal cracks. Climb straight up the face using traditional pro (up to a #3 Friend). No anchors; walk off to the rear, then down the corridor between the Truancy Cliff and Jane's Wall.

80 **Playing Hooky 5.10a**
FA: Greg Mayer – Fall 1991
Begin eight feet left of **Ditch Day** at the base of a scoop/groove with three bolts. Wander up the face past the bolts, then move left to the chain anchor.

81 **Doctor's Orders 5.10b**
FA: Greg Mayer – Fall 1991
Climb the line of three bolts six feet left of **Playing Hooky** to the same chain anchor.

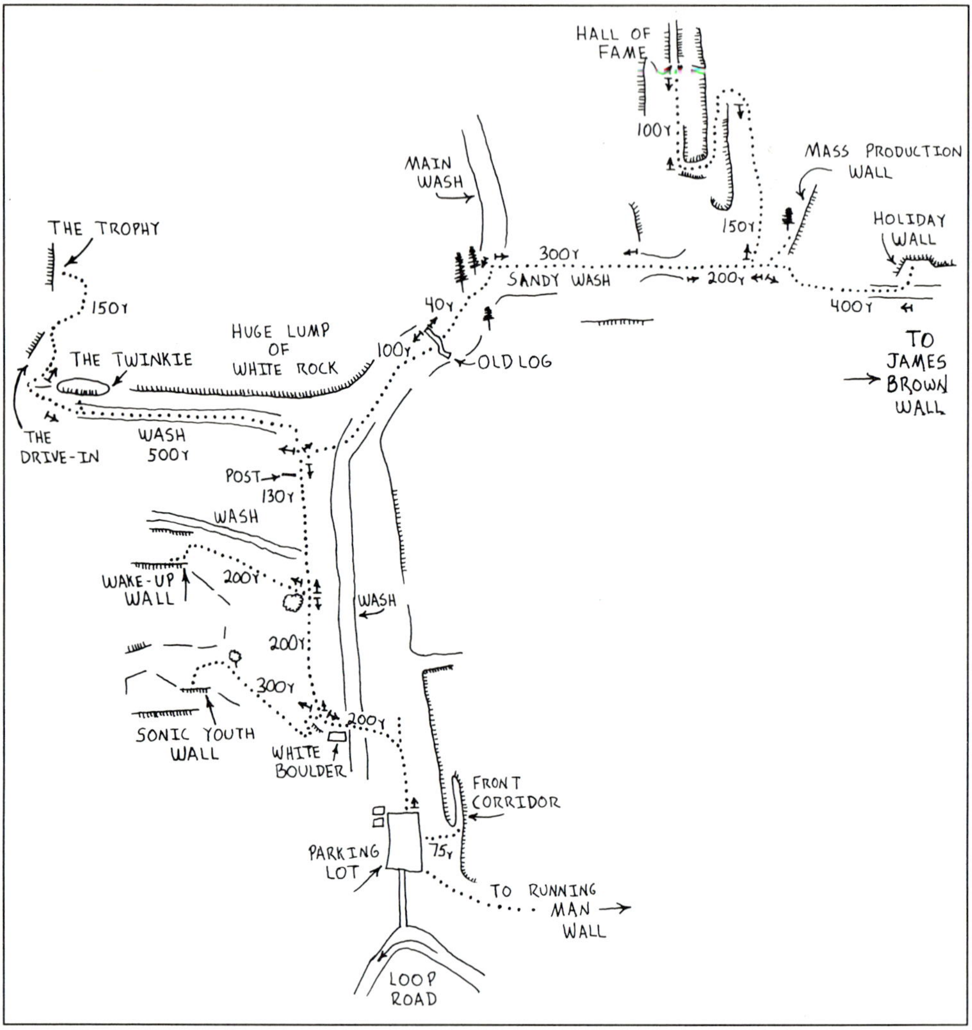

Sandstone Quarry Overview Map (not to scale).

SANDSTONE QUARRY AREA

This area has many worthwhile crags, containing climbs of all difficulties. The approaches range from 1 to 25 minutes, and most of the climbs are in the shade. Follow the scenic loop road 2.7 miles, and park in the large Sandstone Quarry parking lot.

The Running Man Wall

This fine and sunny cliff is southeast of the parking lot, in the direction of the second pull-out. From the southeast corner of the quarry parking lot, walk 50 yards down an old roadbed. Trend left along a faint path, aiming for the outermost section of exposed white rock (about 275 yards). Continue east on this trail along the right (south) slope of a small canyon, then drop down left (north) between two red outcrops to the bottom of the drainage. You'll pass a mushroom-shaped boulder just above the drainage bottom. Walk 50 yards down the drainage, passing two pine trees, then veer left (north) and scramble 100 yards up red slabs to a huge terrace with a large, black block above. Angle right (east) on the terrace for 125 yards to the cliff, which faces the loop road. It is characterized by a long, low roof running along the majority of the crag.

Routes are described from left to right, with the majority of the routes in this guide located near the right edge of the formation. Two ropes are needed to get off most routes.

1 **Boschton Marathon 5.12b**
FA: Geoff Wiegand – circa 1987
This route is not actually on The Running Man Wall, but is on the front of the large, black block mentioned in the approach description. It has six bolts, and a slightly tricky downclimb from the summit.

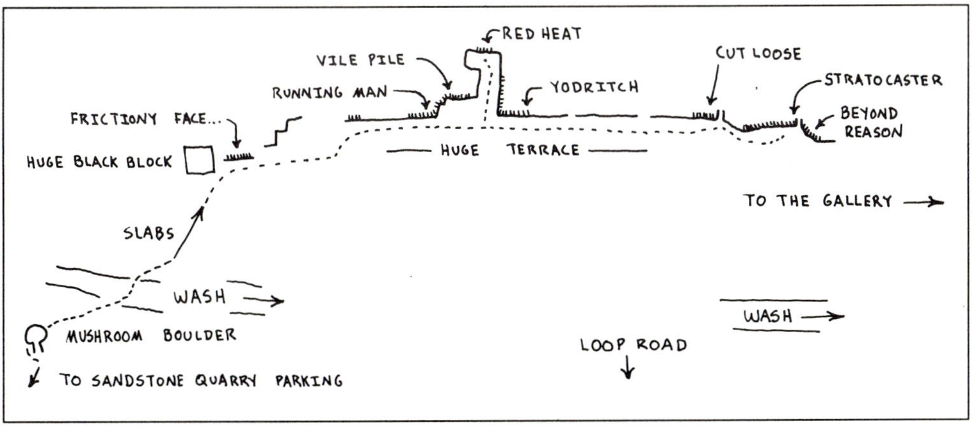

Running Man/Stratocaster Map

2 **Frictiony Face, Panty Waist** 5.8+ 👍
FA: Danny Meyers, Brad Stewart – February, 1989
This route is not actually on The Running Man Wall either, but is just right of the huge black block mentioned in the approach description. Start 20 feet up, on a ledge right of the huge block, and behind a large cat's claw bush. This classic route has six bolts, and ends at a two-bolt belay station 80 feet up.

3 **Calico Terror** 5.11 👎
FA: Mike Ward, Paul Van Betten – December, 1987
Sounds appealing, huh? This is near the left edge of The Running Man Wall. Climb past two bolts into a varnished, right-leaning crack, which is followed up and right past one more bolt to a two-bolt rap station.

4 **There Goes The Neighborhood** 5.11+
FA: Greg Mayer – 1989
Start atop a block and cheater stones 15 feet right of a tree that is near the right edge of the long, low roof. Climb past 11 bolts with black, homemade hangers to an anchor. Bring a # 1.5 Friend.

5 **New Traditionalists** 5.11c/d
FA: Mike Tupper – 1989
Begin 20 feet right of **There Goes The Neighborhood** below a line of bolts with SMC hangers. Power past 11 bolts on very smooth rock to the anchor. There are also bolts leading left from the third bolt on this route into a left-leaning crack (**The**

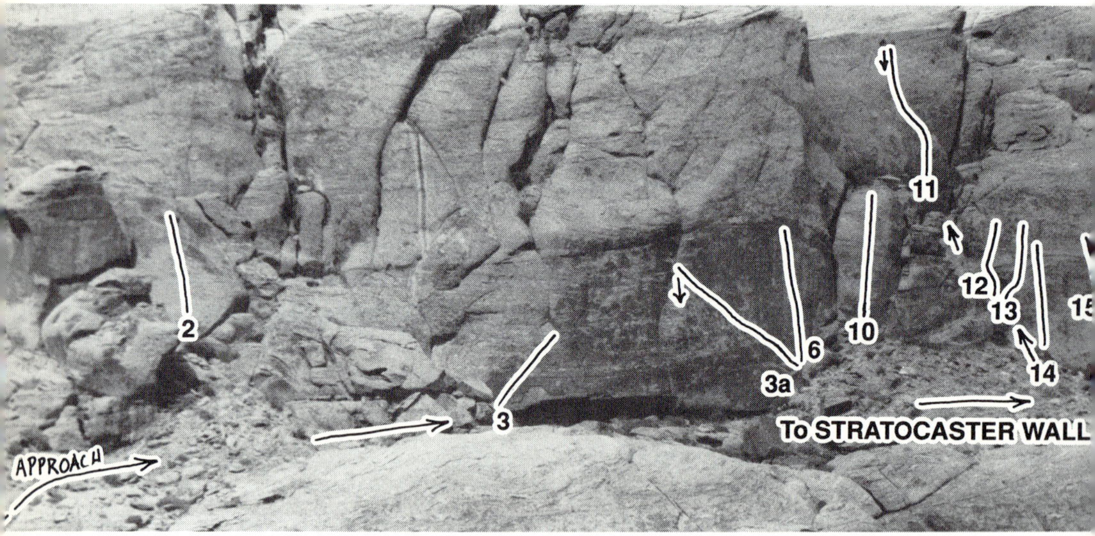

The Running Man Wall as seen from the loop road

2 Frictiony Face, Panty Waist 5.8+ 👍
3 Calico Terror 5.11 👎
3a The Predator 5.10+ R
6 Running Man 5.11 👍
10 Vile Pile 5.10
11 Red Heat 5.10+ 👍
12 Synthetic Society 5.11a/b
13 Plastic People 5.10b
14 Fibonacci Wall 5.11+
15 Northern Lights 5.11d

Predator, 5.10+, R), and a superfluous bolt with a homemade hanger just left of the start of the route.

6 **Running Man 5.11** 👍
FA: Paul Van Betten, Sal Mamusia, Mike Ward – November, 1987
Definitely better than the movie! One of the classic pitches at Red Rocks. Start 40 feet uphill and to the right of **New Traditionalists** below an obvious vertical seam system that trends slightly up and left. Use your Schwarzenegger-like muscles to power past 10 bolts to a bolt anchor. You may want to bring a few TCUs and small wires to supplement the bolts.

7 **Graveyard Waltz 5.11c/d PG** 👍
FA: Mike Tupper – 1989
Rather sporty. Start at the same spot as **Running Man,** but climb straight up past nine bolts with homemade hangers.

8 **Commando 5.11d**
FA: Louie Anderson, Bart Groendycke – 1992
Begin 10 feet right of **Graveyard Waltz** at the left edge of a low ceiling that is just left of a right-facing corner. Nine bolts lead to a three-shut anchor. At press time, an unfinished route started up a right-facing corner just right of **Commando.**

9 **Galloping Gal (aka Idaho Cowgirls) 5.11a/b**
FA: Folks from Spudland (Idaho) – 1990
Being tall helps on this one. Rope up 45 feet right of **Commado,** and three feet left of a left facing chimney/corner. Climb past 10 bolts to a chain anchor.

10 **Vile Pile 5.10**
FA: Mike Ward, Danny Meyers, Jessie Baxter – Fall 1989
Bring some TCUs and Friends. Start five feet right of **Galloping Gal** and zip past six bolts to the top of the block. Either lower off the last bolt, or scramble down the gully to the right (the approach to **Red Heat**).

11 **Red Heat 5.10+** 👍
FA: Nick Nordblom, Mike Ward, Danny Meyers – Fall 1989
Scramble 100 feet up the obvious gully 100 feet right of **Vile Pile** to ledges. Climb a right facing varnished groove past five bolts, then continue up the face past more bolts to an anchor in a hueco. Nine bolts total; bring some units; plan on a two rope rappel.

12 **Synthetic Society 5.11a/b**
FA: Mike Ward, Louie Anderson, Bart Groendycke – December, 1990
Scramble 40 feet up the **Red Heat** gully. On the right (east) wall of the gully, climb past the left edge of a ceiling and seven bolts to a chain anchor.

13 **Plastic People 5.10b**
FA: Louie Anderson, Bart Groendycke – December, 1990
Start as for **Synthetic Society,** 40 feet up the **Red Heat** gully. Trend out right to the arête, then up to the chain anchor, clipping eight bolts enroute.

14 **Fibonacci Wall 5.11+**
FA: Paul Van Betten, Don Welsh – 1987
If you're not a math major, you'll need to look this one up in the dictionary. The name should go with a 5.8 climb. No hooks were used on the FA – all the bolts were placed free on the lead. Climb the rounded arête on the right edge of the **Red Heat** gully past seven bolts.

15 **Northern Lights 5.11d**
FA: Unknown – circa 1991
Begin 40 feet down and right of the **Red Heat** gully on a slab, and just right of a rounded overhang at the base of the cliff. Stick clip the first bolt, then zoom past eight bolts to chains, keeping 10 feet left of a vertical crack (which has been climbed, and is a somewhat scary 5.10).

16 **Yodritch 5.11 R**
FA: Paul Van Betten, Mike Ward – Fall 1987
Start 30 feet right of **Northern Lights** at a line of bolts. Climb up and right past three bolts on a slab to a varnished crack (traditional pro here), then past one more bolt in steep rock to the belay. The second pitch has only one bolt, and is runout 5.8 to the top.

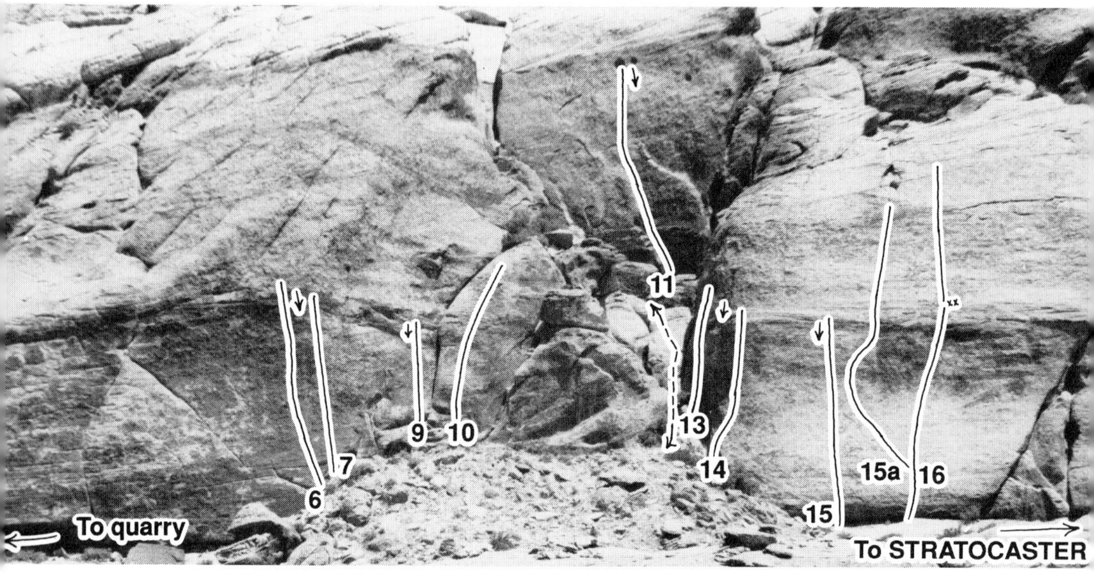

The Running Man Area

6 **Running Man 5.11** 👍
7 **Graveyard Waltz 5.11d PG** 👍
9 **Galloping Gal (aka Idaho Cowgirls) 5.11a/b**
10 **Vile Pile 5.10**
11 **Red Heat 5.10+** 👍
13 **Plastic People 5.10b**
14 **Fibonacci Wall 5.11+**
15 **Northern Lights 5.11d**
15a **5.10 Crack**
16 **Yodritch 5.11 R**

The Stratocaster Wall

This excellent cliff can be approached from either the second pullout, or Sandstone Quarry. It is about 400 yards right (east) of The Running Man Wall, on the same level. You'll pass at least a dozen routes between **Yodritch** and the left edge of this wall, none of which are described in this guide. The Stratocaster Wall has two sections, the leftmost of which is characterized by a deep chimney/corridor on its left side and a large roof in the center. Routes are described from left to right.

17 **Cut Loose 5.11–**

FA: Jay Smith, Nick Nordblom – Spring 1988

A good-looking route. Jam and lieback up the dihedral 20 feet right of the last route to the roof that is 40 feet up. Traverse out right past two bolts (crux) to a chain anchor.

18 **Footloose 5.11b**

FA: Unknown – 1991

Start 40 feet right of **Cut Loose,** at the right edge of the buttress and just left of a rotten, gray gully with huge huecos. Climb a short arête, then up the steep, blank face past a total of seven bolts.

19 **The Choad Warrior 5.12c**

FA: Dan McQuade, Leo Henson – Spring 1992

Steep! Rope up 75 feet right of the last route at the left side of an amphitheater, and eight feet left of a rotten, gray, right-slanting crack. Follow five bolts to a ledge, then climb out a huge bulge past six more bolts.

20 **Marshall Amp 5.11**

FA: Bob Conz, Shelby Shelton, Jay Smith, Paul Van Betten – March, 1991

Begin 50 feet right of **The Choad Warrior** and 30 feet left of the deepest part of the cave at a right slanting crack. Large holds get you to a ledge 20 feet up. Climb huecos past seven bolts to a belay station. 150 ft., 5.11.

21 **Stratocaster 5.11+**

FA: Jay Smith, Nick Nordblom – Spring 1988

You'll be wired after doing this one! Bring a variety of gear and two ropes. Start 65 feet right of the previous route (V1) at the base of a chimney with a prominent black waterstreak.

P1 Climb the chimney/corner to a pod 20 feet up, then move left (bolt) and go up to a belay station. 80 ft., 5.10, R.

P2 Follow cracks and huecos up the right arête of the wall, using bolts and natural gear for pro. Belay in the big hueco. 100 ft., 5.11+.

Descent: Rappel the route.

V1 Stratocaster Direct 5.12a

FA: Dan McQuade – 1991

Begin 15 feet left of **Stratocaster,** and just right of the deepest part of the cave. Power past five bolts to join **Stratocaster** at its first bolt.

22 **Beyond Reason 5.13b**

Installed by Craig Reason and Dan McQuade – completed in spring 1992

A worst-case example of bolting. Start 15 feet right of **Stratocaster** and climb past 15 (!) bolts to a three-bolt anchor that is 40 feet up.

23 **The Bristler 5.12–**

FA: Sal Mamusia, Paul Van Betten – 1987

Richard Harrison's term for a bolt, amongst other things (i.e.: "The Black Corridor is chock full of Bristlers"). This route climbs out the overhanging corner just right of **Beyond Reason** past two bolts, then up and over the next corner. Traverse right to a tree and rappel.

24 **Telecaster 5.11**

FA: Jay Smith, Paul Crawford – circa 1988

Climb the overhanging crack/corner 10 feet right of **The Bristler,** then follow the left facing arch/roof around left to a notch. Join **The Bristler** through the notch, then go right to the rappel tree.

Note: Directly below the Stratocaster Wall is another cliff with a prominent black water streak on it. There are at least three climbs here, all apparently done by Dave Wonderly or Wendell Broussard. Left to right, they are 5.9 (left-facing corner to face), 5.8 (water streak), and 5.10– (corner to thin, curving crack; two pitches, the second is 5.8 R/X). These routes are probably best approached from wash level.

The Front Corridor

Walk 75 yards due east from the parking lot to this obvious north-south corridor. Routes in this corridor are good, but certainly not the best sport climbs at Red Rocks. Some may need traditional gear to supplement the bolts mentioned. The climbs are described from right to left as you enter the corridor; some on the right (east) wall get sun in the afternoon.

25 **Sicktion 5.9**

FA: Nick Nordblom, Randy Marsh – Fall 1988

Start at the mouth of the corridor on the right (east) wall, by an oak tree and below a flake 10 feet up. Follow a vertical seam past three bolts to the top. Belay in a large recess (TCU, #2.5 & 3 Friends), then walk off right.

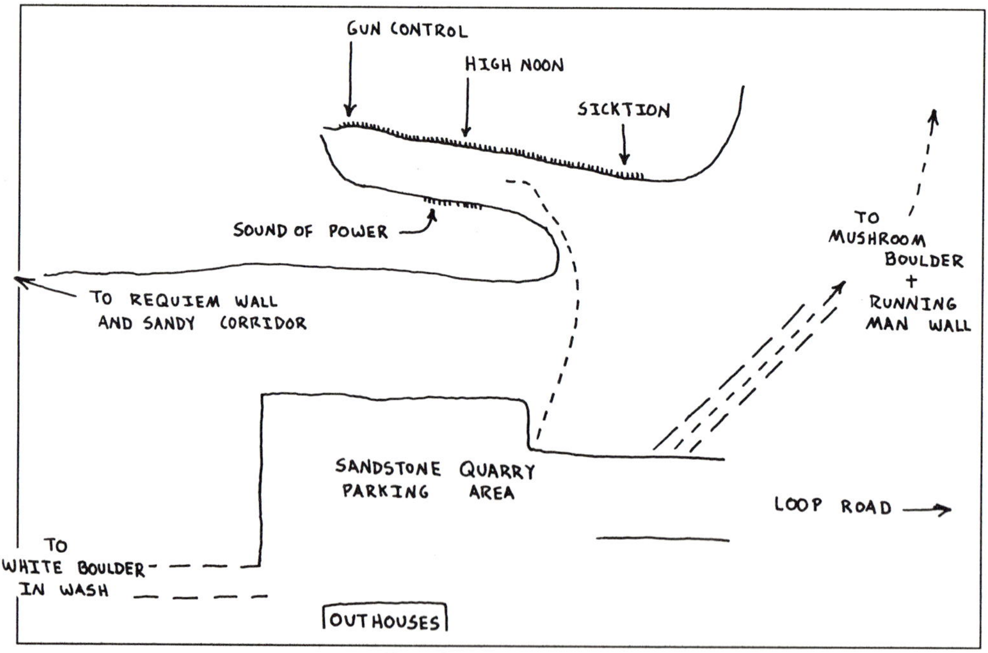

The Front Corridor

26 **Prescription Gription 5.10 R**
FA: Nick Nordblom, Jenni Stone – Spring 1988
Begin 20 feet left of the previous route. Climb past two bolts to a left-leaning seam/corner, then up a vertical crack, passing one more bolt. Bring a #2.5 Friend or bigger for the belay. Walk off right.

27 **Friction Addiction 5.10 PG/R**
FA: Bob Conz, Shelby Shelton – Spring 1988
Start at the right edge of a tree clump 15 feet left of **Prescription Gription.** Power past three bolts, then follow a seam up left. Follow this past two more bolts. Bring a #2.5 Friend or bigger for the belay. Walk off right.

28 **Affliction For Friction 5.11a R**
FA: Mike Ward, Danny Meyers – Fall 1989
Begin at a horizontal oak tree in a clump of four trees that is 10 feet left of **Friction Addiction.** Make a difficult mantel, then climb past two bolts, angling way left (dicey crux) to a seam. Continue up the seam past three more bolts. Bring a #2.5 Friend or bigger for the belay. Walk off right.

29 **Crumbling Community 5.10 PG**
FA: Paul Van Betten, Danny Meyers – 1989
Start 15 feet left at a grey water streak. Dance up the streak past a low bolt to a seam, then follow a left-leaning crack to its top. Angle up right past two more bolts to the top. Walk off right.

30 **A Thousand New Routes 5.11 R**
FA: Paul Van Betten, Nick Nordblom – Summer 1987
Climb the left-leaning diagonal crack, then go up right from the last bolt to the belay station. Three bolts.

31 **High Noon 5.11 R**
FA: Nick Nordblom, Jenni Stone – Spring 1988
Begin 10 feet left of **A Thousand New Routes,** below a right-facing corner with varnish on its right side. There are six bolts on the route. Rappel with two ropes.

32 **Hair Today, Gone Tomorrow 5.11a**
FA: Nick Nordblom, Paul Van Betten – Spring 1988
Start 25 feet left of **A Thousand New Routes**, near a shrub. Climb along a left trending seam past seven bolts, the first being a Metolius about 30 feet up. A 120-foot rappel will get you back to the ground, or you can traverse off right.

33 **To Bolt Or Toupee 5.10c**
FA: Mike Ward, Paul Van Betten – Spring 1988
Rope up 40 feet left of **Hair Today . . .**, and 30 feet right of the end of the corridor. Climb up to a right-facing corner capped by a ceiling, then follow bolts up and right to the rappel anchor. There are seven bolts.

34 **Gun Control 5.11b**
FA: Bob Conz, Shelby Shelton, Nick Nordblom – Summer 1988
Start 10 feet left of **Gun Control,** and 20 feet right of where the corridor narrows down. Follow bolts up into a large scoop, then exit out the left side (crux) to the belay anchor. There are eight bolts. Rappel with two ropes.

The next two routes share a common start, and are in the shade all day. They are on the left (west) wall of the corridor, directly across from **High Noon.**

35 **Churning In The Dirt 5.12b**
FA: Mike Tupper, Craig Reason – November, 1988
The lefthand route, ending at a chain anchor.

36 **Sound Of Power 5.12a**
FA: Craig Reason, Mike Tupper – November, 1988
The righthand route, following thin flakes to a chain anchor.

Sandy Corridor

There are dozens of climbs in this corridor, but only five routes are described in this guide. To reach this area, walk 150 yards north from the parking lot, staying close to the base of the obvious, west-facing cliff on your right, and walking past numerous quarried blocks. Continue 50 yards across slabs, then turn right (east) into the first corridor (the Sandy Corridor). Walk to the back of the corridor, then scramble up the drainage about 100 yards, passing a few pine trees. Just before the red rock ends on the left (north) wall of the canyon, head up left on a ramp towards two HUGE detached boulders. The southwest face of the right (east) boulder is the Requiem Wall. The approach takes about 15 minutes; the routes are in the shade in the early morning. The three routes on this crag are described from left to right.

37 **Integrity Of Desire 5.12a**
FA: Mike Tupper – Spring 1991
Start 10 feet right of the gap between the huge boulders below a vertical white seam that begins in a corner. Six bolts lead to chains.

38 **Flying Cowboys 5.12d**
FA: Don Welsh – Spring 1991
Rope up 45 feet right and around the corner from **Integrity of Desire.** Start up a vertical seam, then move left and up to the cold shut anchor. Six bolts total.

39 **Plastic Pistol 5.12c**
FA: Don Welsh – Spring 1991
Begin six feet right of the last route and 20 feet left of the east edge of the boulder. Climb past five bolts to shuts.

40 **Chrysler Crack 5.9**
FA: Randy Grandstaff, Jon Martinet – 1970s
Judging by the graffiti at the base of the route ("Jesus is Love" & "God Loves U"), this route should be named Christ Crack. This fine offwidth (some might say those two words shouldn't appear in the same sentence) is high on the right wall of the gully, across from and above the Requiem Wall. Bring BigBros, Big Dudes, or be brave! To approach this route, walk 150 yards north from the parking lot, past numerous quarried blocks. Continue 50 yards across slabs, then turn right (east) into the first corridor (the Sandy Corridor). Walk to the back of the corridor, then scramble about 200 yards up the canyon to a large, left-leaning pine tree (this is about 30 yards before the canyon chokes off). Turn right (south) and go up a gully for 50 feet until it narrows into a corridor. Scramble out right (west) onto a ledge, then continue up and right past bulges and ledges for 150 feet to the base of the route. The climb ascends an amazing varnished corner with a pine tree at its base. Descend off left.

41 **Wild, Wild West** **5.12b/c** (Harder if you're tall)
FA: Geoff Weigand – circa 1987
Climb the bolted face right of **Chrysler Crack,** stick clipping the first bolt.

View of Sandstone Quarry from the parking area.

Sonic Youth Cliff

This crag faces north, and really can't be seen from the parking lot, although the rock formation is clearly visible. From the parking lot, walk 200 yards northwest in the main wash toward an old roadway, passing a white boulder. Turn left about 50 yards from the boulder, at the right end of a low, white rock formation. Follow a faint path up a hill, then cross a plateau about 300 yards to some pine trees. Angle slightly left toward a canyon with a large, steep, brown wall on its right. The Sonic Youth Cliff is on your left and is about 100 yards from the pines. It is dark brown, overhanging, and in the shade all day. Most of the routes do not have rappel anchors, and finish on a ledge system dividing the cliff into lower and upper tiers. Routes are described from left to right.

42 **Hooligans** **5.11c**
FA: Greg Mayer – July, 1992
Begin about 25 feet left of a bush, and just right of a left-leaning crack/ramp. Follow six bolts to a rap station that is about 15 feet below a bush on a ledge.

43 **GBH (Great Bodily Harm)** **5.11d**
FA: Richard Harrison, Kevin Biernacki, Paul Van Betten, Don Borroughs – September, 1989
Named for a band, not the scary nature of the climb! Start about ten feet left of a bush, and near the left end of the ledge system at the base of the cliff. Climb past numerous holes and six bolts to the ledge. Walk and scramble off right.

Sonic Youth Wall

42 Hooligans 5.11c
43 GBH (Great Bodily Harm) 5.11d
44 Black Flag 5.11c
45 Loki 5.12a/b
46 Agent Orange 5.12b
47 Sonic Youth 5.11+ 👍
48 Everybody's Slave 5.11c 👍
50 Crankenstein 5.10c 👍

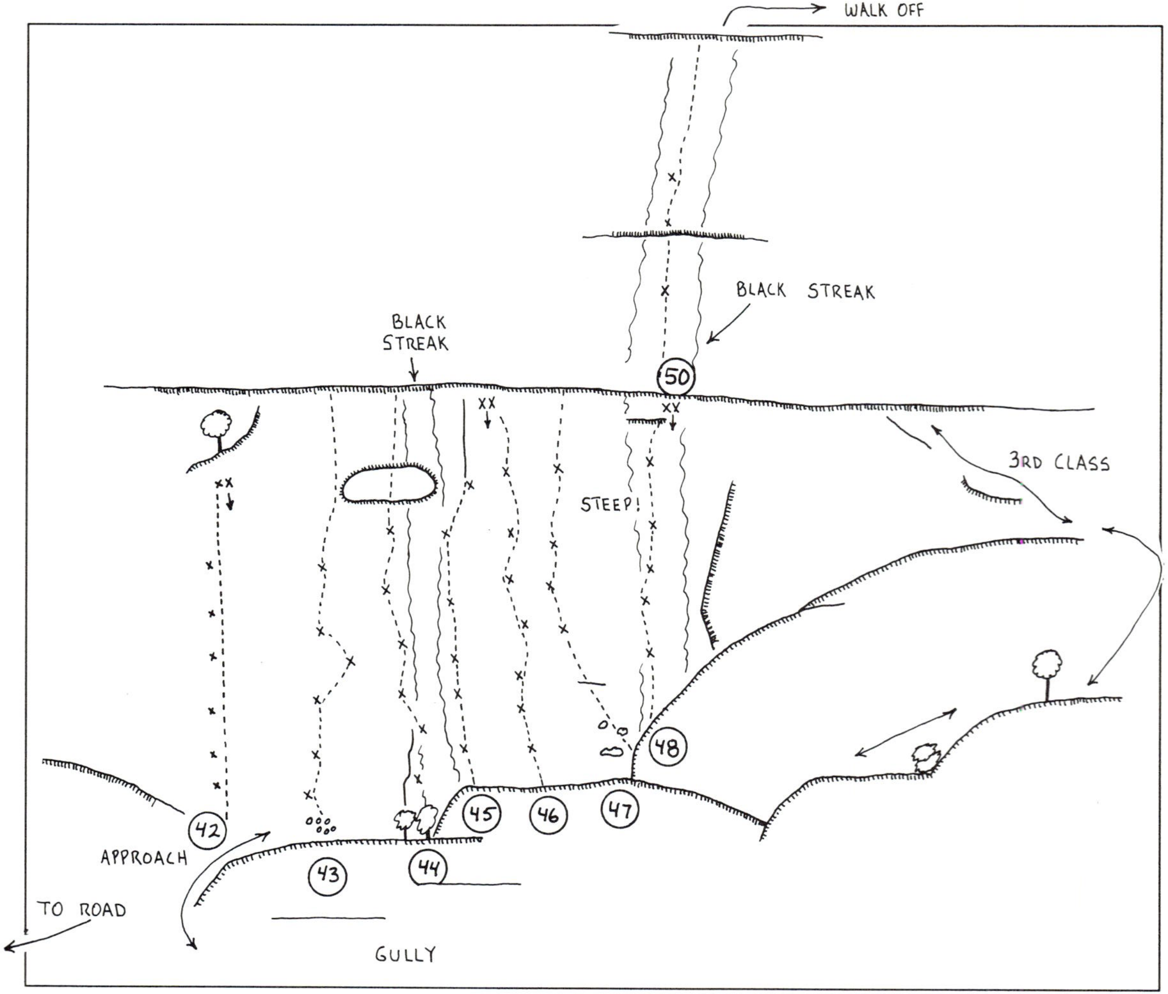

44 **Black Flag 5.11c**
FA: Paul Van Betten, Bob Conz – June, 1989
Rope up 15 feet right of **GBH,** at the right side of a bush. Ascend the cliff, passing five bolts enroute.

45 **Loki 5.12a/b**
FA: Don Welsh – April, 1991
Named for a sci-fi movie character that was half black and half white. Begin five feet right of **Black Flag,** at the right edge of an obvious black streak. Climb past seven bolts to a chain anchor.

46 **Agent Orange 5.12b**
FA: Paul Van Betten, Bob Conz – June, 1989
Start 10 feet right of **Loki** and cruise past seven bolts to the top.

47 **Sonic Youth 5.11+**
FA: Paul Van Betten, Sal Mamusia, Bob Conz – May, 1989
Begin 20 feet right of **Agent Orange** at an assortment of huecos near the left edge of a black streak. Bring a couple of small Friends and TCUs to give you the courage to reach the first bolt and the top! Four bolts lead to the ledge system. Walk off right.

48 **Everybody's Slave 5.11c**
FA: Don Welsh – April, 1991
A very good route - luckily, the holds get bigger the higher you get! Rope up about eight feet right of **Sonic Youth,** in the middle of a black streak, then climb past five bolts to a chain anchor.

49 **Seka's Soiled Panties 5.11**
FA: Richard Harrison, Paul Van Betten – September, 1989
This climb is left of **Crankenstein,** and has one bolt in the bulge. Bring gear up to a #1.5 Friend. Walk off right.

50 **Crankenstein 5.10c**
FA: Danny Meyers (rope solo) – April, 1988
Well worth doing. Scramble up to the ledge system that splits the cliff, then climb the central black water streak past three bolts. This route is directly above **Everybody's Slave.** Walk off right (west).

51 **Slam Dancin' With The Amish 5.9+**
FA: Paul & Pauline Van Betten – June, 1989
This route had to be included for the route name alone! Begin to the right of the **Crankenstein** water streak and climb a small right-facing corner past two bolts over the bulge. Walk off right.

Note: If you continue about 100 yards up the canyon from the Sonic Youth Wall, you'll come to the Toast and Broast Cliff and the Numbers Wall. The Toast and Broast is the higher, prominent cliff, and the Numbers Wall is down and slightly left (west). Numerous routes have been done on both crags by Paul Van Betten, Richard Harrison and Sal Mamusia, but they aren't described in this book. There are also numerous climbs further up canyon.

The Wake Up Wall

As the name implies, you have to get there early (at least in winter) to have much sunshine. The routes are short, and all have rappel/lowering anchors. This crag caused an uproar between the two local climbing factions due to the generic, grid-like nature of the routes. To get there, walk 200 yards northwest in the main wash from the parking lot to an old roadway, passing a white boulder. Follow the roadway about 200 yards to an obvious oak bush on the left side of the trail. Turn left off the road and follow a faint footpath up over a dirt hump (about 200 yards). Angle slightly left (a wash is on your right) into a corridor with a larger brown and white wall on its left side. The base of the cliff is flat, white rock. The climbs will be described from left to right as you approach.

52 **First Born 5.10b/c**
FA: Ed Prochaska – 1990
Start in a pit eight feet right of boulders at a right trending flake, and climb past five bolts to the anchor.

53 **Just Shut Up And Climb 5.11b/c**
FA: Randy Faulk, Rick Denison – June, 1991
The steepest route on the cliff. Begin 40 feet right of **First Born** and clip five bolts as you climb past the right side of a hole.

54 **Shape Of Things To Come 5.11a**
FA: Greg Mayer – Winter 1989
Rope up 70 feet right of **Just Shut Up . . .**, and just right of an obvious left-leaning ramp. Power past three bolts to the anchor.

55 **The Healer 5.11d**
FA: Greg Mayer – Spring 1990
Start eight feet right and climb past four bolts to a shared belay with **Rise & Whine.**

56 **Rise & Whine 5.12a**
FA: Mike Tupper – Spring 1990
Climb along seams five feet right of **The Healer,** clipping four bolts enroute.

57 **Pain Check 5.12a**
FA: Bill Boyle – Spring 1990
Begin eight feet right of **Rise & Whine** and hobble past five bolts to the rap station.

58 **Good Mourning (aka The Burrito) 5.11b/c**
FA: Bill Boyle – Spring 1990
A four-bolt route that begins eight feet right of **Pain Check.**

59 **Native Son 5.11c**
FA: Mike Tupper – Spring 1990
Stroll past five bolts, starting at a pocket ten feet to the right of **Good Mourning.**

60 **Where Egos Dare 5.12a**
FA: Greg Mayer – Summer 1991
Begin as for **Native Son,** but climb up right, passing the left side of a large hole and four bolts.

61 **XTZ 5.9**
FA: Greg Mayer – Spring 1990
The easiest route on the cliff, but not too aesthetic. Rack up 25 feet right at the base of a right-leaning ramp. Climb past three bolts to the rappel anchor.

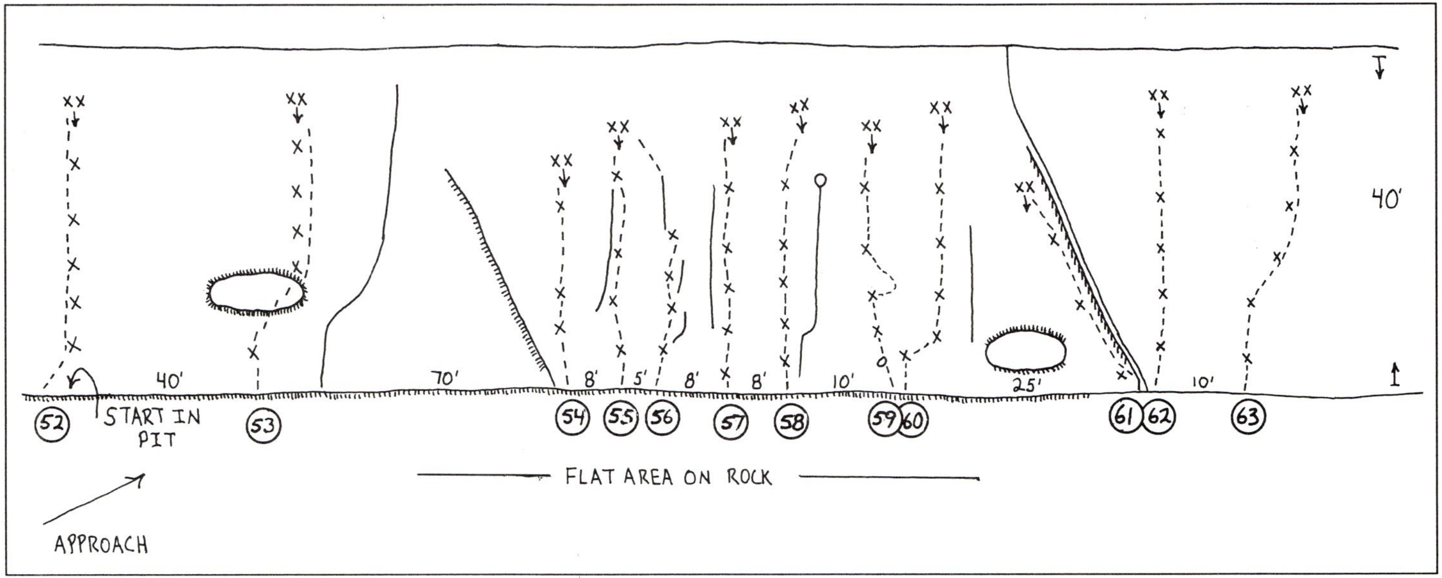

Wake-Up Wall

52 First Born 5.10b/c
53 Just Shut Up And Climb 5.11b/c 👍
54 Shape Of Things To Come 5.11a
55 The Healer 5.11d
56 Rise & Whine 5.12a
57 Pain Check 5.12a
58 Good Mourning (aka The Burrito) 5.11b/c
59 Native Son 5.11c
60 Where Egos Dare 5.12a
61 XTZ 5.9 👎
62 Onsight Flight 5.12b
63 Stand And Deliver 5.12b

62 **Onsight Flight 5.12b**
FA: Don Welsh – Spring 1990
Start four feet right of the ramp and fly past five bolts.

63 **Stand And Deliver 5.12b**
FA: Mike Tupper – Spring 1990
Rope up 10 feet right of **Onsight Flight.** Climb past five bolts that trend slightly right.

The Twinkie

These routes aren't all that great, but you walk right by them to get to good routes. This small, white formation gets sun all day and is visible from the parking area. It is north of the lot, at the left end of the biggest lump of white rock. The approach directions given here aren't the most direct way to the crag, but by following them, you shouldn't get lost. From the parking area, walk 200 yards northwest in the main wash to an old roadway, passing a white boulder. Follow the roadway to its end (a bit over 300 yards), passing an oak bush, a small drainage, and a cedar post. Turn left (northwest) and walk about 500 yards up the wash, paralleling the big white lump, to The Twinkie. Routes are described right to left, and begin in the wash.

64 **Like Mom Used To Make 5.11c/d**
FA: Anthony Williams, John & Ralph Day – Winter 1988
Start just left of an easy-looking bulge at the base of the cliff, below four bolts. The route begins with difficult moves, and finishes in a very short crack. There is a rappel anchor on top.

65 **Flake Eyes 5.10+**
FA: Anthony Williams, John & Ralph Day – Winter 1988
Begin 10 feet left of **Like Mom Used To Make,** behind a bush. Climb up and slightly left past three bolts. There are belay bolts on top. Walk off the rear of the formation, then around left to regain the base of the route.

66 **Short But Sweet 5.10 R/X**
FA: Anthony Williams, John & Ralph Day – Winter 1988
Start 30 feet left of **Flake Eyes** at a right-leaning ramp/corner, just left of a low cave. Climb to the top of the corner, then move up and right about 10 feet to the first bolt (scary). Continue past one more to the top. Belay from bolts, then walk off as for the previous route.

The Avian Wall

These routes are on a north-facing wall just below The Trophy. All are on primarily white rock, and have anchors to lower from. Walk 200 yards northwest from the parking lot in the main wash to an old roadway, passing a white boulder. Follow the roadway a bit over 300 yards to its end, passing an oak bush, a small drainage, and a cedar post. Turn left (northwest) and walk about 500 yards up the wash, paralleling the big white lump, to The Twinkie. Walk just past The Twinkie, then turn right toward a smooth, brown wave of rock (The Drive-in). Go east up the canyon about 100 yards to the cliff, which makes up the right (east) wall of the canyon. The Trophy (described next) is 200 feet up slabs to the left. Routes are described from right to left as you approach up the gully.

67 **Spotted Owl 5.11a**
FA: Don Burroughs, Alan Busby – March, 1992
Tastes just like chicken! Start 20 feet right of a large oak tree at a flat sandy spot. Climb up along vertical seams, clipping five bolts before you reach the chain anchor.

68 **Thunderbird 5.11a/b PG**
FA: Don Burroughs, Alan Busby – March, 1992
Not your typical crimper - this one requires a bit of technique. Begin in a pit 80 feet left of the last route, and follow six bolts along a vertical seam to chains.

69 **Coyote Moon 5.9**
FA: Don Burroughs, Dr. Alan Busby – March, 1992
Start 15 feet left of **Thunderbird** at a block in the pit, and eight feet right of an oak tree. Zip past four bolts to chains.

70 **Spotted Eagle 5.10a**
FA: Don Burroughs, Alan Busby – March, 1992
Rope up 25 feet left of **Coyote Moon,** at the left end of the pit and 10 feet right of a large, right-facing flake. Clip four bolts on your way to the chains.

The Trophy

This sunny cliff redefines the word steep! As with the approach for The Twinkie, these directions aren't the most direct way to the crag, but by following them, you shouldn't get lost. From the parking area, walk 200 yards northwest to an old roadway, passing a white boulder in the main wash. Follow the roadway for a bit over 300 yards to its end, passing an oak bush, a small drainage, and a cedar post. Turn left (northwest) and walk about 500 yards up the wash, paralleling the big white lump, to The Twinkie. Walk just past the Twinkie, then turn right toward a smooth, brown wave of rock (The Drive-in). Go east up the canyon about 150 yards to the obvious, overhanging wall on the left (north) side of the canyon. Routes are described from left to right. Total approach time is about 15 minutes.

71 **Fifi Hula 5.11a**
FA: Don Burroughs, Alan Busby – January, 1992
This sunny route isn't on the main Trophy wall, but about 150 feet left, in the middle of a large white face. Start 40 feet left of a gray waterstreak and climb past six bolts to a chain anchor. There is at least one route, a bolted arête, to the left of **Fifi Hula.**

72 **Shark Walk 5.13a**
FA: Mike Tupper – February, 1992
Start just right of a cave and a scrub oak at the left (west) end of the main cliff. Climb past six bolts to the anchor.

73 **Indian Giver 5.12c**
FA: Mike Tupper – January, 1992
Begin six feet right of **Shark Walk,** and climb past five bolts to a chain anchor.

74 **Midnight Cowboy 5.13a**
FA: Mike Tupper – March, 1992
Start 40 feet right of **Indian Giver.** Angle up and left past two bolts, continue left past five bolts, then up past two more bolts.

75 **Twilight Of A Champion 5.13a**
FA: Mike Tupper – February, 1992
Start as for **Midnight Cowboy.** Angle up and left past two bolts, then straight up past six more bolts to a chain belay.

76 **Pet Shop Boy 5.12d**
FA: Mike Tupper – February, 1992
Named after Tupper's hairdo. Begin 10 feet right of the last two routes. Stick clip the first bolt, then climb straight back (!) past five more bolts.

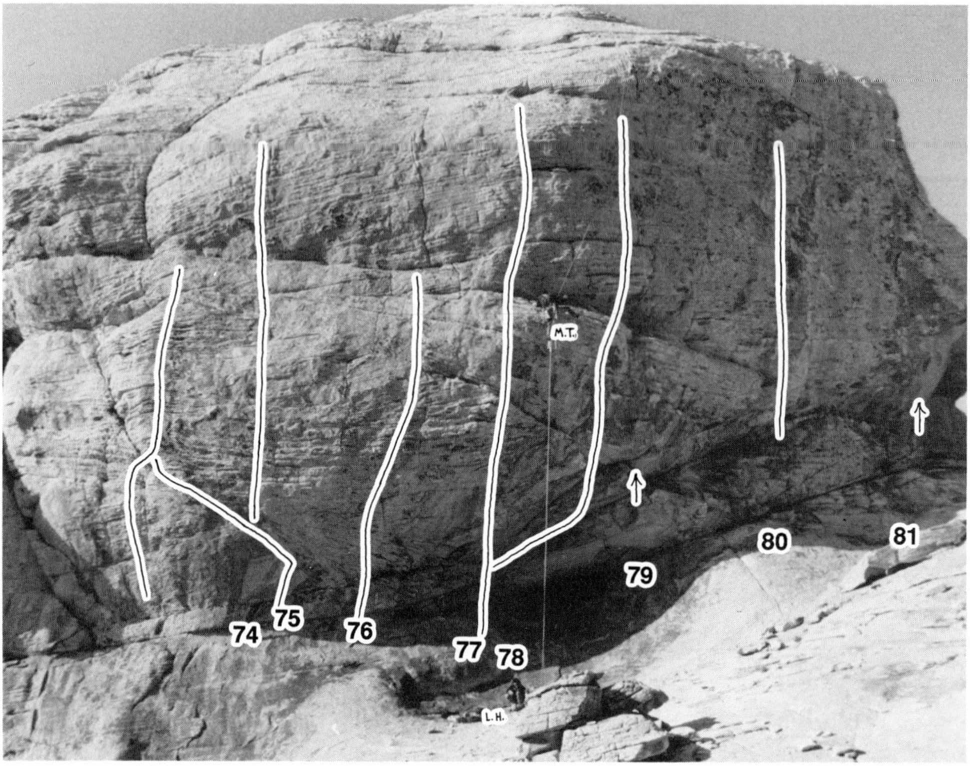

The Trophy

74 **Midnight Cowboy** 5.13a
75 **Twilight Of A Champion** 5.13a 👍
76 **Pet Shop Boy** 5.12d 👍
77 **Keep Your Powder Dry** 5.12b 👍
78 **The Trophy** 5.12c
79 **Caught In The Crosshairs** 5.12a/b
80 **Dodging A Bullet** 5.12a
81 **Meatlocker** 5.?

77 Keep Your Powder Dry 5.12b 👍

FA: Mike Tupper – January, 1992

Rope up 60 feet right of the last route, at the left side of the central cave. Follow nine bolts up very overhanging rock to chains.

78 The Trophy 5.12c

FA: Mike Tupper – January, 1992

This makes **Fear and Loathing** look like a slab climb! Starting eight feet right of **Keep Your Powder Dry,** climb out the right side of the central cave along a horizontal crack. Ten bolts will get you to the anchor.

79 Caught In The Crosshairs 5.12a/b

FA: Greg Mayer – November, 1992

Uncompleted as of press time. Begin 30 feet uphill of the central cave on a ledge. Power past seven bolts to the safety of the anchor.

80 **Dodging A Bullet** **5.12a**
FA: Greg Mayer – Spring 1991
Start about 45 feet right of the central cave, and climb along vertical seams, clipping five bolts enroute.

81 **Meatlocker** **5.?**
FA: ? – after November, 1992
As of press time, this route still had a red ribbon on the first bolt, indicating that the route hadn't been redpointed yet. Begin at the very right edge of the cliff below a flat ceiling. Five bolts lead to chains.

Mass Production Wall

From the Sandstone Quarry parking area, walk 200 yards northwest to an old roadway, passing a white boulder in the main wash. Follow the roadway 250 yards past a bush and a small drainage to a cedar post in the road. Angle right (northeast) into the obvious, pebbly wash, and follow it between two rock formations. Cross over an old log after about 100 yards, and pass some pine trees after another 40 yards. The main wash will curve left (north) at this point, with a subsidiary wash continuing east. Follow the sandy subsidiary wash east about 300 yards, then continue straight east along the same wash through a canyon with red rock for another 300 yards. Just before the red layer of rock ends, you'll see Mass Production Wall uphill to the northeast. The cliff is in the shade most of the day, and is primarily a white-colored rock with pine trees at its base. The approach takes about 15 minutes from the parking area. Routes are described right to left, running uphill from the approach.

82 **Some Assembly Required** **5.10c/d**
FA: Greg Mayer – Spring 1991
Start behind a gnarled pine tree and climb up along parallel, left leaning seams, then up the face right of a cave. Six bolts to chain anchors.

83 **Kokopeli** **5.10b/c**
FA: Don Burroughs, Alan Busby – April, 1992
Named for the hunchbacked flute player commonly seen in Native American rock art. Begin 50 feet uphill of **Some Assembly Required** below the right center of a cave. Face climb past bolts, then out the ceiling at a right facing corner to chains.

84 **Advanced Route Stealing** **5.8** **R/X**
FA: Todd Swain, Jeff Rickerl – April, 1992
Begin 100 feet uphill of **Some Assembly Required** behind two pine trees. Wander up the face using minimal traditional pro to the chain anchor on top. The chain anchor was installed by Greg Mayer at the time he did the other routes here.

85 **Battery Powered** **5.9**
FA: Greg Mayer – Spring 1991
Rope up 10 feet left of **Advanced Route Stealing,** and 10 feet right of a right-facing corner. Climb past six bolts to the chain anchor.

86 **Trigger Happy** **5. 10a**
FA: Greg Mayer – Spring 1991
Start 90 feet uphill of **Battery Powered** below a seam leading through the left edge of a large varnished patch shaped roughly like Australia. Scamper past five bolts to a chain anchor.

87 **Hit And Run 5.9**

FA: Greg Mayer – Spring 1991

Begin 10 feet left of **Trigger Happy** behind a pine tree with a broken top. Climb past five bolts to a chain anchor, keeping just right of a seam/crack.

Note: Numerous climbs have been done on the red layer of rock mentioned in the approach description. All are on the left (north) side of the canyon as you are approaching the Mass Production Wall and the other crags in this area.

The Hall of Fame

From the Sandstone Quarry parking area, walk 200 yards northwest to an old roadway, passing a white boulder in the main wash. Follow the roadway 250 yards past a bush and small drainage to a cedar post in the road. Angle right (northeast) into the obvious, pebbly wash, and follow it between two rock formations. Cross over an old log after about 100 yards; 40 yards beyond are some pine trees. The main wash will curve left (north) at this point, with a subsidiary wash continuing east. Follow this sandy subsidiary wash east about 300 yards, then continue east through a canyon with red rock another 300 yards. Just before the red layer of rock ends, you'll see The Mass Production Wall uphill to the northeast. For the Hall of Fame, head up left (north) along a gully 300 yards to the base

Mass Production Wall and The Hall of Fame

83 **Kokopeli 5.10b/c**

86 **Trigger Happy 5.10a**

of a large, white, south-facing cliff with a steep gully/cleft running north-south. From the base of the cleft, contour around left (west, then north) on ledges above one cliff band and below another for 100 yards (there should be cairns marking the way along this section). Scamper 50 yards up the first gully you reach, and you should be at the lower entrance to the Hall of Fame. The Hall runs in a north-south direction; all routes are on the right (east) wall. They are in the shade all day, although it's very easy to reach sunshine to warm up on cooler days. The approach to this cliff takes an additional ten minutes from The Mass Production Wall, or a total of 25 minutes from the parking area. Routes are described right to left, running up The Hall from the approach.

88 **Yearnin' And Learnin' 5.10d/11a**
FA: Don Burroughs, Alan Busby – April, 1992
Begin about 15 feet inside the corridor, below two lines of bolts with a common start. Climb up and right past four bolts to chains.

89 **Repeat Offender 5.10d**
FA: Greg Mayer – Spring 1991
Start as for **Yearnin' And Learnin'**, but climb slightly left past six bolts to a chain anchor. Move left, then back right between the second and third bolts. If you climb straight between these bolts, the route is 5.11c.

90 **Armed And Dangerous 5.10d**
FA: Phil Bowden – Spring 1991
Begin six feet left of **Repeat Offender.** After a difficult lieback move, climb past huecos to the left side of a bulge. Follow a total of six bolts to the chain anchor.

91 **Bad Reputation 5.11b**
FA: Phil Bowden, Guy Pinjuv – Spring 1991
Climb the face 15 feet left of **Armed and Dangerous.** Go past six bolts to the same chain anchor. There is a difficult ceiling down low, but the crux is up higher.

92 **Innocent Bystander 5.10a**
FA: Greg Mayer – Spring 1991
Start 30 feet uphill of **Bad Reputation** and power past five bolts to a chain anchor.

93 **Ms. Adventure 5.7**
FA: "Chucky" Mayer – Spring 1991
Begin 30 feet left of **Innocent Bystander,** and about 20 feet downhill from the upper entrance to the corridor. Climb past three bolts to the anchor. The crux is off the ground.

94 **Sand Illusion 5.11c**
FA: Greg Mayer – Spring 1991
This route climbs a prominent arête about 150 yards to the west of The Hall of Fame. It faces southeast, and has three bolts and a chain anchor.

The Holiday Wall

This crag has a number of very good sport routes that are in the sun most of the day. Total approach time is about 20 minutes. From the Sandstone Quarry parking area, walk 200 yards northwest to an old roadway, passing a white boulder in the main wash. Follow the roadway for 250 yards past a bush and small drainage to a cedar post in the road. Angle right (northeast) into the obvious, pebbly wash, and follow it between two rock formations. You'll cross over an old log after about 100 yards, and reach some pine trees 40 yards farther. The main wash will curve left (north) at this point, with a subsidiary wash continuing east. Follow this sandy subsidiary wash east about 300 yards, then continue straight east through a canyon with red rock another 300 yards. Just before the red layer of rock ends, you'll see The Mass Production Wall uphill to the northeast. Continue up the main drainage beyond The Mass Production Wall, heading slightly right to gain a trail that contours along the hillside. About 200 yards beyond the end of the red rock, the trail drops down into a drainage. and the red rock appears again. Continue up the valley 200 yards to The Holiday Wall, which is on the left (northeast). Routes are described from left to right.

95 **The Grinch 5.12c/d**
FA: Mike Tupper – Christmas 1990
Start near the left edge of the wall and 50 feet right of a medium-sized oak at smooth, overhanging, varnished rock. Climb past three bolts (there were four, but the first is missing) to chains.

96 **Death Before Decaf 5.12b**
FA: Don Welsh – January, 1991
Bolted by Kevin Lawler and Sandy Carrick, then led by Welsh much later. Begin 20 feet uphill of **The Grinch** on a red slab. Fire past six bolts to chains.

97 **Gift Rapped 5.11b**
FA: Karen Peil – Christmas 1990
"Given" to Peil by Tupper as a Christmas present! Start 10 feet uphill of **Death Before Decaf** behind a pine tree, at a shallow, left-facing corner. Clip six bolts as you climb along seams to a chain anchor.

98 **Red Sky Mining 5.11a**
FA: Karen Peil – December, 1990
Climb past seven bolts to chains. Start 10 feet right of **Gift Rapped,** and behind a gnarled pine tree.

99 **Red Storm Rising 5.11b**
FA: Karen Peil – December, 1990
Begin as for **Red Sky Mining** and climb up along a left facing flake/corner past five bolts to chains. A bit loose and creaky.

100 **When The Cat's Away 5.11b** 👍
FA: Greg Mayer – December, 1990
Rope up 15 feet right of **Red Storm Rising** at the base of a buttress with a small ceiling at the bottom. Pull the ceiling and clip six bolts as you climb up small, opposing flake systems.

101 **Saddam's Mom 5.11d**
FA: Karen Peil – December, 1990
Closely related to **The Grinch.** Begin eight feet right of **When The Cat's Away** at the right arête of the buttress. Shoot past six bolts to a chain anchor.

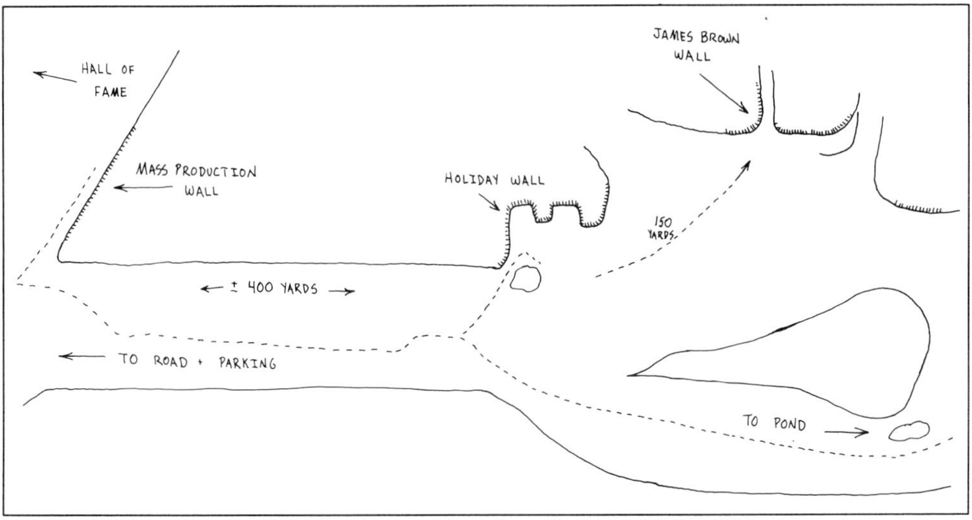

Holiday Wall Area

102 **Moments To Memories 5.11a PG**
FA: Greg Mayer – December, 1990
Start 40 feet right of **Saddam's Mom,** and 30 feet right of a striking dihedral (a future testpiece) at the left arête of a short buttress. Climb the arête past four bolts to chains.

103 **Fast Moving Train 5.11b**
FA: Greg Mayer – December, 1990
Begin just right of **Moments . . .** and climb past five bolts up the right arête of the buttress.

JAMES BROWN AREA

From the Sandstone Quarry parking area, walk 200 yards northwest to an old roadway, passing a white boulder in the main wash. Follow the roadway 250 yards past a bush and small drainage to a cedar post in the road. Angle right (northeast) into the obvious, pebbly wash, and follow it between two rock formations. You'll cross over an old log after about 100 yards, and reach some pine trees 40 yards beyond. The main wash curves left (north) at this point, with a subsidiary wash continuing due east. Follow this sandy subsidiary wash east about 300 yards, then continue east through a canyon with red rock another 300 yards. Just before the red layer of rock ends, you'll see The Mass Production Wall uphill to the northeast. Continue up the main drainage beyond The Mass Production Wall, heading slightly right to gain a trail that contours along the hillside. About 200 yards beyond the end of the red rock, the trail drops down into a drainage, and the red rock appears again. Continue up the valley 200 yards to The Holiday Wall, which is on the left (northeast). The James Brown Area is 150 yards diagonally up right (east) from the right edge of the Holiday Wall, and 200 yards above wash level. The cliff forms the left side of a corridor, and is characterized by a prominent brown waterstreak on the left arête of the corridor. Total approach time is about 25 minutes to this sunny crag. Routes are described from left to right.

104 **James Brown 5.11b**

FA: Randy Marsh, Pier Locatelli – Winter 1991

Dance up the brown waterstreak on the left arête of the corridor, clipping seven bolts enroute to chains.

105 **Brand New Bag 5.10d**

FA: Randy Marsh, Pier Locatelli – Winter 1991

Paper or plastic? Start 20 feet right and uphill of **James Brown,** and just left of a bush. Four bolts lead to chains.

106 **Soul Power 5.11c/d**

FA: Randy Marsh, Pier Locatelli – Winter 1991

To complete this without falling, you'll have to be the hardest working person in rock climbing! Begin 10 feet uphill of **Brand New Bag,** between two bushes. Climb past eight bolts to a chain anchor.

Note: If you continue up the main canyon from The Holiday Wall about 500 yards, you'll come to an idyllic little pond (Calico Tank).

Photo: Randy Marsh

Dan McQuade climbs his route, The Choad Warrior, 5.12c.

WILLOW SPRING

While not as in vogue as The Gallery or Wall of Confusion, Willow Spring offers many short routes of good quality. The turnoff for Willow Spring is 7.3 miles along the scenic loop road. This spur road is paved for 6/10 of a mile – after that it's four-wheel-drive territory all the way through to the town of Pahrump.

Most of the routes are one pitch long, though at times you may need two ropes to get back to your gear easily. Those longer convenience rappels are noted. The typical rack for Willow Spring includes a set of Friends, TCUs and wired stoppers - it's mostly a traditional area.

A rather crude picnic area on the right is at the end of the pavement. There are a few picnic tables under the big cottonwood trees, a natural spring (no potable water though), and an outhouse. Just to the right of the outhouse building is some excellent bouldering, but stay off the Native American rock art!

LOST CREEK CANYON/HIDDEN FALLS

After turning off the scenic loop road into Willow Spring, you'll come to a dirt pullout on your left at 2/10 of a mile. This is the parking for Lost Creek Canyon and Hidden Falls. Follow the obvious trail about 300 yards, passing a spring enroute to the mouth of the canyon. To the left (southeast) are routes **N' Plus Ultra** through **Buffalo Balls.** These routes are in the shade all day. Routes **The Threat** through **Heatwave** are to the right of the dry waterfall. These routes get sun in the morning, then move into the shade in the afternoon.

1 **N'Plus Ultra 5.10-**

FA: (TR) Joe Herbst – 1975 First Lead: Randy Grandstaff – 1976

This route sits on the second tier of cliff bands, about 300 yards left (southeast) of the trail. Turn off the trail at the spring, and follow a faint path towards the cliff. Approach by scrambling up an easy gully with a pine tree at the base. The route climbs out a huge roof via a fist crack. Bring multiple #4 Friends. Descend by walking off right (northwest) around to the base of the roof, then back down the approach gully.

2 **The Abdominizer 5.11**

FA: Paul Van Betten, Richard Harrison, Shelby Shelton – April, 1990

No spare tires allowed. Climb the roof just left of **N'Plus Ultra** along flakes. Two bolts in the roof provide protection.

3 **Pillar Talk 5.7 R**

FA: Joe Herbst – 1970s

Turn off the trail to Hidden Falls at the spring (as for **N'Plus Ultra**) and follow the faint trail about 200 yards to the base of a pillar with an obvious hand-and-fist crack on its right side.

P1 Climb the crack to a roof (large protection needed; V1), then hand traverse left (scary) to the arête. Climb up the easy face and belay in one of many cracks. 100 ft, 5.7.

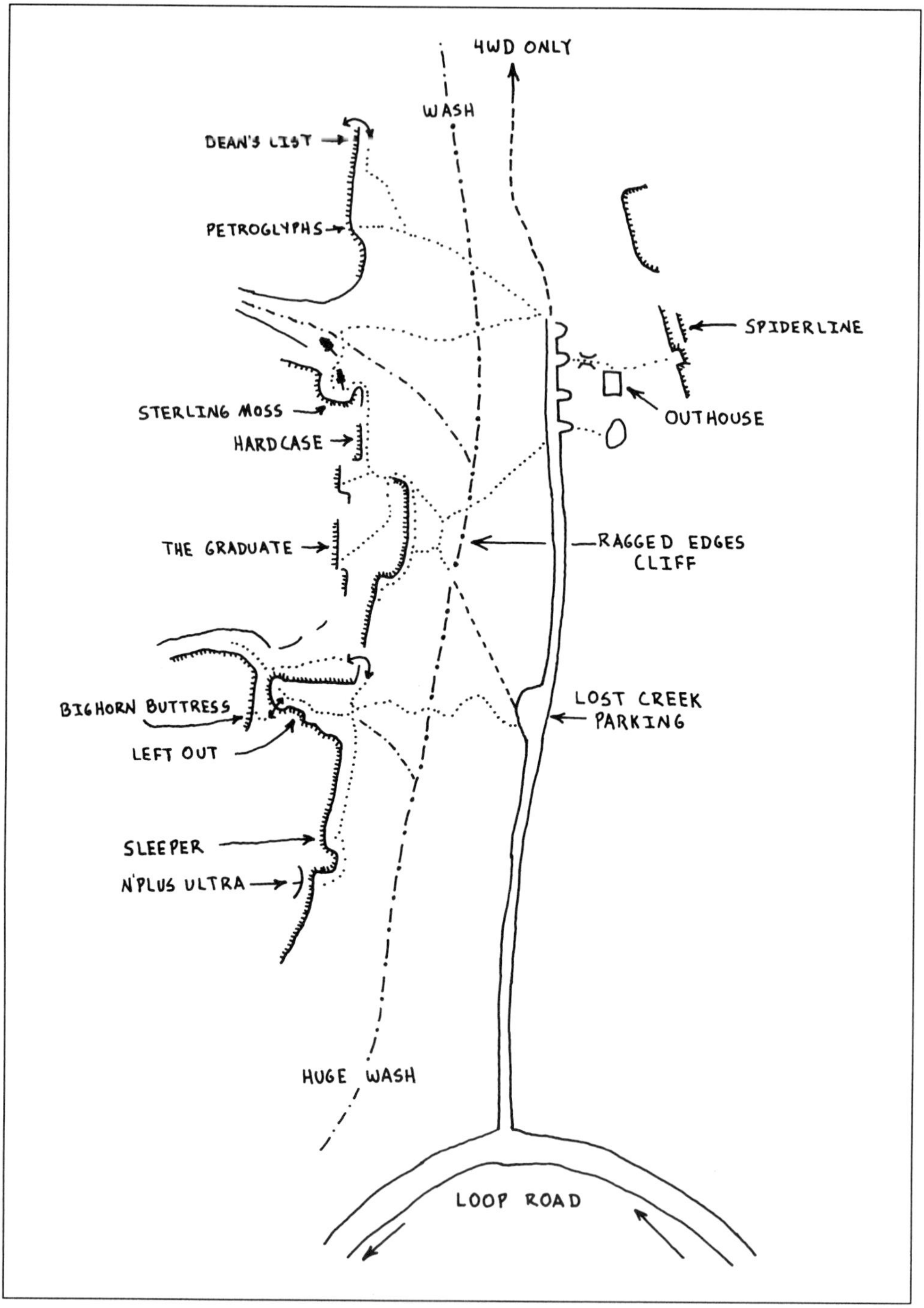

Willow Spring Map

Hidden Falls area as seen from the trailhead at Lost Creek

3 Pillar Talk 5.7 R
5 Sleeper 5.9
7 Left Out 5.10+
16 Grippitty Gravity 5.10
20 Captain Crunch 5.10- X
23 Heatwave 5.10- R

P2 Continue up the easy face to the top of the pillar. 80 ft., 5.4 R.

V1 Continue up the crack through the roof above, then rejoin the regular route. Large Friends needed. 5.10–.

Descend by walking right (west) and rappeling with two ropes from a pine tree atop **Sleeper.**

4 **Big Iron 5.11b/c**
FA: Paul Van Betten, Bob Conz – Summer 1990
Climb the steep face past seven bolts just around the corner and to the right of **Pillar Talk.** Rappel **Sleeper** with two ropes.

5 **Sleeper 5.9**
FA: Wendell Broussard, Rocky Paravia – 1981
Start 30 feet right of **Pillar Talk,** below an obvious finger crack leading to a pine tree. Climb flakes to a bulge that is split by a crack about 50 feet up. Pull the bulge (crux), and follow the crack to top. Rappel from the pine tree with two ropes.

The next five routes are on the varnished buttress just left of the trail to Hidden Falls, and at the mouth of the canyon. They are in the shade all day.

6 **Killer Clowns 5.10+**
FA: Paul Van Betten, Sal Mamusia, Richard Harrison, Kevin Biernacki – September, 1989
Climb an easy ramp on the left edge of the steep, varnished wall to an alcove 20 feet up. Struggle up through a bombay slot, then up the face and cracks above to the top. Descend by scrambling over the highest part of the buttress, then down a gully just right (south) of the varnished wall.

7 **Left Out 5.10+**
FA: (TR) Unknown First Lead: Joe Herbst – circa 1975
This excellent route climbs a thin crack on the left side of the varnished face. Not to be left out! Climb steep huecos just left of the obvious central crack on the forma-

tion, then up the thin crack to its top. Climb the easier face to the top of the formation. Descend as for **Killer Clowns.**

8 **Black Track 5.9**

FA: Joe Herbst – early 1970s

The obvious line on the wall, and a good follow-up climb to **Ragged Edges.** Climb the central crack on the wall to a ledge at two-thirds height. Either rappel with one rope from the chain anchor, climb the short offwidth to the top, or climb the steep face directly above past two bolts (5.11c).

9 **Bigfoot (aka Buckets and Bolts) 5.9+**

FA: Unknown – 1990

A very good face climb just right of **Black Track.** Climb the steep face past four bolts to the chain anchor.

10 **Buffalo Balls 5.11c**

FA: (TR) Bob Yoho – 1989 First Lead: Don Burroughs, Alan Busby – May, 1992

Follow four bolts up the steep face just right of **Bigfoot.**

11 **Bighorn Buttress 5.11 PG**

FA: Nick Nordblom, Jenni Stone – Spring 1987

As of press time, I hadn't done this supposedly excellent route. It is on the left (south) side of the upper Lost Creek Canyon, and starts about 300 feet up and left of the dry waterfall (**The Threat**). The route climbs a large, inobvious, triangular buttress in four pitches. The start of the route faces the road, but the majority of the climbing faces right, toward the Ragged Edges Cliff. Bring gear up to a #3 Friend, and some long slings.

P1 Climb a black face past a horizontal crack with a bush growing out of it, then follow a seam to a bolt. Follow a crack through a bulge to the belay ledge. 140 ft., 5.10–, PG.

P2 Continue up the crack, exiting right to a bolt. Step around the arête, passing two bolts (crux), then climb a corner to the belay. Watch out for rope drag. 150 ft., 5.11.

P3 Climb up past a couple of left-facing corners, and finish the pitch by face climbing past a bolt to a two-bolt belay. 80 ft., 5.9.

P4 Go up right past a bolt, turn a small roof into a right-facing corner, and follow this up to the top. Belay on the summit. 80 ft., 5.10.

Descent: Rappel the route with two ropes.

The next routes all are located on the other side of Hidden Falls, and are described starting at the falls and moving right (north). The routes are in the sun in the morning.

12 **The Threat 5.10+**

FA: Joe Herbst, Randy Grandstaff – 1975

An obvious, water polished crack is just to the right of the dry falls. Move left into the crack (bolt; crux), then up this past another bolt to the top. The easiest descent is to walk left (east) along ledges and scramble down the gully to the right of the **Black Track** buttress. It is also possible to walk off right (north) by **Heatwave,** then circle back around the base of the cliff.

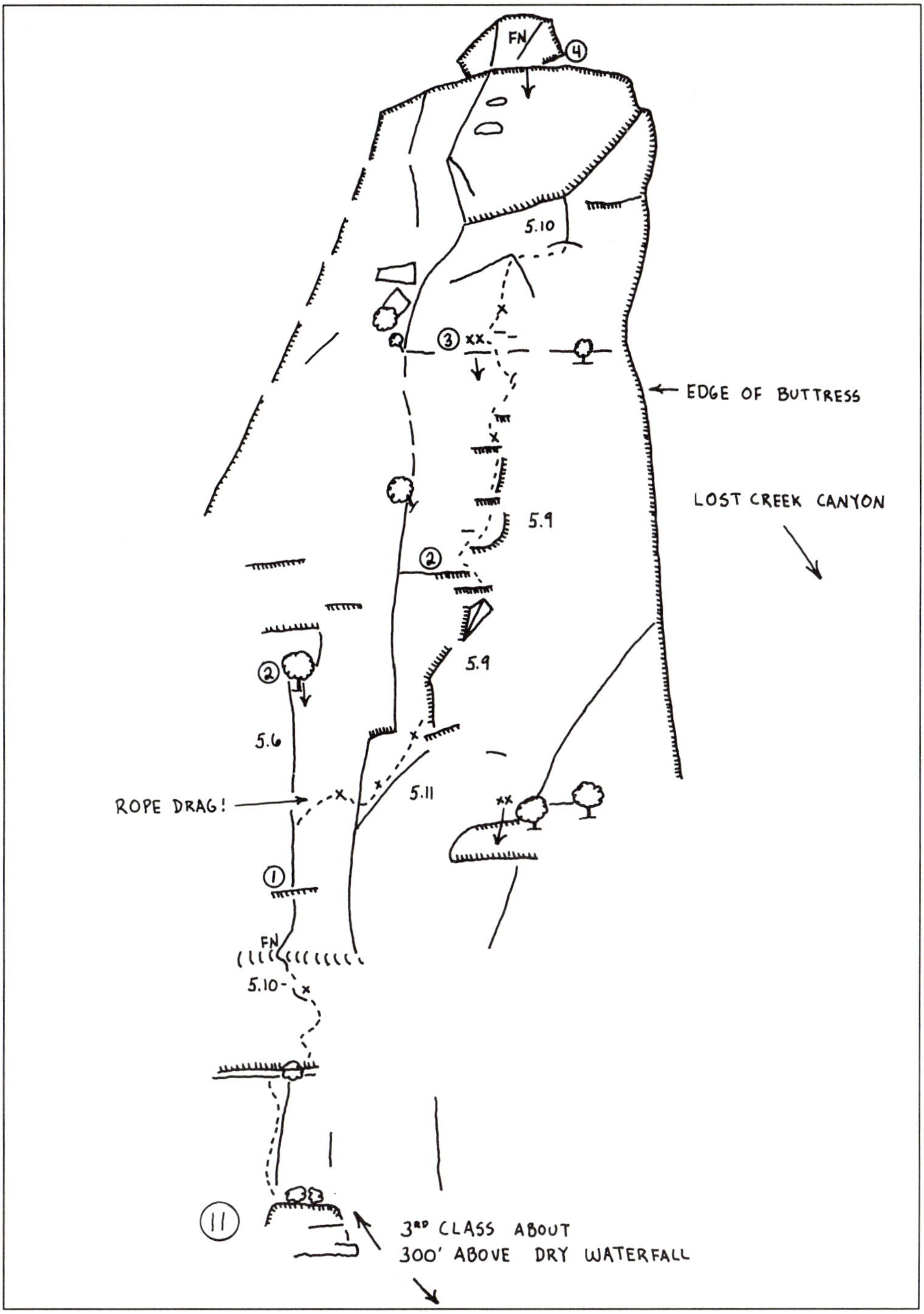

Bighorn Buttress, 5.11 PG

13 **Flight Line 5.12c**
FA: Paul Van Betten, Richard Harrison – Summer 1990
Climb smooth flakes 10 feet right of **The Threat** to a very smooth wave of rock above. Clip the doubled bolts and surmount the wave to gain the top. Don't expect to get this route without a big investment in time - it's technical and tricky

14 **Mind Bomb 5.11+ PG**
FA: Paul Van Betten, Richard Harrison – Summer 1990
A good route - if you can get off the ground! Climb the three-bolt arête 50 feet right of the falls, and just right of a cave. Bring some natural gear.

15 **Little Big Horn (aka Little Big Man) 5.9+**
FA: Jay Smith, Randy Grandstaff, Doug MacDonald – 1981
Walk 100 feet to the right of **Mind Bomb,** past three ugly cracks, to the point where the trail enters the trees. Start in the trees and climb a left-facing corner past an overhang (crux), to the varnished face and the top.

16 **Grippitty Gravity 5.10**
FA: Jon Martinet, Randy Grandstaff – mid 1970s
A short crux leads to an easy dihedral above. Start atop boulders 100 feet right of **Little Big Horn,** and below a low roof split by a crack. Climb out the roof (crux), then up the low-angled, varnished corner above. Finish up easy cracks and a short face.

17 **Sportin' A Woody 5.11+**
FA: Paul Van Betten, Sal Mamusia, Bob Conz – February, 1990
Another good-looking, left-facing corner protected by bolts and RPs is about 120 feet right of **Little Big Horn.**

18 **Captain Hook 5.11 R**
FA: Paul Van Betten, Jay Smith – Fall 1988
A large, steep face with two bolt routes on it is roughly 160 feet to the right of **Little Big Horn.** This climbs the left side of the face past two bolts to a thin seam/flake. Follow the seam/flake to the top.

19 **Captain Curmudgeon 5.11- R**
FA: Nick Nordblom, Jenni Stone, Paul Van Betten – Spring 1986
Climb loose flakes up the center of the steep face just right of **Captain Hook,** passing three bolts enroute.

20 **Captain Crunch 5.10- X**
FA: Nick Nordblom, Jenni Stone – Fall 1988
Bring a few small wires (not that you'll get many in!). Climb the right edge of the buttress, ending on the shoulder. Scary and loose.

21 **Tuckered Sparfish 5.10b**
FA: Paul Van Betten, Don Borroughs – June, 1992
Rope up 20 feet right of **Captain Crunch** on the next buttress, and climb past four bolts to a tree on the top.

22 **Rock Rastler 5.12+ R**
FA: Paul Van Betten – Summer 1985
Climb a hand crack to a roof, then struggle up an offwidth to the top.

Lost Creek Area

15 **Little Big Horn (aka Little Big Man) 5.9+**
16 **Grippitty Gravity 5.10**
17 **Sportin' A Woody 5.11+**
18 **Captain Hook 5.11 R**

23 **Heatwave 5.10- R**
FA: Paul & Pauline Van Betten – 1988
This is at the far right (north) end of Lost Creek Canyon, and 200 feet right of **Captain Curmudgeon.** Climb the center of a slabby face past three bolts. The hiking trail leading into upper Lost Creek Canyon passes just to the right of this route. It may also be used as the descent.

RAGGED EDGES AREA

The Ragged Edges Cliff is probably the most obvious cliff in the Willow Spring area. Either park as for Lost Creek Canyon, or continue down the spur road toward Willow Spring 3/10 of a mile (5/10 total from the scenic loop road). A large, varnished wall with an obvious vertical crack system in the center is on the left side of the road. This crack is the classic **Ragged Edges.** After deciding where to park, follow one of the clearly defined trails to the base of the cliff. The following routes are shaded most of the day.

24 **Kemosabe 5.10- PG**
FA: Sal Mamusia, Richard Harrison, Paul Van Betten, Wendell Broussard – 1983
An exciting climb. Bring small gear. Begin at the base of an arch 100 feet left of **Ragged Edges.** Climb the face and thin cracks up the arête of the arch to a bolt. Continue up the arête (scary), or weenie out and traverse off left, then up to the top. Walk off to the right (west) as for **Ragged Edges.**

Ragged Edges Area

The Graduate Cliff

39 **Walk To School 5.7**

40 **The Graduate 5.10-**

41 **Acid Jacks 5.11**

42 **Circle Jerks 5.11d**

Ragged Edges Cliff

24 **Kemosabe 5.10- PG**

25 **Tonto 5.5**

26 **Vision Quest 5.12d**

27a **Bodacious 5.10**

28 **Plan F 5.11- PG**

29 **Ragged Edges 5.8**

30 **Chicken Eruptus 5.10 PG**

31 **Gun Boy 5.11+**

32 **Sheep Trail 5.9+/10– PG**

36 **Sheep Dip 5.11- R/X**

25 Tonto 5.5

FA: Joe & Betsy Herbst – 1972

Climb the obvious crack in the slab that is 90 feet left of **Ragged Edges,** and just right of the arch mentioned in **Kemosabe.** At the top, move out right onto the face, or continue up the crack past a roof (5.7).

26 **Vision Quest 5.12d**
FA: Paul Van Betten, Sal Mamusia – October, 1988
Start 75 feet left of **Ragged Edges**, and just right of an ugly chimney/corner (**Theme Book**, 5.9). Climb up a short crack, then move slightly right to a bolt. Continue up the overhanging wall past three more bolts to a chain anchor. The second pitch climbs a left-leaning crack to the top (5.10). The two ring bolts below were placed by Craig Reason in a failed attempt to do a direct start.

27 **Bodiddly 5.10 PG**
FA: Robert Finlay, Richard Harrison – 1985
A very good route, but a tiny bit scary. Start 30 feet left of **Ragged Edges** on the left, front corner of the wall. Climb up the arête and face to a bolt, then follow more bolts up left (V1) past a steep flake. Continue up the easy face above. Walk off right as for **Ragged Edges.**

V1 Bodacious 5.10
FA: Sal Mamusia, Richard Harrison, Wendell Broussard – Spring 1983
From the second bolt on **Bodiddly**, it is possible to traverse straight left, then up past a bolt to rejoin the route. This was how this section of rock was first climbed; **Bodiddly** is the straighter (and perhaps more logical) line.

28 **Plan F 5.11– PG**
FA: Sal Mamusia, Richard Harrison, Paul Van Betten, Nick Nordblom – April, 1983
The initial finger crack is often done by itself; folks rap off the bolt in the **Ragged Edges** crack. Begin eight feet left of **Ragged Edges** below an obvious finger crack. Jam up the crack (5.10-), then angle left up the smooth, slippery face past a few bolts to the top.

29 **Ragged Edges 5.8** 👍
FA: Joe Herbst – early 1970s
THE classic route in Willow Spring. Bring lots of large gear. Climb the central crack on the varnished wall. The route is a full rope length, so bring an extra long rope to reach the belay tree, or #1.5 and 2 Friends for a belay just below the top. Walk off to the right (west), then back along the base of the crag.

30 **Chicken Eruptus 5.10 PG** 👍
FA: Richard Harrison, Wendell Broussard, Paul Van Betten, Sal Mamusia – Spring 1983
Named to commemorate Broussard's meal from the previous night! An excellent, sporty route for solid 5.10 leaders. Start five feet right of **Ragged Edges** and climb up a right-leaning ramp 40 feet to horizontal cracks. Move out right to the nose, then climb straight up the face past a bolt to the summit. Bring #1.5 and 2 Friends for the belay.

31 **Gun Boy 5.11+ PG**
FA: Paul Van Betten, Sal Mamusia, Richard Harrison, Danny Meyers – March, 1991
Start 30 feet right of **Ragged Edges** in a yellow band of rock. Climb past one bolt to a rounded, brown dihedral. Continue straight up the face, keeping just left of a black streak and passing two more bolts to the top. Bring small RPs.

32 **Sheep Trail 5.9+/10– PG** 👍
FA: John Bachar, Mike Lechlinski, Richard Harrison – Spring 1983
Wonderful climbing, but make sure you're solid at the grade. This was originally rated 5.8! Begin 40 feet right of **Ragged Edges** at a black streak in a clearing in the

vegetation. Weave up past numerous horizontals to a shallow, left-facing corner about 50 feet up. Continue basically straight up the face, exiting the brown rock at a short, vertical crack. Belay on the terrace (small to medium Friends), then walk off right.

33 **Dense Pack 5.10 PG**
FA: Nick Nordblom, Robert Finlay – Spring 1984
Another excellent sporty route. Traverse out left on a ledge system 150 feet right of **Ragged Edges** to a right-facing corner. Lieback and stem up the corner, then swing out left (V1). Weave up the varnished face above, angling slightly left. Belay on the terrace above, then walk off right.

V1 Twelve Pack 5.10+
FA: Paul Van Betten, Luis Saca – April, 1990
From the top of the corner on **Dense Pack,** follow an undercling flake out right, then climb up the face past one bolt to the terrace.

34 **Why Left 5.11b**
FA: Sal Mamusia, Paul Van Betten, Luis Saca – August, 1992
Begin about 30 feet right of **Dense Pack** below a line of bolts. Climb up and left past four bolts to the terrace.

35 **Why Right 5.11b**
FA: Paul Van Betten, Sal Mamusia, Luis Saca – August, 1992
Clip the first two bolts on **Why Left,** then climb up and right past two more. Walk off right on the terrace.

36 **Sheep Dip 5.11- R/X**
FA: (TR) Randy Marsh – 1981 First Lead: Richard Harrison, Robert Finlay – 1986
Start as for **Dense Pack,** at a black water streak about 150 feet right of **Ragged Edges.** Climb up the black streak on obvious holds (placing a #4 Friend in the horizontal) to a white, left-facing corner. Follow this up to the terrace.

Note: More topropes have been done to the right of these climbs, but aren't included in this guide.

The Graduate Cliff

This crag is 100 yards directly above **Ragged Edges**, and has huge, bulging roofs on its right side. It's easiest to approach these routes by walking up past the right side of the Ragged Edges Cliff. All three hard routes have rappel anchors, and start partway up the cliff on a varnished, water-streaked slab. The routes are in the shade in the afternoon, and are described from left to right.

37 **Walk To School 5.7**
FA: Jon Martinet, Randy Grandstaff, Scott Gordon – 1975
Climb the straight-in crack 40 feet left of **The Graduate** and 10 feet right of large white blocks at the mouth of a corridor.

38 **The Graduate 5.10-**
FA: Randy Grandstaff, Jon Martinet, Scott Gordon – 1975
Making the **Dean's List** isn't necessary to do this fine route. This climb forms the left margin of the varnished wall, and climbs a large, right-facing corner. There is a rappel anchor above the ceiling that is at the top of the corner. Bring a good selection of gear.

39 **Acid Jacks 5.11**

FA: Richard Harrison, Kevin Biernacki, Jerry from Colorado – Summer 1989

Start 20 feet right of **The Graduate** on the varnished slab below a line of bolts. Bring small gear to supplement the four bolts on the route, and belay at the same anchor as **The Graduate.**

40 **Circle Jerks 5.11d**

FA: Paul Van Betten, Richard Harrison, Kevin Biernacki – Summer 1989

Power past six bolts, starting 25 feet right of **Acid Jacks** and just left of some white corners above the varnished slab. There is a two-bolt belay over the roof.

The next three routes are 150 yards right and about 50 feet above the top of the Ragged Edges Cliff. They are to the right (northwest) and slightly below the Graduate Cliff. **Hard Case** is easy to spot from the road - it climbs a left-leaning crack on a cliff that has a brown upper section, and white lower section. Approach by walking up the bushy slope just right of the Ragged Edges Cliff.

41 **Territorial Imperative 5.10 R/X**

FA: Kurt Reider, Randy Grandstaff – 1980

This scary but excellent route is to the left of **Space Case** and **Hard Case,** and climbs

The Graduate Cliff

36 Sheep Dip 5.11- R/X
37 Walk To School 5.7
38 The Graduate 5.10-
39 Acid Jacks 5.11
40 Circle Jerks 5.11d
41 Territorial Imperative 5.10 R/X
42 Space Case 5.7
43 Hard Case 5.8
45 Sterling Moss 5.10

a black water streak on small edges. Bring small RPs - with a bit of luck (and talent), you can get some in just before the crux, which is between first and second bolts. Walk off left.

42 **Space Case 5.7**
FA: Unknown – 1970s
Originally done without the bolt. Begin 20 feet from the left edge of the **Hard Case** face, and climb past a bolt into a crack that leads up and slightly left. Walk off left.

43 **Hard Case 5.8**
FA: Joe Herbst, Matt MacMackin – circa 1975
Start 60 feet right of **Space Case,** below an obvious, varnished, left-leaning crack with a ceiling 20 feet up. At the top of the crack, go up the face and over a bulge.

The next two routes are down and right of **Hard Case,** and can be approached from that route, or from the end of the paved Willow Spring road. To approach from **Hard Case,** traverse 75 feet down and right on a rock rib, then scramble left (west) around some corners. To approach from the end of the pavement, walk 200 yards west into an obvious drainage that has three large pine trees on its left side. Scramble up to the highest pine tree (about 200 feet above the drainage bottom) and rack up.

44 **Soylent Green Jeans 5.9+/5.10-**
FA: Paul & Pauline Van Betten – 1985
Bring small gear, including tiny TCUs. Start at a clean right-facing corner left of **Sterling Moss,** and just above the huge pine tree. Climb the corner past a small pine tree, pull the roof left of **Sterling Moss,** then join that route into the upper corner.

45 **Sterling Moss 5.10**
FA: Richard Harrison, Randy Grandstaff, Wendell Broussard, Nick Nordblom, Sal Mamusia – Spring 1982
Named for a famous race car driver. Begin 30 feet right of the huge pine tree. Friction up the smooth, gray face to a bolt 30 feet up. Traverse right, then straight up to an overlap (pro). Move slightly right into a small right-facing flake/corner. Go up to a slab beneath an overlap, and make difficult moves over the overhang into the upper corner, which is followed to the top. Walk left to descend.

Sumo Greatness Slab

Walk 200 yards up the dirt road from the end of the pavement on the Willow Spring road. About 200 yards to the left (southwest) is a cliff band with a prominent black water streak in its center, and a smooth, slabby face at its right end. The next three climbs are located about 180 feet right of the water streak, on the slabby face, and are in the shade all day. There is Native American rock art about 30 feet right of the water streak, and like all rock art, it should not be climbed on or disturbed in any way. Dozens of routes have been done to the left of the black streak, including the classic corner of **Peaches** (5.5), and the overhanging face just left, called **Buckety Goodness** (5.11–).

46 **Sumo Greatness 5.9+ R**
FA: Richard Harrison, Nick Nordblom, Sal Mamusia, Paul Van Betten – Winter 1982
Start behind a pine tree, at a right-leaning crack/groove with dark varnish on its left side. This is about 150 feet right of the rock art. Climb 40 feet up the crack/groove, then angle right to a bolt. Climb up past a white splotch to another bolt, and then to the top. Descend off to the right.

47 **Ice Climb 5.9+ R**

FA: John Long, Lynn Hill, Doug Robinson, Randy Grandstaff – 1981

Slippery. Bring some TCUs and wires. Start 20 feet right of **Sumo Greatness** at a short, overhanging wide crack. Climb the face just left of the crack, then follow the thinner, right diagonalling crack to a red band. Clip a bolt, then go up a short seam through a bulge (fixed pin) to an alcove (#3 Friend). Step left and finish up the face above. Descend off to the right.

48 **Dean's List 5.11 PG**

FA: Paul Van Betten, Richard Harrison, Wendell "the Dean" Broussard, Druce Finlay (8 years old!) – 1990

Can you make the grade? Bring some small wires to protect the moves to the first bolt. You'll also need very thin fingers for the pockets past the last bolt. Start 45 feet right of **Sumo Greatness** atop boulders. Move out left onto a ledge above some low roofs, then angle back right on the slab to a bolt at the right edge of the dark streak. Face climb past two more bolts to the top. Descend off to the right.

Outhouse Wall

To access this cliff, park at the end of the pavement on the Willow Spring road. A south-facing cliff is on the north (right) side of the road, and above the outhouse building. Go 50 yards directly uphill to an alcove formed by a huge detached boulder. Many other routes have been done here, but only these two are described. This cliff is in the sun all day.

49 **Tricks Are For Kids 5.10- PG/R**

FA: Joe Herbst, Randy Grandstaff – 1975

Bring your bag of tricks for this one. Start in the alcove above the outhouse building and climb a flake to a ledge at 20 feet. Continue up the left-leaning corner/crack above (cheater stones may be needed to get off the ledge), moving right when the crack doglegs. Walk off right (south).

50 **Spiderline 5.7 PG**

FA: Unknown – 1975

Start in the alcove as for **Tricks Are For Kids,** and climb an easy wide crack on the left to a platform 40 feet up. Climb the left edge of the varnish above, finishing at a notch in a small ceiling. Walk off right (south).

Photo: Mike Ward Collection

Mike Ward tackles Breakaway in Icebox Canyon.

ICEBOX CANYON

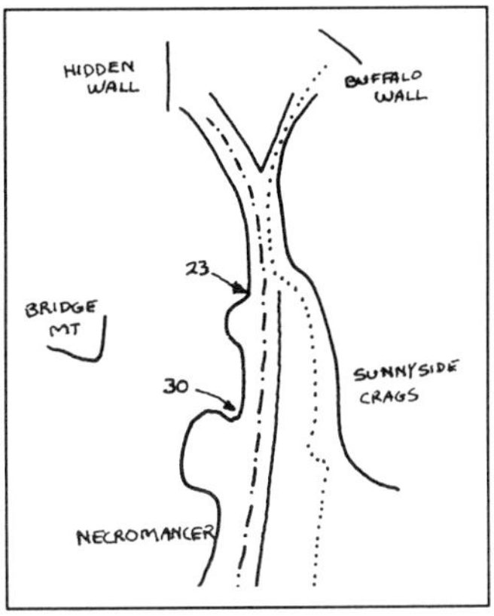

The Icebox Canyon routes described here are primarily one-pitch routes, although numerous multi-pitch routes exist. Drive 7.8 miles along the scenic loop road to the Icebox Canyon parking area. A well-maintained trail leads from the parking lot into the canyon; the majority of routes are within 25 minutes of the road.

Sunnyside Crag

Prominent orange roofs are seen at the bottom of the right (north) wall of the canyon as you view it from the parking lot. The climbs start about 200 yards to the left, further into the canyon, where the trail comes closest to the cliff. Approach time is about 20 minutes to this sunny cliff. Routes are described from right to left.

Icebox Canyon as seen from the trailhead

Bridge Mountain
20 The Northeast Arête 5.8
The Necromancer
34 Sensuous Mortician 5.9
Smears for Fears Area
29 Rojo 5.11+ PG/R
30 Smears For Fears 5.11 PG/R
31 Lebanese JoJo 5.9+
Refridgerator Wall
26 Amazing Grace 5.9
25 Earth Juice 5.10+ PG/R
23 Unfinished Symphony 5.11

1 **Whipper 5.10**
FA: Unknown – circa 1987
This route ascends a prominent roof crack about 100 feet left of a boulder with pine trees behind it. Climb the crack out a roof, then up the vertical crack to an anchor. Rappel with one rope.

2 **Backlash 5.11**
FA: Paul Van Betten, Jay Smith – October, 1987
Begin 45 feet left of **Whipper** at a crack system through a large, bulging roof and just right of a nose. Climb the flake/right-facing corner to a two-bolt anchor.

3 **Whiplash 5.12–**
FA: P1 Paul Van Betten, Jay Smith – October, 1987
FA: P2 Paul Crawford, Paul Van Betten – Spring 1988
Rope up as for the last route, but head out left around a corner/nose to a left-leaning crack. Belay above the crack in an alcove. A second pitch has been done, and follows thin cracks on an arête to an anchor under a roof (5.10+). Rap the route in two 75-foot rappels.

4 **Meteor 5.11**
FA: Unknown FFA: Les Hutchinson, Paul Van Betten – 1988
FA: P2 Jay Smith, Paul Van Betten – 1988
The second pitch was done at a later date, and is named **Meteorite.** Start in a cave 40 feet left of **Whiplash,** up on a ledge.

P1 Power out of the cave along an obvious roof crack to a belay stance in a shallow left facing corner. 60 ft., 5.11.

P2 Climb the vertical seam, then move right into a more pronounced crack/corner system. Climb up toward a roof, then angle about 30 feet up and right to an alcove under the roof. Pull the roof to broken ground and fixed gear (supposedly). 5.10+.

Descent: Rappel with two ropes.

5 **Cold September Corner 5.8**
FA: Joe Herbst, Stephanie Petrilak, Bill Bradley – Fall 1978
An obvious, right-facing dihedral is 20 feet to the left of **Meteor.** This has been climbed for two pitches, but no more is known. If you climb to the top of the crag, it appears you can descend off to the left (as for **Shady Ladies**).

6 **Shady Ladies 5.7**
FA: Jineen Griffith, Barbara Euser – May, 1978
Start 75 feet left of **Cold September Corner** at a varnished dihedral that is just left of a brown face with one bolt on it. Stem up the dihedral to a roof, then traverse out left to a rap station (two-rope rappel). The first-ascent party apparently continued upward for three more pitches. If you elect to do this, descend by heading left and rappeling from boulders and trees.

7 **Van Allen Belt 5.9?**
FA: Unknown – 1980's
Begin 20 feet left of **Shady Ladies** in an alcove below a dark-colored prow. Climb a crack system about 50 feet, then move left to the arête (V1) and up a crack system to a belay ledge. Rappel with two ropes.

V1 Move right and go up a shallow, left-facing dihedral to the anchor.

Sunnyside Crag, north wall

18 **Buffalo Wall** 5.11- A3+
16 **Tarantula** 5.12– 👍
14 **Gotham City** 5.12- PG/R 👍
7 **Van Allen Belt** 5.9?
5 **Cold September Corner** 5.8
1 **Whipper** 5.10

8 **Quark 5.10**
FA: Jay Smith – 1980s
The bolts were added after the first ascent. Start 75 feet left of **Van Allen Belt** at a cave with at a very nice-looking varnished nose just to its left. Climb past two bolts and horizontal cracks, then up left to a chain anchor.

9 **Tie Me Tightly 5.10**
FA: Nick Nordblom, Jenni Stone – 1988
Start 20 feet left on varnished rock with numerous pockets and huecos. Climb 15 feet up, then move right to a right-facing flake. Climb the flake, then move right and up to the chain anchor on **Quark.** Either rap from there, or continue up a crack and the face to a two bolt belay anchor.

10 **Mercedes 5.11-**
FA: Jay Smith – 1988
Begin as for **Tie Me Tightly,** but climb straight up the steep face past four bolts to a ceiling. Either move right to the chain anchor, or continue to the anchor above.

11 **Water Dog 5.11+**
FA: Paul Van Betten, Jay Smith, Paul Crawford – October, 1987
Rope up 10 feet left of **Mercedes** at a thin, slightly left leaning crack that is 10 feet right of a corner. Follow the crack up to a thread at the roof, then up and left through more ceilings to an obvious fixed anchor.

V1 Pit Bull Climb the crack just left of **Water Dog.** It joins the regular route at the thread.

V2 Hot Dog Toprope the thin arête/flake just left of **Pit Bull.**

12 **Water Logged 5.9?**
FA: Unknown – circa 1987
The obvious dihedral four feet left of **Hot Dog.** Rap from the **Water Dog** anchor with one rope.

13 **Mister Masters 5.9+**
FA: Paul Van Betten, Danny Meyers – 1987
This route may be used to set up a toprope for the next three routes. Start just left of the obvious dihedral and climb a varnished face up and left to the arête. Traverse left to a fixed anchor in the horizontal crack.

14 **Gotham City 5.12– PG/R**
FA: Paul Van Betten, Robert Finlay – October, 1987
The next three routes climb the front of an appealing, varnished buttress that is just left (west) of **Water Logged.** This route climbs the right side of the face using a thin seam for protection. It goes to the communal anchor in the horizontal crack.

15 **Spring Break 5.11+**
FA: Paul Van Betten, Sal Mamusia – Spring 1986
Ascend the center of the buttress along a thin, vertical seam, then go up the face past horizontal cracks, keeping just left of a right-curving fissure.

16 **Tarantula 5.12–**
FA: Paul Van Betten, Sal Mamusia – Spring 1986
Get Peter Parker to lead this one! The FA party found a tarantula in a horizontal crack about 40 feet up. This route climbs the left arête of the varnished buttress, following very thin seams to the communal belay.

Note: A bolted route has been attempted to the left of **Tarantula,** but as of press time, it hadn't been completed. The route has been dubbed **Hideous Taco,** after the talented Japanese climber Hidetaka Suzuki.

17 **Crossfire 5.11**
FA: Jay Smith, Nick Nordblom – 1989
Begin at a thin left-leaning crack about 40 feet left of the **Tarantula** arête and 20 feet right of a dirty, broken corner. Follow the left-leaning crack to a ceiling, then up past a bolt to horizontals. Move right into an obvious left-facing corner, and follow this to its top. Continue up the short, plated face to the anchor. A two-rope rappel will get you to safety.

The Buffalo Wall

According to the first (and apparently only) party to climb this wall, it is much steeper and more difficult than the Rainbow Wall in Juniper Canyon. Approach by hiking up the canyon beyond the Sunnyside Crags. Take the right (north) fork of the canyon up to the base of the wall. The approach up the north fork may require technical climbing. This cliff supposedly looks like a buffalo (hence the name), and is characterized by a huge, dark section of rock in its middle.

18 **Buffalo Wall 5.11- A3+**
FA: Richard Harrison, Paul Van Betten, Sal Mamusia – March 1991
The first ascent took three days of climbing, and used portaledges. The route climbs

the center of the wall, finishing on the "hump" of the buffalo. The free-climbing crux was a flaring offwidth arch on pitch three. There are nine pitches total. To descend, hike north to the dirt road running from Willow Spring toward Pahrump.

Hidden Wall

Like the Buffalo Wall, this cliff is not easy to get to, and may only have been climbed once (after reading the description, I can see why!). It apparently sits quite a distance up the south fork of Icebox Canyon, and is visible only from the loop road in the vicinity of White Springs or the Sandstone Quarry.

19 **Blitzkrieg 5.10+ R**
FA: Richard Harrison, Sal Mamusia – 1982
Follow prominent water streaks up the middle of the wall for seven pitches. There are no bolts on the route. To descend, hike north, then down all the way through Icebox Canyon.

Bridge Mountain

This mountain separates Icebox and Pine Creek Canyons. Numerous routes have probably been done, but information was available for only one. To approach this route, you first need to somehow climb the Frigidaire Buttress, then wander up through "the Maze" to the base of the arête. Obviously, this is a big undertaking.

20 **The Northeast Arête 5.8**
FA: Sal Mamusia, Richard Harrison – 1982
Three pitches up the obvious, white arête lead to the top of the mountain. Hike off north to the dirt road leading out from Willow Spring to Pahrump.

Refrigerator Wall

This is the largest cliff described in Icebox Canyon. The routes are in the shade most of the day (hence the name), and have about a 25-minute approach. To reach this section of the canyon, follow the trail from the parking lot past the Sunnyside Crag. The trail will drop down into the wash, at which point you cross the wash and head about 100 yards up the bushy hillside on the left (southwest) side of the canyon. The routes are described from right to left; the first four routes are on the right side of a nose about 100 yards right of three obvious pine trees.

21 **Weenie Juice 5.10**
FA: Richard Harrison, Paul Van Betten, Wendell Broussard, Sal Mamusia, Lynn Cronin – 1983
This excellent route is about 300 yards up canyon from **Unfinished Symphony** and the point where the trail drops down into the wash. Climb a gray, right-facing lieback flake that turns into an arch. Bring large gear, and two ropes to rappel from the bolt anchor.

22 **Music To My Fears 5.10**
FA: (pitches 1&2) Robert Finlay, Brad Ball – 1984
Only two pitches of this route will be described, although at least five have been done. Nick Nordblom, Paul Van Betten, Jay Smith and Paul Crawford have all turned back on the upper pitches due to loose rock and poor protection.

Within the most vegetated area to the right of the obvious pine trees, scramble up to a prominent white block that lies to the right of the obvious drainage/gully (the start of **Unfinished Symphony**).

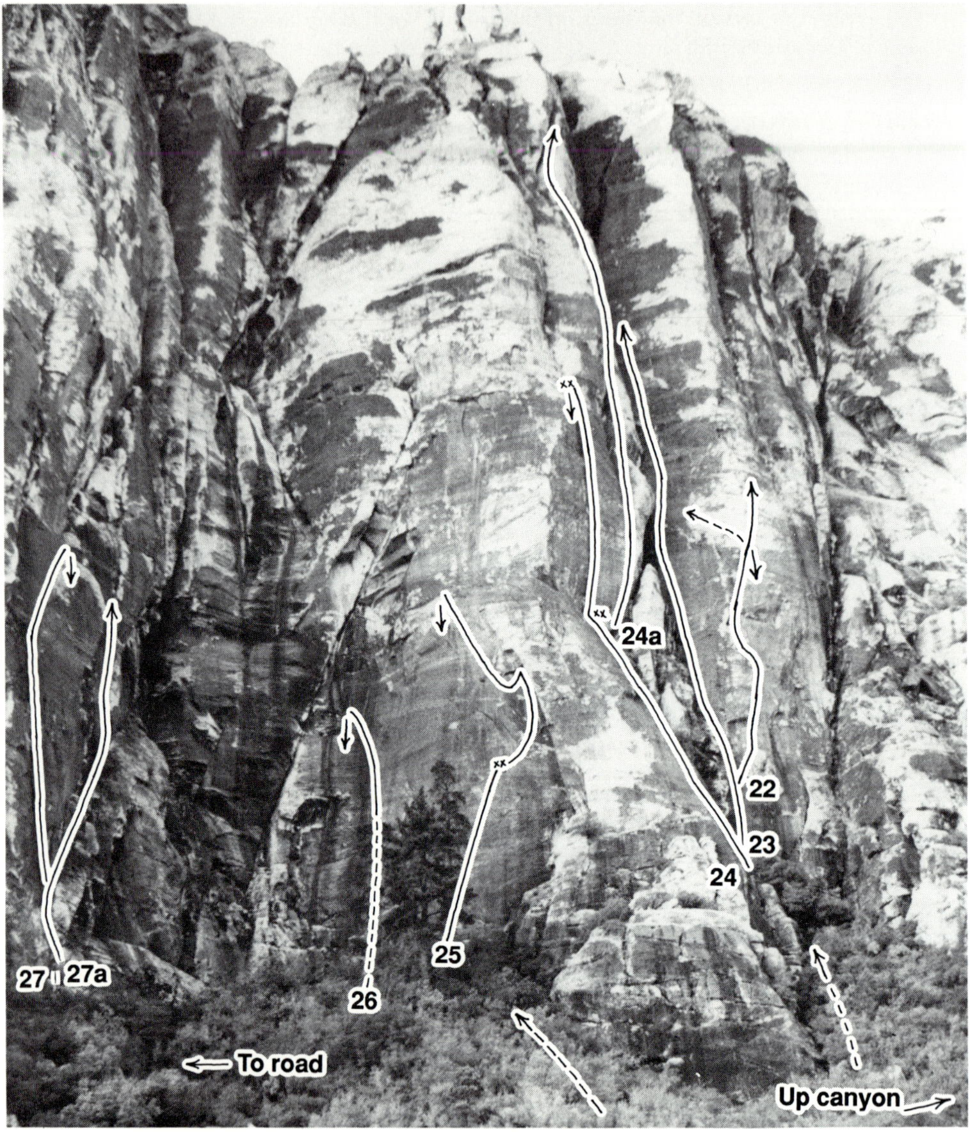

Refrigerator Wall

27 **Greased Lightning** 5.10-
27a **Swing Shift** 5.10
26 **Amazing Grace** 5.9
25 **Earth Juice** 5.10+ PG/R
24 **Breakaway** 5.10+
24a **Unnamed** 5.10 X
23 **Unfinished Symphony** 5.11
22 **Music To My Fears** 5.10

P1 From the top of the block, climb a thin crack up to large, loose, white blocks and belay. 80 ft., 5.9.

P2 Follow the obvious cracks left, then up, then left again, to the top of the crack systems. Belay on a ledge to the left, toward the **Unfinished Symphony** chimney. 150 ft., 5.10.

Descent: Either traverse left into **Unfinished Symphony** and rappel (two ropes may be needed), or continue up the loose, scary arête directly above the first two pitches (no fixed anchors).

23 Unfinished Symphony 5.11

FA: Ross Hardwick, Joe Herbst, Andre Langenbacher – Fall 1978

You'll be singing the blues if you don't like wide cracks! Bring lots of large gear and two ropes.

Start on the right side of a nose, about 100 yards right of three obvious pine trees, at the highest point of the vegetated hillside. This is directly below a gully leading to a prominent chimney system.

P1 Climb the drainage/gully past numerous ledges to a belay below the obvious chimney/corner. 150 ft., 5.9.

P2 Move right into the corner, then follow this past a bulge to a large, sloping ledge. 5.8.

P3 Worm up a chimney to an alcove (5.8), then continue up the nasty offwidth above to a belay stance.

P4 Follow the corner/crack to a belay under a huge roof.

P5 Three bolts lead up the central, overhanging crack. 5.11.

Descent: Rappel the route with two ropes.

Note: The prominent crack system just left of **Unfinished Symphony** has been climbed for six pitches, and has red bolt hangers on it. The Uriostes climbed the first five pitches (5.10-), and Bob Conz and Nick Nordblom added another pitch (5.10 X) before traversing into **Unfinished Symphony** and rappeling.

24 Breakaway 5.10+

FA: Danny Meyers, Mike Ward – Summer 1991

This excellent route climbs the very prominent black water streak to the left of **Unfinished Symphony**. Bring two ropes to rappel with. Start at the base of the **Unfinished Symphony** gully/drainage.

P1 Climb a broken corner to a low-angled face with three or four bolts. Belay on a small ledge at the base of the black water streak. 180 ft., 5.8.

P2 Zoom up the water streak past 11 bolts to a two-bolt belay at the base of a corner system. 140 ft., 5.10+.

Descent: Rappel the route.

The next two routes are on the right side of a small amphitheater, and directly behind three prominent pine trees. Both routes climb the smooth, varnished wall that is left of a nose and huge left-facing flake/corner.

25 Earth Juice 5.10+ PG/R

FA: Kurt Reider, Chris Robbins, Augie Klein – circa 1979

A route to get your juices flowing. Start right of the large pine trees and left of a ramp system that leads up right into the huge corner.

P1 Climb the varnished face past bolts to a crack. Follow the crack to a bolt, then move left to a belay station. 150 ft, 5.10+

P2 Go up a steep corner to a bolt, downclimb, then head up and left on a blunt prow to a belay stance below a white ceiling. 140 ft., 5.10+, PG/R.

Descent: Rappel with two ropes.

Note: There is a line of bolts between **Earth Juice** and **Amazing Grace.** The route was attempted long ago, and now appears to lead over to the first **Earth Juice** belay. Reportedly, the pitch is 5.10.

26 **Amazing Grace 5.9**
FA: Danny Meyers – 1985
Another great pitch. Begin to the left of the large pines and climb the varnished face past two bolts to a small ledge at the base of a shallow left-facing flake/corner. Ascend the flake/corner to its top, then traverse left to a belay anchor at the base of a thin light-colored water streak. Rappel with two ropes.

27 **Greased Lightning 5.10-**
FA: Nick Nordblom, Randy Marsh – 1989
A prow with a lightning bolt crack that leads to a ledge is across the amphitheater from **Amazing Grace** (toward the road). This route is supposedly just left of **Swing Shift** (the prominent crack system leading to clean, light-colored corners near the top of the wall (5.10; 7 pitches). Rappel from a bolted belay anchor with two ropes.

SMEARS FOR FEARS AREA

The next four routes are just above wash level, and directly across from the Sunnyside Crag. Follow the trail from the parking area for about 15 minutes, then turn left and drop into the wash. The routes are at the right (west) edge of a large amphitheater that is clearly visible from the road. Most of the routes are one pitch, and are described from right to left. You'll need to scramble up through a short, bushy section to reach the starting ledge for the routes.

28 **Romeo Charlie 5.10+**
FA: Sal Mamusia, Robert Finlay – 1989
The rightmost route, this starts on a ledge about 100 feet right of **Rojo** at a right-leaning crack just right of a mossy section of cliff. Climb the right-leaning crack, then up the face along a rounded arête that divides brown and black rock. Pull over a bulge, and angle slightly up and right to a fixed anchor on a mossy slab. Rappel with two ropes.

29 **Rojo 5.11+ PG/R**
FA: Paul Van Betten, Sal Mamusia – 1989
Rope up on a wide, flat ledge below a smooth, varnished face. A prominent, right-facing corner marks the left edge of this face. Climb a right-leaning crack/corner to its top, then face climb to a shallow right facing corner. Climb the corner (bolt) and the smooth face above (two bolts) to a bolted anchor. Rap with two cords.

30 **Smears For Fears 5.11 PG/R**
FA: Sal Mamusia, Mike Ward, Robert Finlay, Paul Van Betten – 1989
A classic one-pitch route, but not for the meek! Start 10 feet left of **Rojo** and 15 feet right of a prominent right-facing corner. The left side of the corner forms a jutting

Icebox Canyon, south wall

The Necromancer
32 **Hop Route 5.8**
34 **Sensuous Mortician 5.9**
35 **Fold-Out 5.8**

Smears for Fears Area
31 **Lebanese JoJo 5.9+**
30 **Smears For Fears 5.11 PG/R**
29 **Rojo 5.11+ PG/R**
28 **Romeo Charlie 5.10+**

prow. Climb a shallow right-leaning dihedral to a bolt 20 feet up, then go up the face past two more bolts to an overlap. Pull over this, and continue past two more bolts to the top (scary!). Rappel from the anchor with dual ropes.

31 **Lebanese JoJo 5.9+**
FA: Sal Mamusia, Bob Conz, "Frodo" Lybarger, Paul Van Betten – 1990
Good rock on this one, but the line is rather weird. Start about 75 feet left of **Smears For Fears** at a loose, right-facing corner below the left edge of a roof. Climb up to a pine tree, then traverse out right above the roof to a belay at a thin crack system. Climb the most obvious line up the varnished face above, then rappel with two ropes.

The Necromancer

This dark, squat formation is on the left (south) side of the canyon, and is clearly visible from the parking area. The formation is on the left side of a huge amphitheater; the routes lead to a huge terrace at the top of the formation. Follow the main trail from the parking lot until you are even with the obvious, orange roofs to the right (north) of the trail (before you reach the Sunnyside Crag). Turn left (south), and go down into the wash. Bushwhack about 150 yards up the opposite hillside to the prominent, dark brown buttress. Routes are described from left to right, beginning at a huge, right-facing corner/flake.

32 **Hop Route 5.7**
FA: Dave Hop, Joe & Betsy Herbst – March, 1975
The first pitch is very good, the rest a bit less interesting.

P1 Climb an obvious hand crack 15 feet right of a white, right-facing corner (V1). Follow the crack as it veers left into the corner, then go up the corner past a couple of chockstones to a belay ledge on the left. 100 ft., 5.7.

P2&3 Continue up easy cracks to the top of the buttress.

V1 You can climb the corner directly – it's a bit harder than the hand crack.

Descent: Walk off left (toward the road).

33 **Black Magic Panties 5.10–**
FA: Nick Nordblom, Jenni Stone, Danny Rieder – 1988
This route starts about 10 feet right of the hand crack on **Hop Route** and climbs up the varnished face past a fixed pin and two bolts. Turn the ceiling above at a hand crack, then move left to the huge ledge on **Hop Route** and finish up that route.

34 **Sensuous Mortician 5.9** 👍
FA: Nick Nordblom, Jon Martinet – Spring 1979
Perhaps the best route on the wall. Begin 20 feet right of the **Hop Route** hand crack at the next crack line. Follow the crack and black water streak to a bolted belay anchor. Bring lots of small gear, and two ropes to rappel with.

35 **Fold-Out 5.8**
FA: Tom Kaufman, Joe Herbst – March 1976
This climbs the rightmost crack system on the buttress. Excellent rock and good protection bring you to a ledge about 130 feet up. Continue up another pitch or two, or rappel from either the **Sensuous Mortician** anchor, or fixed slings on the **Fold-Out** ledge. If you do go to the top of the buttress, walk off left (toward the road).

PINE CREEK CANYON

Many fine routes are located in this beautiful canyon. To reach the trailhead, drive 10.3 miles along the scenic loop road. The parking lot has a sign, and is just off the road on your right. There are outhouses at the parking lot, and the trail is well-maintained to the point where the Pine Creek drainage splits.

From the parking lot, follow the obvious trail past an old homestead into the canyon proper (about a 15-minute walk). Ahead, the canyon is split into north and south drainages by a pyramid-shaped formation called the Mescalito. The first routes described in this chapter are on the right (north) side of the canyon well before it is split by the Mescalito.

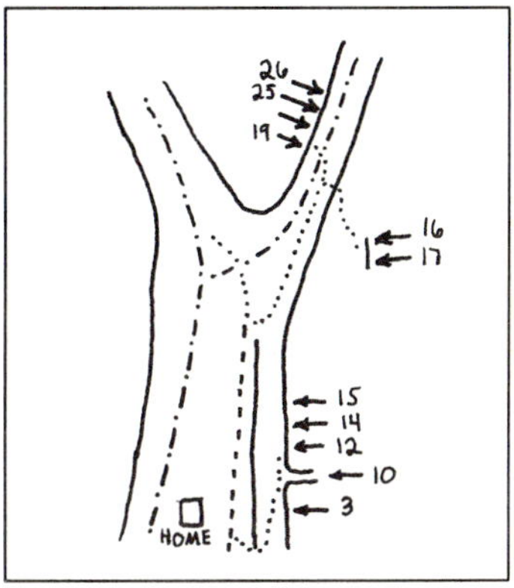

The north side of Pine Creek Canyon as seen from the old homesite

Straight Shooter Wall
5 Forget Me Knot 5.11
3 Straight Shooter 5.9+ 👍
Beer and Ice Gully
10 Terminal Velocity 5.13– 👍

Brass Wall
12 Mushroom People 5.10+
14 Topless Twins 5.10-

Straight Shooter Wall

As you enter the Pine Creek drainage, a short, red cliff band appears on the right. The Beer and Ice Gully is the huge, obvious cleft in the right wall of the canyon and the Straight Shooter Wall encompasses the climbs on the right side of this gully. To approach the Straight Shooter Wall and Beer and Ice Gully, head off the trail at the homestead, and skirt the right (east) end of the red cliff band. You also can hike directly up to the Beer and Ice Gully itself, but this entails a bit of dicey soloing through the center of the red band. A well-beaten path runs along the base of the canyon wall in this area, which gets sun all day. The routes are described from right to left. The first routes described are about 400 feet right of the Beer and Ice Gully on a smooth, black face.

1 **The Lazy Fireman 5.11a**
FA: Cameron Robbins, Randy Marsh – Spring 1991
A boulder/prow that protrudes from the cliff is at the right end of the smooth, black face described above. A short, overhanging dihedral with two bolts is on the left (west) face of this prow. Continue up the face above the dihedral past two more bolts to a chain anchor.

2 **Sidewinder 5.11–**
FA: (TR) Unknown – 1980s First Lead: Rick Dennison, Daryl Ellis – April, 1991
Start 20 feet left of the previous route, and just right of a striking finger crack that goes up the smooth, black wall. Climb the slippery face past five bolts, following small flakes and seams to a rappel anchor.

3 **Straight Shooter 5.9+**
FA: Joe Herbst – circa 1975
Climb the perfect, smooth, finger crack splitting the black face to an anchor 50 feet up.

4 **Slabba Dabba Do 5.11a**
FA: Mike Tupper – Winter 1985
Begin about 10 feet left of **Straight Shooter** and smear up the glassy face past three bolts with homemade hangers to the ledge 50 feet up.

5 **Forget Me Knot 5.11**
FA: Mike Tupper – Winter 1985
Shades of Lynn Hill! Start 20 feet left of **Straight Shooter** at a thin, vertical seam. Climb the seam, then up the face past one bolt to a ledge (5.11, possible belay here). Continue up the right-leaning crack on the upper wall to a rap anchor (5.11–). The crack is named the Bird Crack, was first climbed by Paul Van Betten, and originally was done as a second pitch to **Straight Shooter.**

Beer and Ice Gully

The Beer and Ice Gully is the huge, obvious cleft in the right wall of the canyon. As you enter the Pine Creek drainage, a short, red cliff band appears on the right. To approach the Beer and Ice Gully, head off the trail at the homestead, and skirt the right (east) end of the red cliff band. You also can hike directly up to the Beer and Ice Gully itself, but this entails a bit of dicey soloing through the center of the red band.

6 **29 Posers 5.11+**
FA: Paul Van Betten, Bob Yoho – 1987
As you enter the Beer and Ice Gully proper, there are a few obvious features on the right wall. This route climbs a flake (Friends) to an overhanging, huecoed face. Power up the face past two bolts and a blind #1.5 Friend placement to a tree. Rappel off the tree back to the ground.

Photo: Randy Marsh

Richard Harrison on a first ascent in Pine Creek Canyon.

7 **This Bud's For You** 5.11–

FA: Paul Van Betten, Bob Conz – 1988

Start 100 yards uphill of the previous route at a left-facing, left-leaning book with a hand-and-finger crack in its back. Climb the corner to a two-bolt belay station (130 feet).

8 **Corona Crack** 5.11+

FA: Paul Van Betten, Sal Mamusia, Bob Conz – Winter 1988

Begin 50 feet left of **This Bud's For You** at a curving, flaring, finger crack. Bring an assortment of gear for this one. This shares the belay with **This Bud's For You.**

9 **Stout Roof** 5.10+

FA: Mike Ward, Paul Van Betten, Bob Yoho – Winter 1987

An acquired taste. Climb a crack through an obvious roof to a ledge.

10 **Terminal Velocity** 5.13–

FA: Mike Tupper, Greg Mayer – March, 1989 (after a year of working on it!)

A big undertaking, but a must for the true crack master. Allow about 45 minutes for the approach. Bring gear up to a #3 Friend, including a full set of TCUs and Sliders or Lowe Balls. Scramble up the Beer and Ice Gully to its very end – this is where the climb begins.

P1 Scramble 20 feet up a chimney/gully, then exit onto the left wall. Climb the face and crack above to a one bolt belay. 160 ft., 5.9.

P2 Exit right from the belay onto a vertical wall, and crank up the "Wheat Thin"-like flake (bolts) to its top. Jog left and climb up a shallow dihedral to a two-bolt belay. 60 ft., 5.11+.

P3 Traverse 15 feet straight right over the lip of a small roof (exposed). Enter a right-facing dihedral, and follow this to another two-bolt belay. 70 ft., 5.11.

P4 Climb a small dihedral for 30 feet (5.12–), then exit left to the base of a striking, thin finger crack. Punch up the crack to a two-bolt belay. 60 ft., 5.13–.

P5 Stem up a slightly overhanging corner past two bolts to a finger crack in the corner. Continue up another 50 feet to the top of the crack. Exit left across a slab to a two-bolt belay. 65 ft., 5.11+.

Descent: Rappel with two ropes as follows: P5 to P4, P4 to P3, P3 straight down 150 feet to a ledge with bolts, ledge with bolts 150 feet to ground.

11 **Chilly Ones** 5.10+ R

FA: Paul Van Betten, Sal Mamusia – 1988

Start directly across the gully from **This Bud's For You.** Climb past three bolts to a hand-and-fist crack that leads to a ledge. Rappel with two ropes.

Brass Wall

This section of cliff is to the left (west) of the Beer and Ice Gully, which is the huge, obvious cleft in the right wall of the canyon. As you enter the Pine Creek drainage, a short, red cliff band appears on the right. To approach the Beer and Ice Gully, head off the trail at the homestead, and skirt the right (east) end of the red cliff band.

12 **Mushroom People** 5.10+

FA: Dave Diegelman, Randy Grandstaff, Greg Child – 1979

Start about 200 feet left of the Beer and Ice Gully, and directly below the left edge of a bushy ledge about 70 feet up. Climb a thin, left-angling seam up slippery black rock to a rap anchor just below a huge hueco. Two ropes are needed for the rappel.

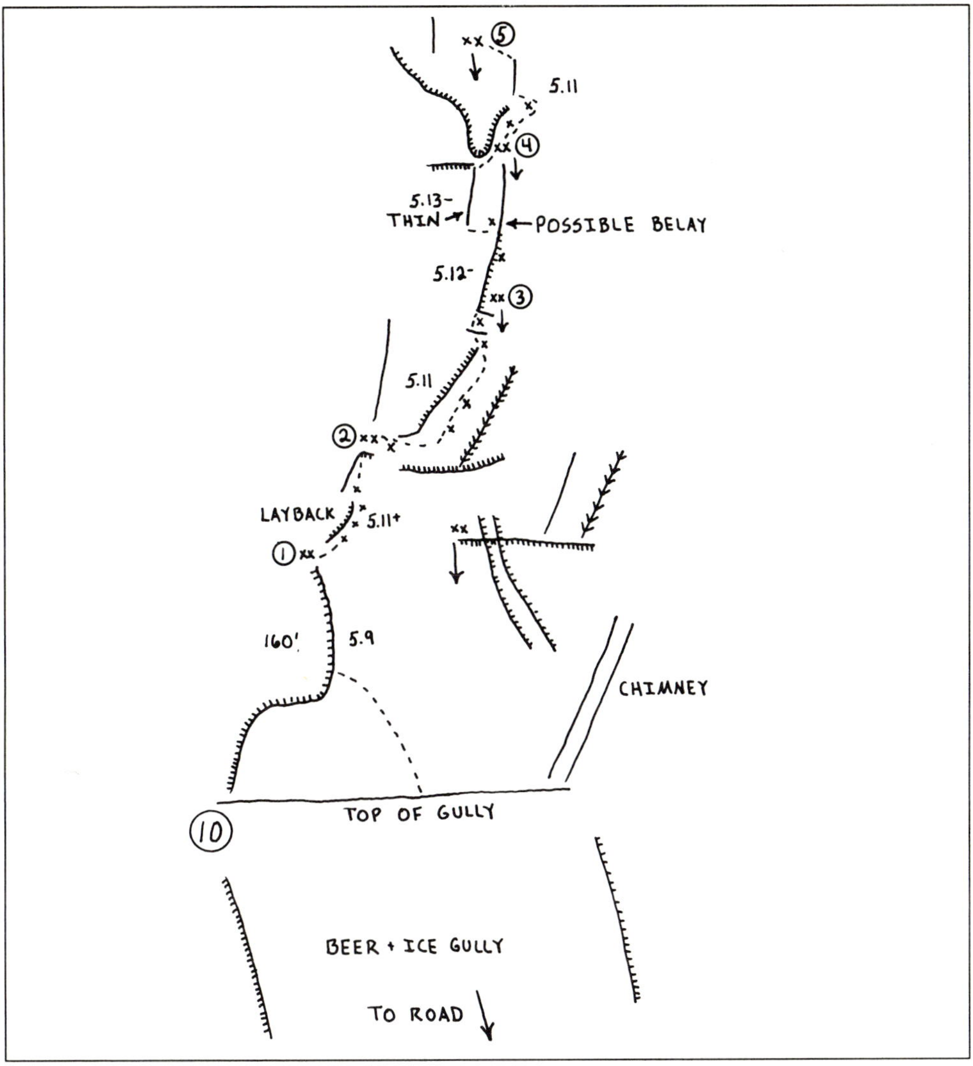

Terminal Velocity, 5.13–

13 **No Laughing Matter 5.10–**
FA: Greg Child, Randy Grandstaff – 1979
Start 70 feet above the ground on the bushy ledge mentioned in the **Mushroom People** description, and climb a thin crack that ends atop pillar in a corner. Rappel.

14 **Topless Twins 5.10–**
FA: Randy Grandstaff, Wendell "the Dean" Broussard – 1980
Rope up 45 feet left of **Mushroom People** below a series of dihedrals that lead to thin, black cracks. Climb the cracks to a rappel station, then zip back to the ground with two ropes. You'll need a good selection of gear for this route.

15 **Sea of Holes 5.10 R**

FA: Nick Nordblom, Jay Smith P1 1980, P2&3 – Fall 1988

The first pitch is **The Black Hole,** and was done before the rest of the route. Begin about 50 feet left of **Topless Twins.** An excellent route.

P1 Start out of a chimney and climb a shallow corner to a two bolt belay. 110 ft., 5.8.

P2 Traverse out left using numerous huecos, then up through the left side of a roof at a crack. Friends in huecos for pro. One-bolt belay on arête. 160 ft., 5.10, R.

P3 Go straight up the black face to a crack in a bulge. Continue up the face to a belay on the shoulder of the buttress. 165 ft., 5.10–.

Descent: You'll find a rap station in the gully. Descend in three rappels.

OUT OF CONTROL AREA

The next few routes are on the right (north) wall of the canyon, but are quite far from the routes previously described. From the parking lot, walk up the trail toward the Mescalito, then take the right (north) fork of Pine Creek. The trail becomes faint and braided at this point, but the best route is to head uphill about 100 feet (above the red band of rock), then go left (west), contouring along the hillside on a trail. Roughly 350 yards up this drainage, and past three huge pine trees, the lowest cliff band on the right is split by a low-angled gully. Head up this gully until you are above the first cliff band, then go right (toward the road) on ledge systems about 100 yards. You should now be even with the front (east) face of the Mescalito. The following routes are described from left to right, and are in the sun all day.

16 **American Ninja 5.10**

FA: Paul Van Betten, Robert Finlay – 1986

Start below a short, clean dihedral in an alcove about 50 feet above the traverse ledge. Climb the corner to rap anchors on the low-angled face above.

17 **Out Of Control 5.10**

FA: Randy Grandstaff, Dave Anderson – 1978

Begin about 150 feet up and right of **American Ninja** at the base of a long, straight hand crack in a smooth, white wall. This crack is about 15 feet left of a huge dihedral. Bring lots of hand-sized gear, and two ropes to rappel with. Follow the crack past a roof to a rap station.

18 **Remote Control 5.9**

FA: Dave Anderson, Randy Grandstaff – 1978

Rope up 15 feet right of **Out Of Control** at the base of a huge corner. Climb the left-facing dihedral (which has a huge, smooth, right wall) for 165 feet to a rappel anchor.

DARK SHADOWS AREA

The next nine routes are on the north face of the Mescalito, the pyramid-shaped formation splitting the canyon into two drainages. The rock is of excellent quality, rivaling the best in Black Velvet Canyon. Bring two ropes to get off all of these shady routes.

From the Pine Creek parking lot, follow the trail into Pine Creek Canyon. When the canyon forks, take the right (north) fork. The trail becomes faint and braided at this point, but the best route is to head uphill about 100 feet (above the red band of rock), then go left (west), contouring along the right hillside of this drainage about 600 yards on one of the many trails that lead to the large, varnished, north face of the Mescalito. Pine Creek runs right along the base of the wall here, and the surrounding vegetation is surprisingly

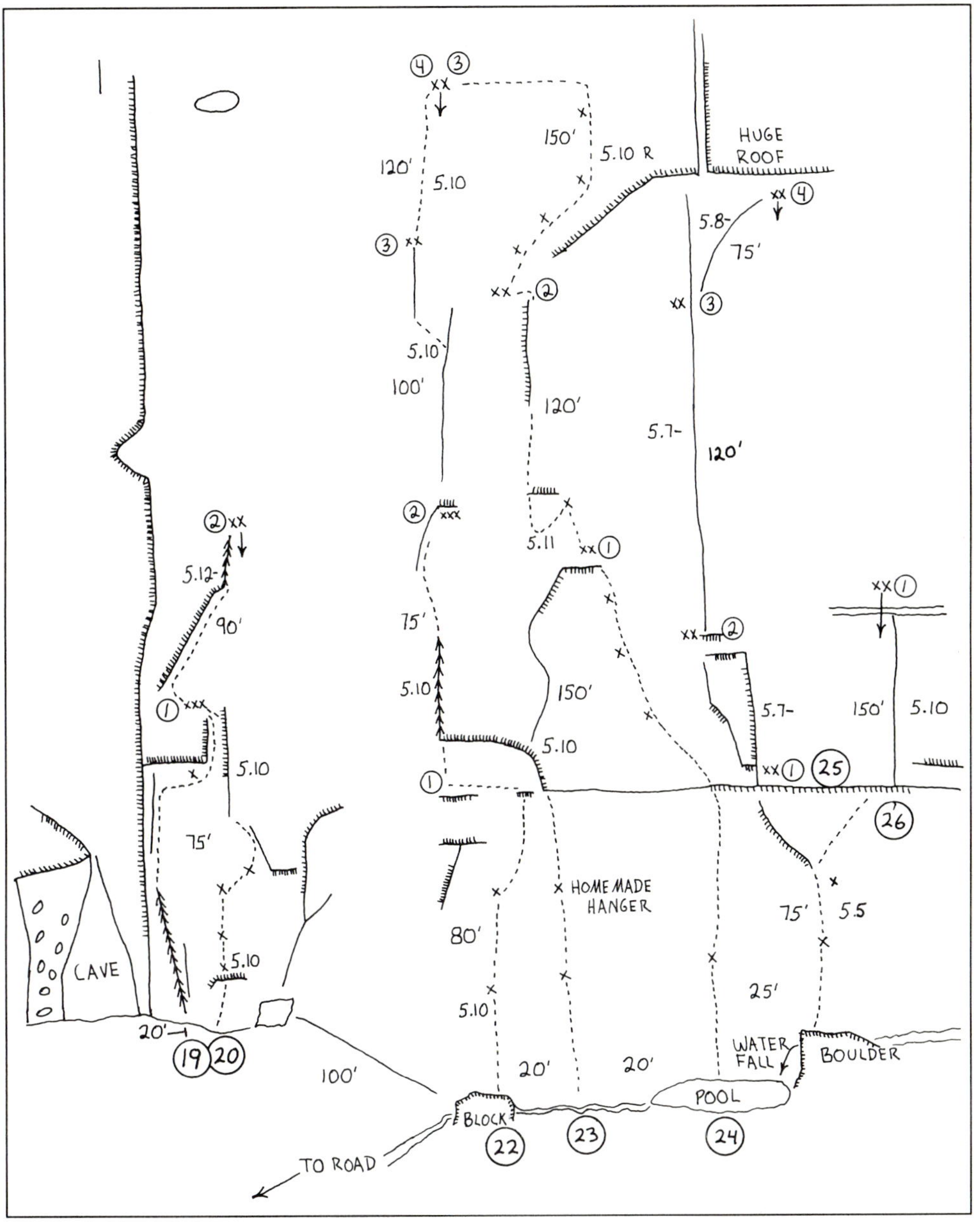

Dark Shadows Area

19 **Lethal Weapon 5.12**
20 **Parental Guidance 5.12– PG**
22 **Risky Business 5.10+ PG** 👍
23 **Excellent Adventure 5.11 R** 👍
24 **Sandstone Sandwich 5.10c**
25 **Dark Shadows 5.8–** 👍
26 **Slot Machine 5.10 PG** 👍

lush and varied. The climbs are described from left to right, as you approach up the creek.

19 **Lethal Weapon 5.12**

FA: Mike Tupper, Greg Mayer – Fall 1989

The left (east) margin of this wall is defined by a huge, right-facing chimney/corner system, the bottom of which forms a cave (**Negro Blanco,** 5.10+). Start 20 feet right of the cave, in a cleared area below several small corners and a huge flake/chimney system.

Climb the easy, bigger dihedral to the base of a gaping chimney, then angle right up a corner to a roof. Traverse right under the roof (bolt), then follow a flake to a belay station.

20 **Parental Guidance 5.12– PG**

FA: Mike Tupper, Greg Mayer – Winter 1988

The first pitch is worth doing by itself. Bring Friends and wires. Start eight feet right of **Lethal Weapon** at a small block leaning against the cliff.

P1 Climb the face to an overlap 15 feet up (bolt), then continue past two more bolts to a stance (bolt). Angle up left to an obvious, vertical flake. At the top of the flake, step left to a communal belay. 75 ft., 5.10.

P2 Face climb past bolts to a right-leaning flake/crack, and pull past this into a shallow dihedral. 90 ft., 5.12–.

Descent: Rap the route.

21 **Short Circuit 5.10**

FA: Mike Ward, Nick Nordblom – July, 1992

As of press time, only the first pitch had been done on this route, although it's expected to go three pitches. Bring TCUs and wires up to a #7 Rock. Start about 20 feet right of **Parental Guidance** and climb a corner past a fixed peg. Continue past five bolts to a two bolt rap anchor.

22 **Risky Business 5.10+ PG**

FA: Mike Tupper, Greg Mayer – Summer 1985

Certainly as good as the movie - maybe better! Begin 100 feet right of **Parental Guidance,** at the point where the stream runs along the base of the cliff and directly in front of some large blocks.

P1 Go up a short, left-facing flake, then face climb past two bolts. Move slightly right to a flake (scary), then easily up left (V1) to a belay at the left end of an arching ceiling. 80 ft., 5.10.

P2 Follow the shallow dihedral above the left edge of the ceiling, then continue along a seam to a belay station under a small ceiling. 75 ft., 5.10.

P3 Step left and climb up and slightly left, passing numerous bolts to another bolted belay anchor. 100 ft., 5.10.

P4 Continue up the varnished wall above to another rap station. 120 ft., 5.10.

V1 It's possible to undercling the arching ceiling at 5.11+ (but who'd want to?).

Descent: Rappel with two ropes.

23 **Excellent Adventure 5.11 R**

FA: Mike Tupper, Greg Mayer – Fall 1989

Perhaps the best route on the wall. Really scary on the last pitch, both for the leader and follower. Start 20 feet right of **Risky Business** at the left edge of the deeper pool at the base of the cliff.

P1 Climb to the right end of the arching ceiling on **Risky Business,** passing two bolts with homemade hangers enroute. Follow the arching ceiling left 15 feet, then pull the ceiling. Intimidating climbing leads left to a crack system. Follow this up and slightly right past an overhang to a belay stance with bolts. 150 ft., 5.10.

P2 Go up from the belay, then make tricky moves down and left (bolts). Climb up the right side of a vague arête, stepping back out left to a belay anchor. 120 ft., 5.11.

P3 Get ready! Follow bolts up and right along the lip of the giant roof, then go straight up (5.10 R). Eventually, you can angle back left to the final rap station on **Risky Business,** and rappel the route. Whew!

24 **Sandstone Sandwich 5.10c**

FA: Bob Conz, George Smith, Jim Lybarger – July, 1990

Don't bite off more than you can chew! A wonderful bolted face climb between the first pitches of **Excellent Adventure** and **Dark Shadows.** Rappel with two ropes from the first belay on **Excellent Adventure,** or continue up that route.

25 **Dark Shadows 5.8–** 👍

FA: Lots of folks – 1973

One of the best 5.8 routes at Red Rocks, and a popular soap opera in its time. The climb goes to the top of the Mescalito, but only the first four pitches are described here. Bring a variety of gear, and be prepared to have fun. Start on a flat boulder atop a small waterfall at the right edge of a pool, and below a huge, black dihedral system capped by a giant roof. Good belay ledges on each pitch.

P1 Face climb up and right past two bolts to a left-leaning ramp that leads to the base of a varnished corner. Two-bolt belay anchor. 75 ft., 5.5, PG.

P2 Climb the clean, varnished, right-facing corner above, moving left to a belay ledge and a bolted belay. 75 ft., 5.7–.

P3 Stem up the beautiful dihedral to a ledge with two different bolted belay anchors. 120 ft., 5.7–.

P4 Climb the right-curving crack in the right wall to another two bolt belay under the giant roof. 75 ft., 5.8–.

Descent: Rappel the route in three rappels, using two ropes.

Note: From the last pitch described on **Dark Shadows,** it's possible to climb out left through the giant roof, using old fixed pegs for pro. This is **Heart Of Darkness** (5.10+). There is a rap anchor right above the roof. The route continues upward, but the pitch described is the most worthy of effort. It was first climbed by Richard Harrison, John Long and Lynn Hill in Spring, 1981.

26 **Slot Machine 5.10 PG** 👍

FA: Bob Conz, Sal Mamusia – July, 1990

A worthwhile pitch that rewards those with small fingers. Start as for **Dark Shadows,** atop a flat boulder at the right edge of the pool at the base of the cliff. Bring small RPs and gear up to a #3 Friend.

Climb easily past two bolts to the base of a left-leaning ramp (as for **Dark Shadows**). Continue straight up a thin seam in a steep, varnished wall, passing one bolt to the two-bolt anchor. Rappel with two ropes. 150 ft., 5.10.

Photo: Ward Collection

Mike Ward on the Original Route, Rainbow Wall.

JUNIPER CANYON

For most routes, it is best to approach Juniper Canyon by parking at the Pine Creek parking area, located 10.3 miles along the scenic loop road. Follow the very well-marked trail down the hill, then angle south across the desert (no trail) to Juniper Canyon. Once you enter the canyon, follow the main drainage to avoid dense scrub oak. The selected climbs are scattered throughout the canyon - each route has its own detailed description to help you find the start.

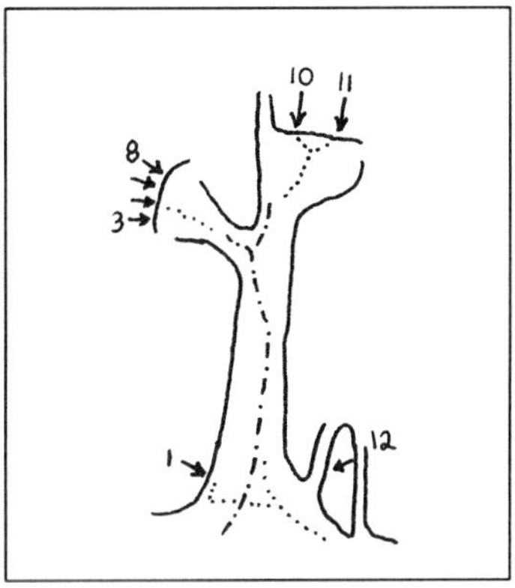

1 **Crimson Chrysalis 5.9**
FA: Jorge & Joanne Urioste – October, 1979

A superb route that requires both crack climbing skills and stamina. Bring two ropes and a good selection of bigger gear. This long, continuous crack system is on

Crimson Chrysalis

the Cloud Tower, at the mouth of Juniper Canyon. From the Pine Creek parking area, follow the very well-marked trail down the hill, then angle south across the desert (no trail) to Juniper Canyon. Once you enter the canyon, head up the left (south) slope of the drainage, aiming for a prominent bushy ramp that leads to the base of a white buttress with a red top (the Cloud Tower). Follow this bushy ramp up and right (west) a couple hundred yards to the top of the ramp, then go down (west) a short way to the base of the route.

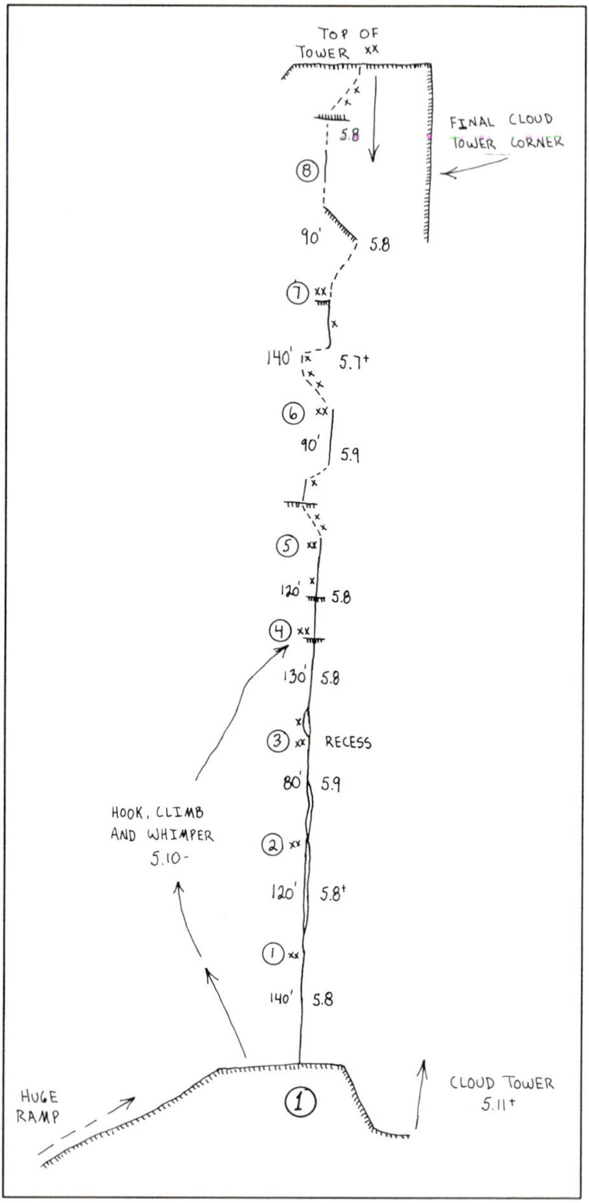

Crimson Chrysalis, 5.9

P1 Climb the obvious crack and right-facing corner to a belay anchor. 140 ft., 5.8.

P2 Continue up the crack/corner past four bolts to another anchor in a recess. 120 ft., 5.8+.

P3 Jam up the same fissure past two bolts to a hanging belay from bolts. 80 ft., 5.9.

P4 Worm up a chimney (bolt), then follow thin cracks through two bulges to a belay ledge. 130 ft., 5.8.

P5 Climb a steep, thin crack past one bolt to a belay station about 40 feet above a ledge. 120 ft., 5.8.

P6 Go up left past two bolts to a ledge at 40 feet. Follow a seam past one bolt, move right to a bolt, then follow a thin crack to the anchor. 90 ft., 5.9.

P7 Move left and climb past three bolts until you are forced back right into a crack. One more bolt will get you to the belay stance in the red rock. 140 ft., 5.7+.

P8 Climb up past a bulge, then angle right to a left-leaning ramp. Climb a steep face and crack above the upper end of the ramp to a belay below an overhang. 90 ft., 5.8.

P9 Power through the overhang, then move about 30 feet right to a depression. Continue past some bolts to the anchor on top. 125 ft., 5.8.

Descent: Rappel with two ropes. Be careful not to get the ropes stuck in the crack.

2 **Cloud Tower 5.11+** 👍

FA: Paul Van Betten, Richard Harrison, Nick Nordblom – Spring 1983

Called **The Astroman of Red Rocks** by some. The final pitch is one of the very best in the area. This climb is on the Cloud Tower, at the mouth of Juniper Canyon. From the Pine Creek parking area, follow the very well-marked trail down the hill, then angle south across the desert (no trail) to Juniper Canyon. Once you enter the canyon, head up the left (south) slope of the drainage, aiming for a prominent bushy ramp that leads to the base of a white buttress with a red top (the Cloud Tower). Follow this bushy ramp up and right (west) for a couple hundred yards to the top of the ramp, then go down (west) a short way to the base of the route.

Start about 100 feet right of **Crimson Chrysalis.**

P1 Climb a left-facing corner to a belay. 150 ft., 5.8.

P2 Continue up the corner, and belay on a bushy ledge. 100 ft., 5.8.

P3 Power up the beautiful straight-in hand crack. 150 ft., 5.10–.

P4 Stem up the right-facing, right-leaning corner with a tips crack in its back to a ledge with two bolts and a loose block. Bring lots of TCUs for this cruxy pitch. 120 ft., 5.11+.

P5 Pull over a roof, then up a hand and fist crack in the middle of a face to a belay ledge. 140 ft., 5.10.

P6 Struggle up an offwidth to the top of the tower. 60 ft., 5.10+.

P7 Climb the incredible right-facing corner with a hand-and-finger crack in its back. The crux is reaching the bolts at the top of the pitch. 160 ft., 5.11+.

Descent: Use two ropes to rappel straight down (not down the route), keeping right of the tower.

The Rainbow Wall

The Rainbow Wall sits high on the left (south) side of Juniper Canyon, and is clearly visible from the Calico Hills and Sandstone Quarry Area. It is characterized by colorful green and black streaks, and huge red arches on the right portion of the cliff. Only one route on the wall will be thoroughly described in this guide (the only one I've done), but topos are included for most of the other recorded routes on the wall. Climbing this formation is not as hideous as it may have been portrayed, although it does require a commitment to hard work. The wall is in the shade most of the day, and the approach takes about four hours if you're hauling gear. Routes are listed from left to right.

3 **Sergeant Slaughter 5.10 A3** 👍

FA: Richard Harrison, Paul Van Betten – Winter 1984

This was the first winter ascent of the wall. Follow the corner systems that parallel the left shoulder of the wall for six pitches to a large ledge. Climb behind a large, detached pillar (5.10), gaining the shoulder of the wall. Follow cracks and corners upward, aiming for an obvious right-facing corner capped by a roof. Bring six Knifeblades; six Lost Arrows; six angles (up to three-quarters of an inch); a double set of wires; TCUs and Friends (bring a BIG Friend); one set of RPs; and one set of HBs.

4 **Emerald City 5.10 A2**

FA: Randy Grandstaff, John Thacker – Spring 1983

The route climbs a series of corners that trend right and lead to the right edge of a large ledge. A big black water streak comes off this ledge. Above, follow either of two

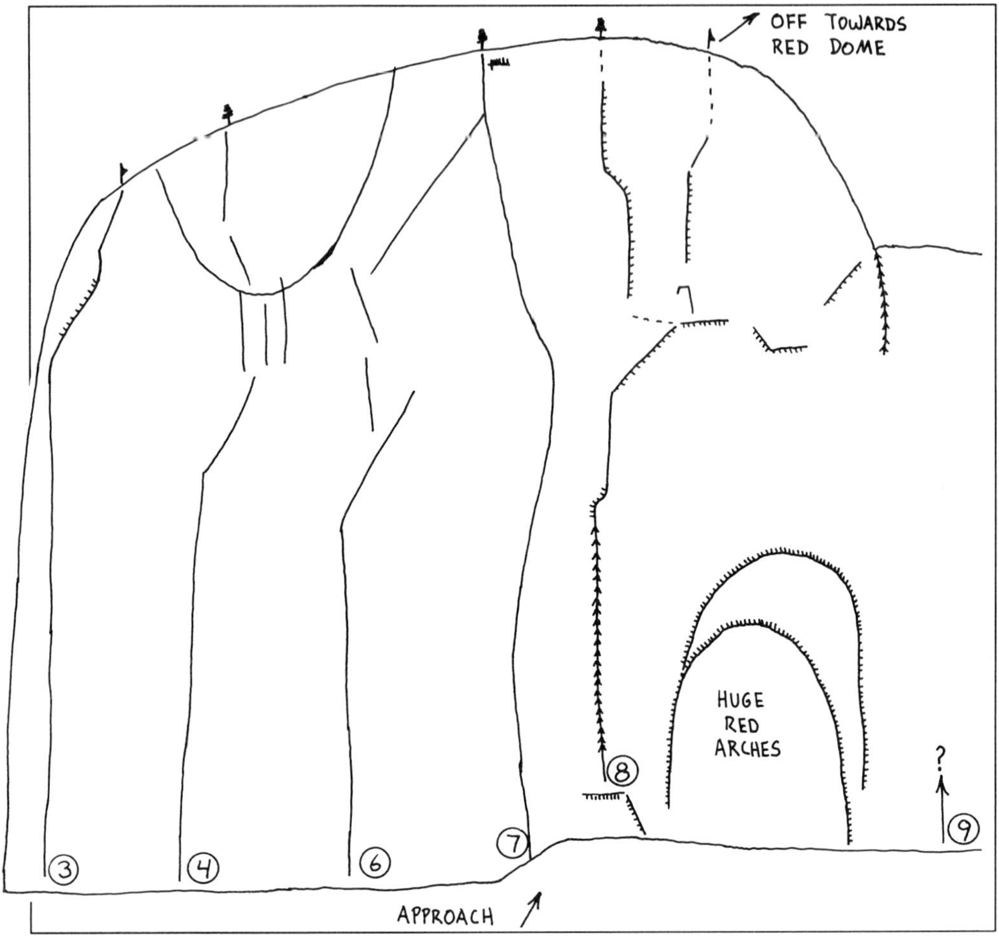

Rainbow Wall Overview

corners that start from the right end of the ledge and lead to a shattered recess. Climb through this to the top. Gear needed: four Knifeblades; four Lost Arrows; two baby angles; double sets of TCUs and Friends; one set of wires and RPs.

5 **Crazy World 5.7 A4**

FA: Bart Groendycke, Todd Alston – May, 1992

The newest and hardest. This climb doesn't go to the top of the cliff, and has fixed rappel stations. The route goes just left of the prominent black water streaks on the wall. The first-ascent party reccommends fixing three ropes, and sleeping at the base of the route. Gear list: seven short thin Knifeblades; 15 RURPs; five Lost Arrows; two hooks, one Fish hook; four three-eights-inch bolt hangers; 25 #1 Copperheads; 30 #2 Copperheads; 20 #3 Copperheads; 10 #4 Copperheads; 25 extra three-eights-inch Copperheads for ladders; three sets of RPs; two sets of Stoppers; three sets of TCUs; two #1 Camalots; one each #2-4 Camalots.

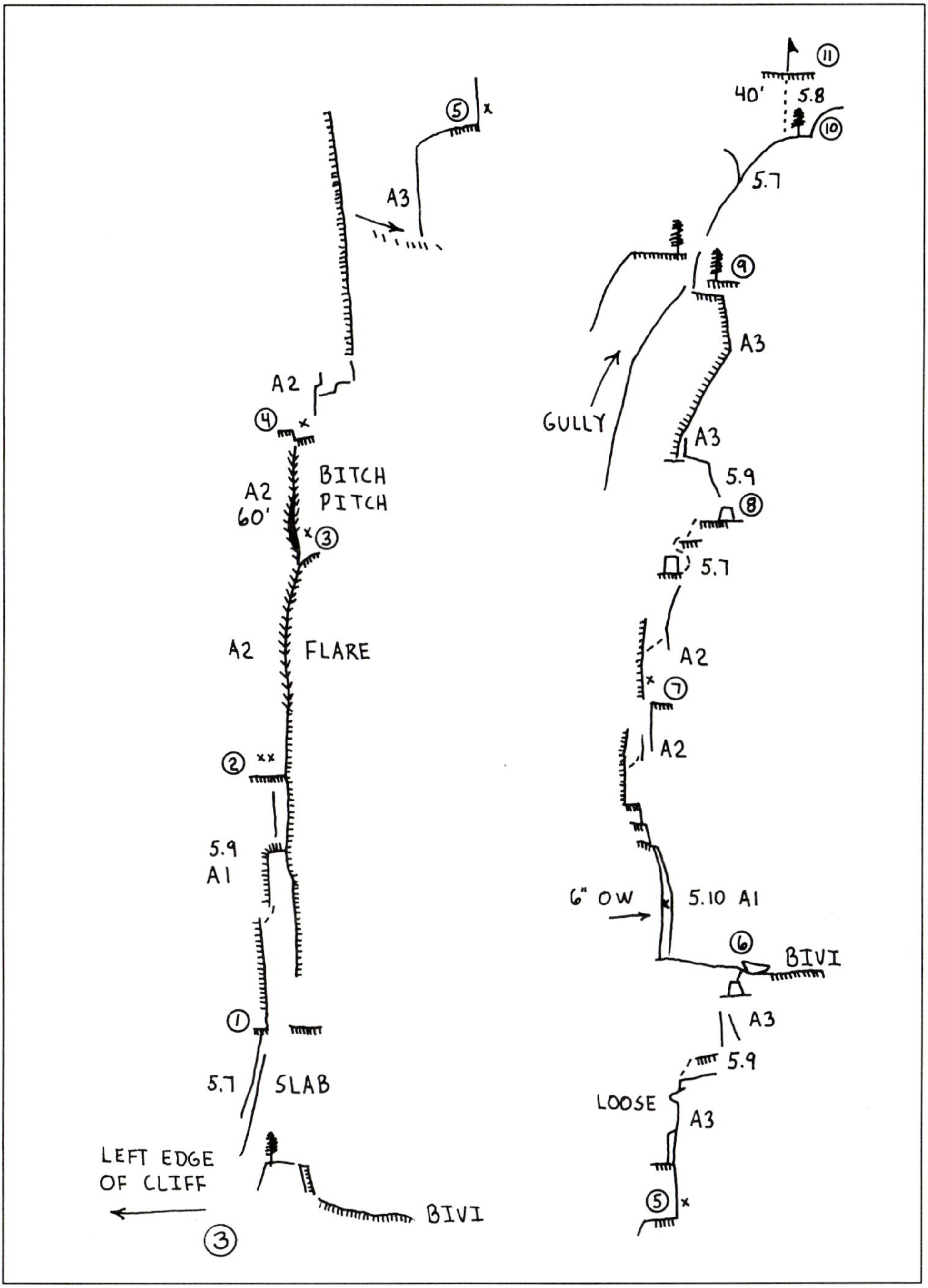

Sergeant Slaughter, 5.10 A3

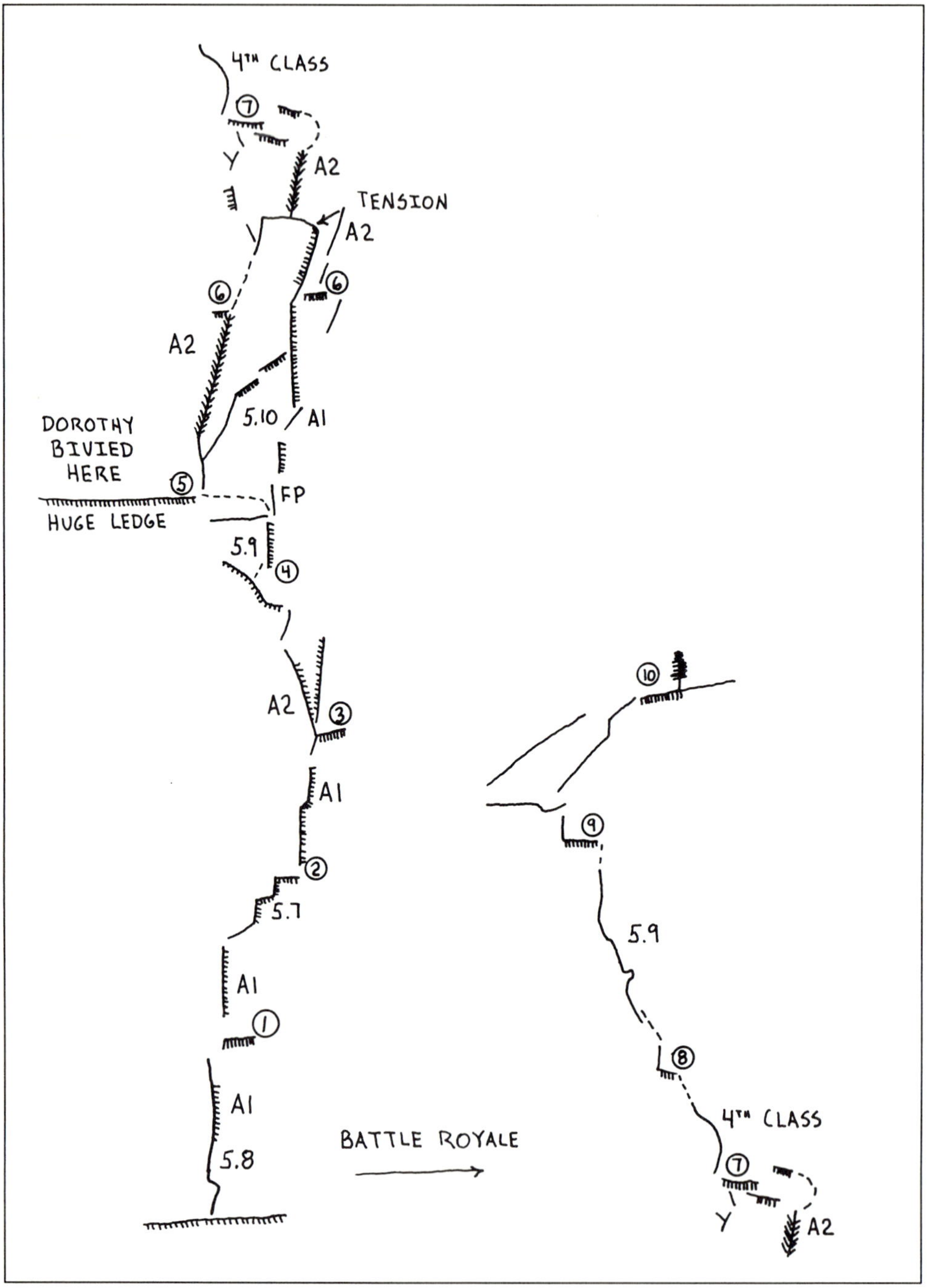

Emerald City, 5.10 A2

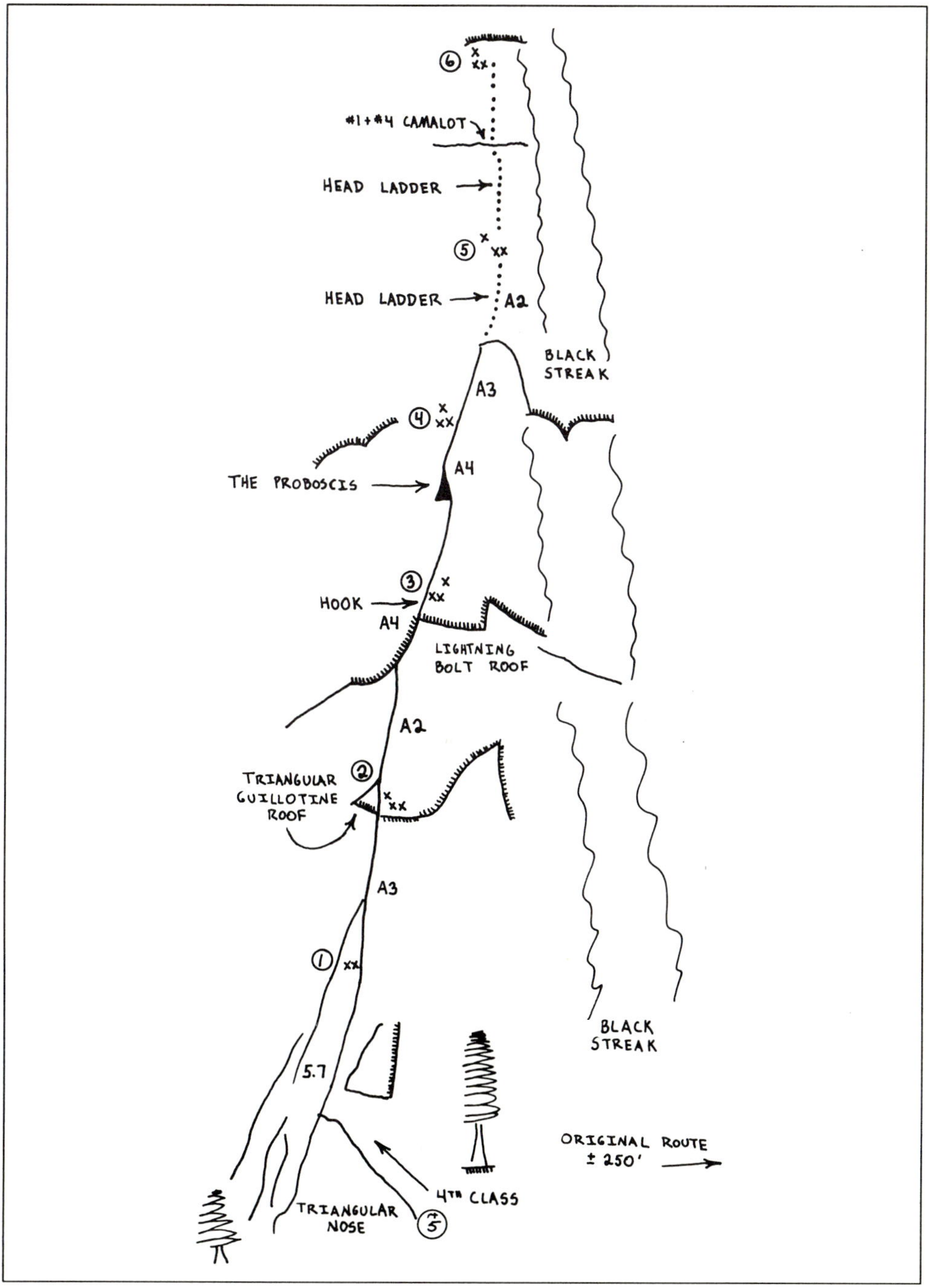

Crazy World, 5.7 A4

6 **Battle Royal** 5.9 A2
FA: Richard Harrison, Nick Nordblom, Wendell Broussard – Spring 1983
Climbs a broken, right-facing corner through the obvious black water streaks. Not recommended.

7 **Desert Solitaire** 5.9 A3+
FA: Nick Nordblom (roped solo) – Spring 1989
The first major crack system left of the **Original Route.** The gear list and rating suggest this is the second hardest route on the wall: You'll need nine Knifeblades; eight Lost Arrows; three small angles; double sets of TCUs, Friends and wires; one set each of RPs and HBs; hooks (including a Bat Hook); one small copperhead; one Crack Tack; one Bird Beak; several rivet hangers. There were a total of 40 holes drilled on the route: 14 belay bolts, 18 rivets, and eight for pro.

8 **Original Route (aka Herbst - Hamilton)** 5.9 A2+
FA: Joe Herbst, Larry Hamilton – April, 1973

This route can be done in a day, but the view of the Las Vegas lights from the bivi ledge can't be beat. Bring a double set of Friends, a #4 Camalot, a double set of TCUs, one set of wires, a double set of RPs, 5 Knifeblades, 5 Lost Arrows, a couple smallish angles, and lots of slings.

Since you can't park overnight on the loop road, hike in from Oak Creek Campground, up the old road toward Oak Creek Canyon, then angle right (north) across the desert (no trail) to the mouth of Juniper Canyon. Follow the drainage upstream for about an hour to a big, white lump of rock with a pine tree on its left side that divides the drainage in two. The Rainbow Wall is up on the left, and the Brownstone Wall is straight ahead (west), at the top of the main canyon. Climb slabs up left (south) for about 600 lung searing yards to the base of the wall. The route starts roughly 100 feet left of the prominent red arches on the right side of the wall, at an obvious dihedral system.

P1 Start left of a pine tree, and wander up the face to a belay ledge with one bolt and a piton. 75 ft., 5.6.

P2 Free climb up, then aid a blank section of the dihedral (three bolts). Continue up to a bolted belay anchor. 75 ft., 5.7 A2+.

P3 Lieback a wide crack (5.8), then aid up the corner to a sloping ledge. 75 ft., 5.8 A2+.

P4 Free and aid up the dihedral past a ledge to a three-bolt belay stance above a wide crack. 75 ft., 5.9 A2.

P5 Free climb up a loose flake, then aid and free up around a ceiling. Belay off nuts and Friends in the dihedral above. 110 ft., 5.7 A2.

P6 Continue up the dihedral past bushes to an easy chimney, and climb this to a ledge with small trees and one bolt. 100 ft., 5.4 A1.

Note: This is the lower left edge of Faith Ledge, a long, multi-stepped ledge that has an adequate bivouac spot at its upper end (at the mouth of the Bat Cave). There is room for two to sit, but if you bring hammocks, the accommodations are better.

P7 Follow broken ledges up right, then climb a left-facing dihedral to a stance just left of a chimney. Belay from TCUs and Friends. 150 ft., 5.8.

P8 Struggle up the short chimney to a ledge (bolt), then traverse around right and climb an easy but dirty face to a long, flat ledge with a huge pine tree on its right end. Belay from two bolts. 100 ft., 5.7.

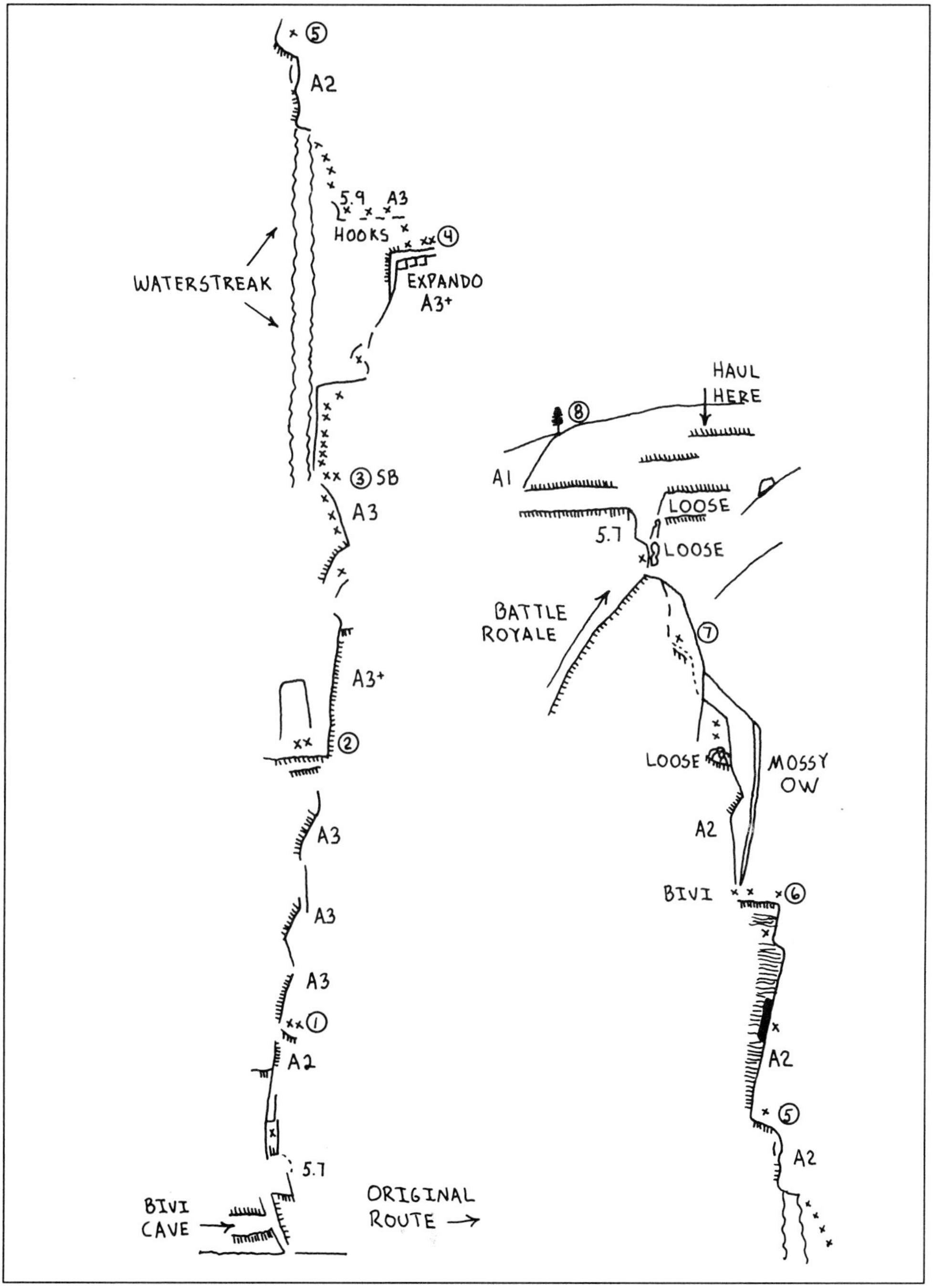

Desert Solitaire, 5.9 A3+

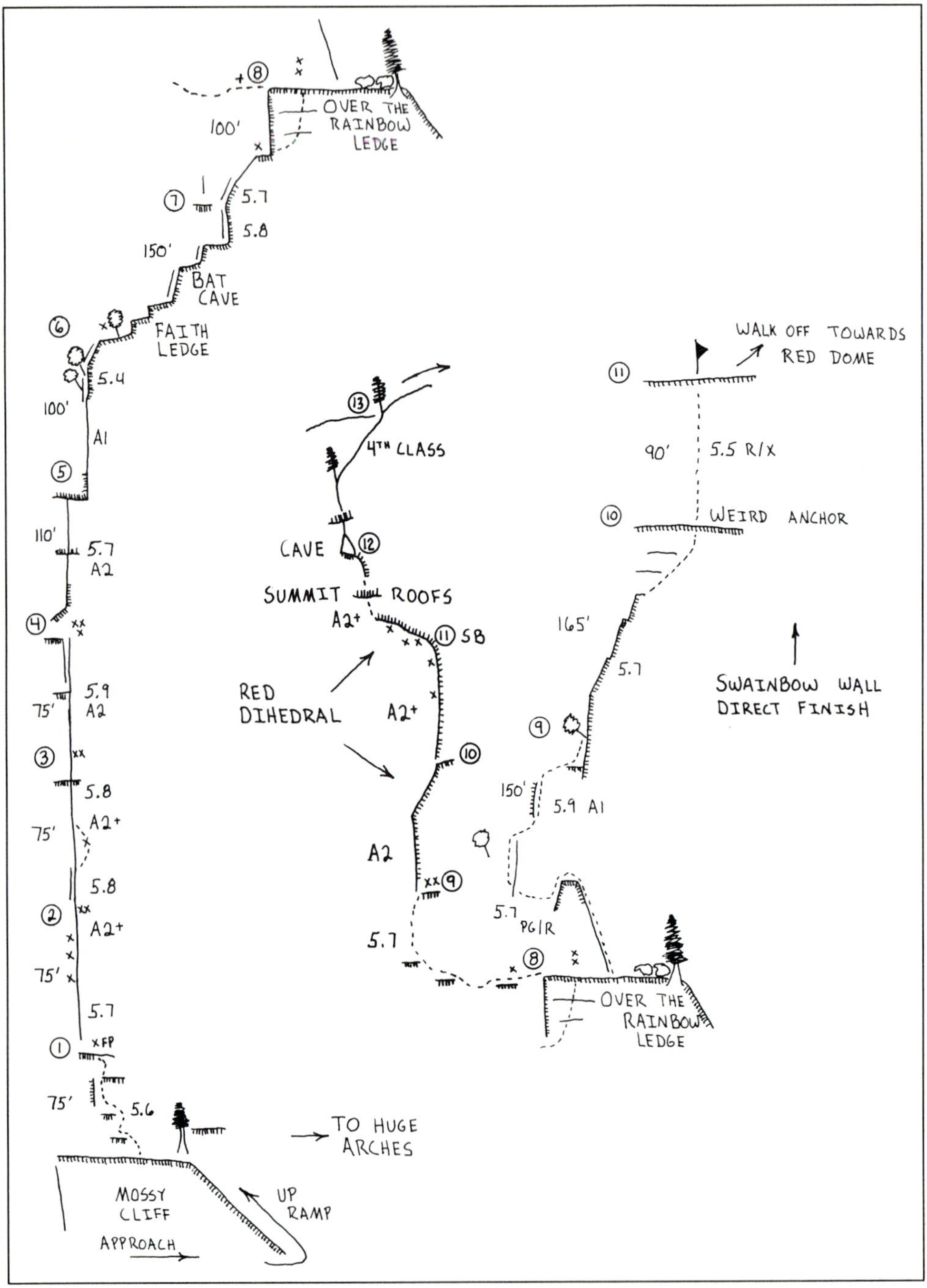

Original Route, 5.9 A2+ PG/R

Note: This is the Over The Rainbow Ledge. It is about 75 feet long, seven feet wide and can sleep three people comfortably. This is the bivi ledge to shoot for – the view is great!

P9 From the left end of the ledge (V1), traverse left (occasionally with tension) on ledges past a bolt, then face climb up to the base of the Red Dihedral and a bolt belay. 5.7.

P10 Aid up the huge, left-facing corner, belaying off gear. A2.

P11 Continue up the arching corner past a couple bolts to a bolted belay. A2+.

P12 Negotiate the summit roofs to a belay in a cave, or if the rope drag isn't bad, continue up to a tree just below the top of the wall. A2+.

P13 Scramble to the top. Fourth class.

V1 The Swainbow Wall 5.9 A1 *PG/R*

FRA: Jeff Rickerl, Mark Hoffman, Todd Swain – June, 1992

A direct (and perhaps the most logical) finish to the route.

P9 From the center of the Over the Rainbow Ledge, climb a shallow, left-leaning dihedral to a pedestal. Traverse down and left to the arête (no pro) then up a low-angled face to an obvious, right-facing flake. Climb the flake, angle right into the big, left-facing corner, then go up the corner past a ledge to a hanging belay from a tree, nuts and Friends. 150 ft., 5.9 A1, PG/R.

P10 Follow the corner past numerous ledges, then step around right and angle up right across a face to a belay on a sloping ledge in white, rounded rock. A difficult belay anchor to set up; you'll need lots of TCUs and Friends. 165 ft., 5.7.

P11 Climb the scary vertical face above to the summit. Good training for the Eiger! 90 ft., 5.5, R/X.

Descent: Not as bad as the approach, but it still takes about three hours. Walk south about 300 yards toward the red domes behind the Rainbow Wall, which are at the rim of Oak Creek Canyon. From the top of the red domes, angle slightly southwest down a ridge with rock outcrops. Curve around left (south) onto white rock, and follow the ridge and slabs down left to the top of the Oak Creek drainage. It should take about 30-40 minutes from the summit of the Rainbow Wall to the top of Oak Creek Canyon. Follow the drainage down and east (toward the road) past numerous waterholes. You'll eventually exit the drainage on its right (south) bank, and follow a trail and the old road back to your vehicle. Not only is this descent quicker than going back down Juniper Canyon, you're much more likely to encounter water in Oak Creek to soak in!

9 The Kor Route 5.? A?

FA: Layton Kor, Alison Sheets – 1989

Supposedly Kor did a route somewhere on the wall to the right of the huge, red arches.

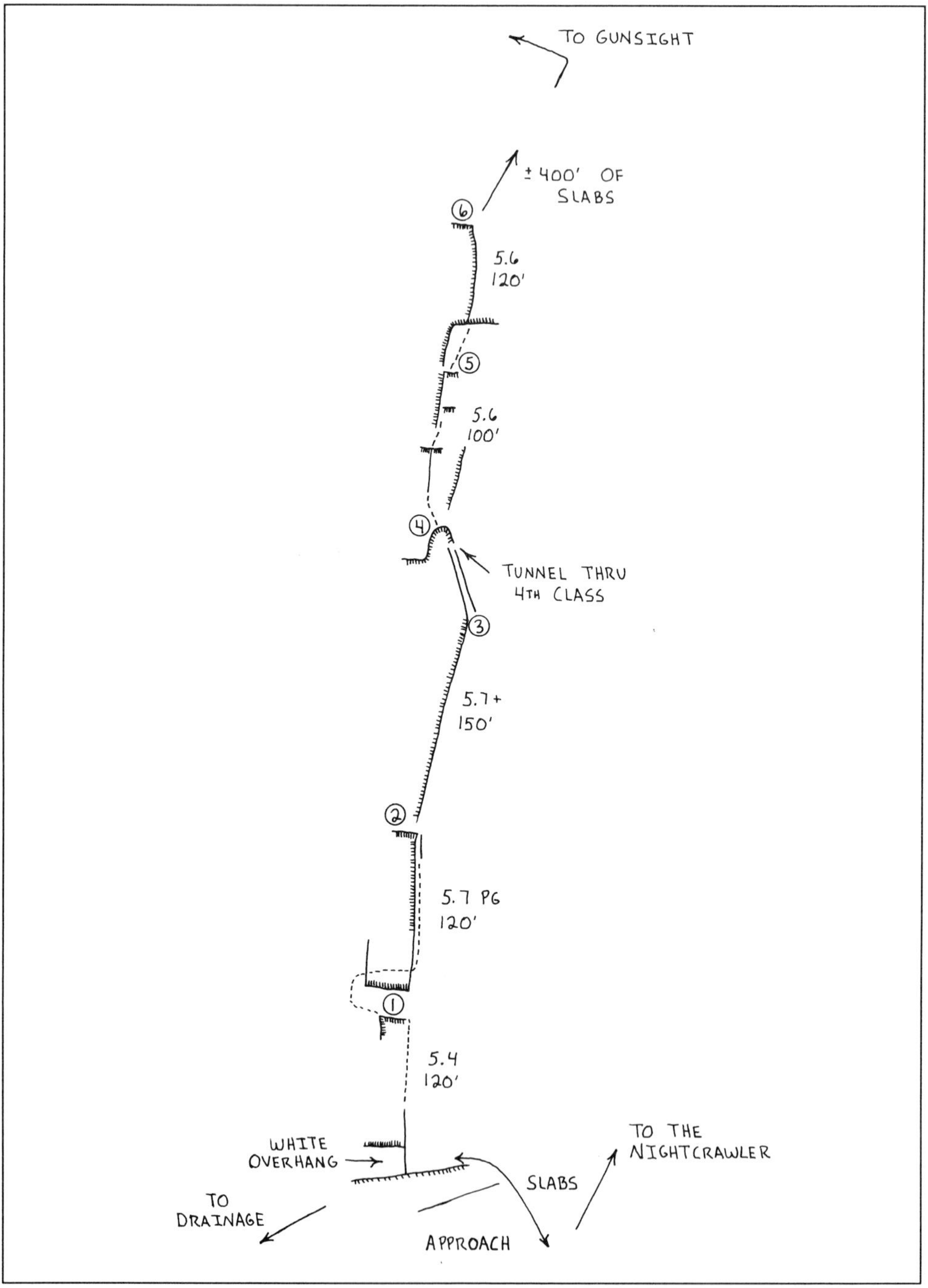

The Black Dagger, 5.7+ PG

Brownstone Wall

10 **The Black Dagger 5.7+ PG**

FA: Joe Herbst, Rick Wheeler – 1977

Take a stab at this one. This route is on the Brownstone Wall – the large, brown wall at the very rear of Juniper Canyon. Bring large gear for pitch three. From the Pine Creek parking area, follow the very well-marked trail down the hill, then angle south across the desert (no trail) to Juniper Canyon. Once you enter the canyon, follow the main drainage to avoid dense scrub oak. About halfway up Juniper Canyon, a big, white lump of rock with a pine tree on its left side divides the drainage in two. The Rainbow Wall is up on the left, and most of **The Black Dagger** is obscured by the white lump. Go through bushes below and right of the white lump (cairn), then up an open talus slope. Follow easy slabs up and left to the top of the right side of the lump. Traverse left (south) across more slabs to the obvious right-facing corner system near the left edge of the Brownstone Wall. The approach takes about 1.5 hours. The route is in the sun most of the day.

Start just right of a white overhang at an easy-looking crack/dihedral. This is directly below the huge corner mentioned in the approach.

P1 Climb the crack and easy face to a belay atop a block that is just below a prominent white roof. 120 ft., 5.4.

P2 An airy traverse left from the block starts the pitch. Climb up to a crack on the left side of the roof (scary), then traverse back right on varnished plates to the main right facing corner system. Continue up the corner system to a ledge below the huge, right-facing corner. 120 ft., 5.7, PG.

P3 Lieback and stem up the magnificent corner for a full pitch. Belay at the base of a chimney. 150 ft., 5.7+.

P4 Wiggle up the very easy and aesthetic chimney, exiting left through a hole to a huge ledge. 80 ft., Fourth class.

P5 From the top of the pillar, climb the plated face to a low-angled, right-facing crack/corner. Belay on the highest ledge, just below a roof. 100 ft., 5.6.

P6 Climb up the face to the roof, then pull over this into the right-facing corner. Follow the corner to a large ledge. 120 ft., 5.6.

Descent: Scramble up about 400 feet of very easy cracks and slabs to the top of the Brownstone Wall. Walk left (south) along the top of the formation to the notch (the Gunsight). A very straightforward but bushy descent down the gully takes you back to your pack.

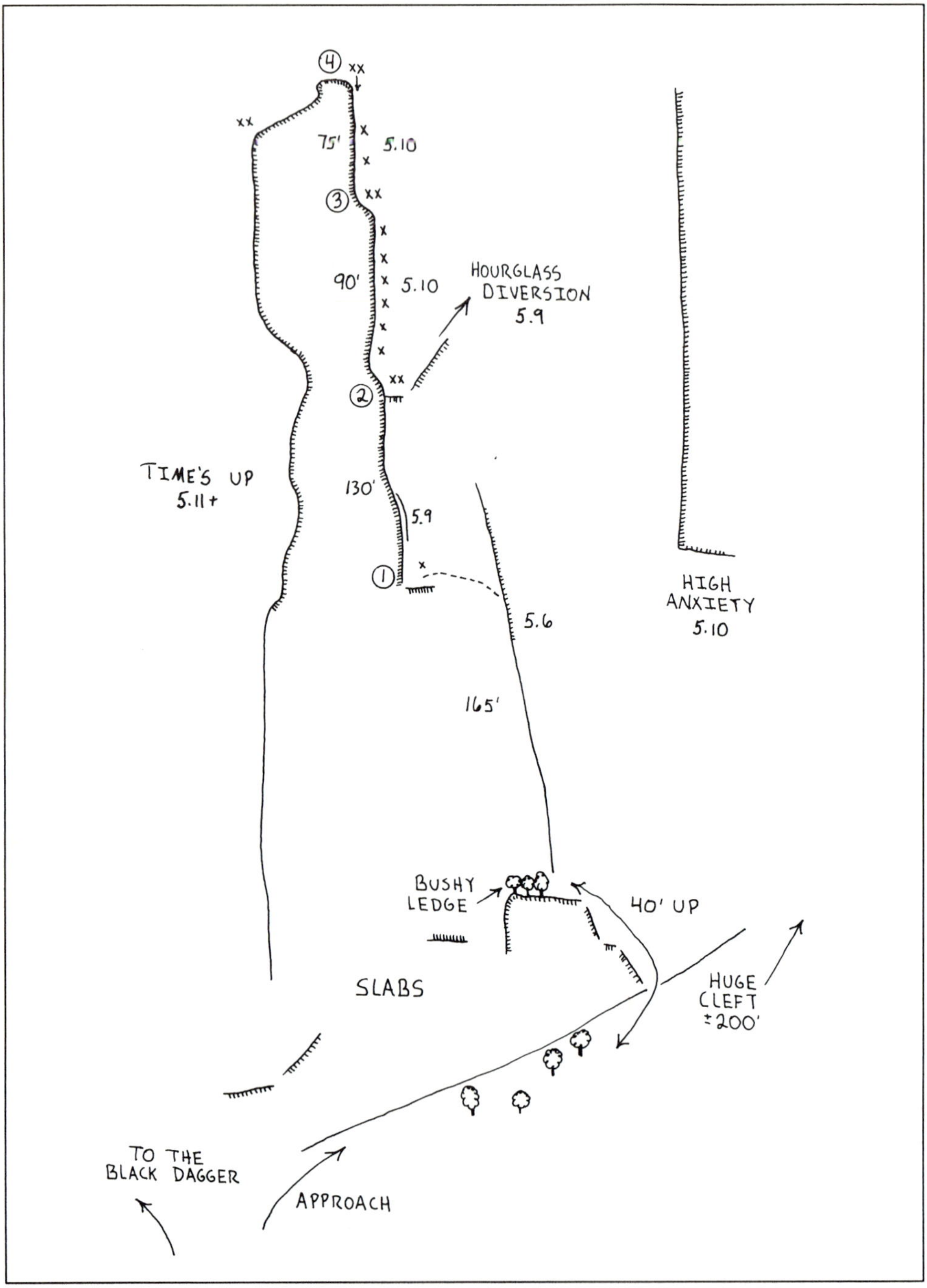

The Nightcrawler, 5.10

11 **The Nightcrawler 5.10** 👍

FA: Jorge & Joanne Urioste – April, 1978

Don't be lured onto this route without a large Friend or two. Like **The Black Dagger**, this route is on the Brownstone Wall – the large, brown wall at the very rear of Juniper Canyon. Approach from the Pine Creek parking area, following the very well-marked trail down the hill, then angling south across the desert (no trail) to Juniper Canyon. Hike up the drainage until it is split by a large, white lump of rock with a pine tree on its left side. The Rainbow Wall is up on the left, and **The Nightcrawler** is about 100 yards right of the white lump, just right of a lone pine tree. The route follows the large, right-facing corner system formed by a huge flake leaning against the wall. Go through bushes below and right of the white lump (cairn), then up an open talus slope. Follow easy slabs up and right to the base of the route. The approach takes about 1.5 hours.

Begin on a bushy ledge about forty feet above the ground, and 200 feet left of an obvious break in the Brownstone Wall. The route is in the sun most of the day, although the corner pitches are shaded.

P1 Follow easy cracks up and slightly left for 140 feet, then traverse about 10 feet left to a one-bolt belay. 165 ft., 5.6.

P2 Climb the huge, right-facing corner system up to a two bolt belay stance, worming up a chimney enroute. 130 ft., 5.9.

P3 Stem and lieback up the amazing corner, passing six bolts to a two-bolt anchor. 90 ft., 5.10.

P4 Continue up the corner past two bolts and more liebacking to the top of the giant Hourglass flake. Two-bolt belay. 75 ft., 5.10.

Descent: Rappel the route in four rappels, using two ropes (watch out for stuck ropes in the crack just below the third anchor).

Rose Tower

12 ***Olive Oil 5.7 PG***

FA: Jorge & Joanne Urioste, John Williamson – February, 1978

A slick route. Bring large gear to protect the last two pitches. Except for the tree atop pitch one, there are no fixed anchors. Approach from the Pine Creek parking lot. Follow the very well-marked trail down the hill, then angle south across the desert (no trail) to Juniper Canyon. Just before you reach the the mouth of Juniper Canyon, head up right into a tree-filled gully to the left (west) of the Rose Tower (a formation separate from the right [north] wall of Juniper Canyon). Scramble about 200 yards up the gully to the base of the route. This approach takes about 45 minutes, and the route is in the sun all day.

Start at the base of a left-leaning chimney/corner with an obvious tree about 150 feet up. The base of the chimney/corner forms somewhat of a cave.

P1 Climb up the left-leaning ramp just left of the ugly chimney/corner to a tree and ledge (rap anchors here). 150 ft., 5.7, PG.

P2 Slither up a short chimney, then climb the obvious finger-and-hand crack about 15 feet right of a large, right-facing corner. Belay in the crack when you run out of rope. 150 ft., 5.7.

P3 Continue up the crack and face, eventually moving left into the right facing corner. Belay on a large ledge just left of the corner. 120 ft., 5.6.

P4 Traverse right about 20 feet and follow the central crack upward. At the end of the pitch, move right into the left facing corner and belay. 150 ft., 5.5.

P5 Continue up the corner 30 feet to a huge ledge on the right. Walk right about 25 feet. 55 ft., 5.4

P6 Angle up and right across the face into the huge dihedral above. Continue up this until you run out of rope. 150 ft., 5.7, PG.

P7 Continue up the corner to the top. 150 ft., 5.6.

Descent: Scramble up slabs about 150 feet, then walk to the top of the Rose Tower. Walk left (west) to a notch, then drop down right (north) into the gully. A typically bushy but easy descent to the valley floor follows.

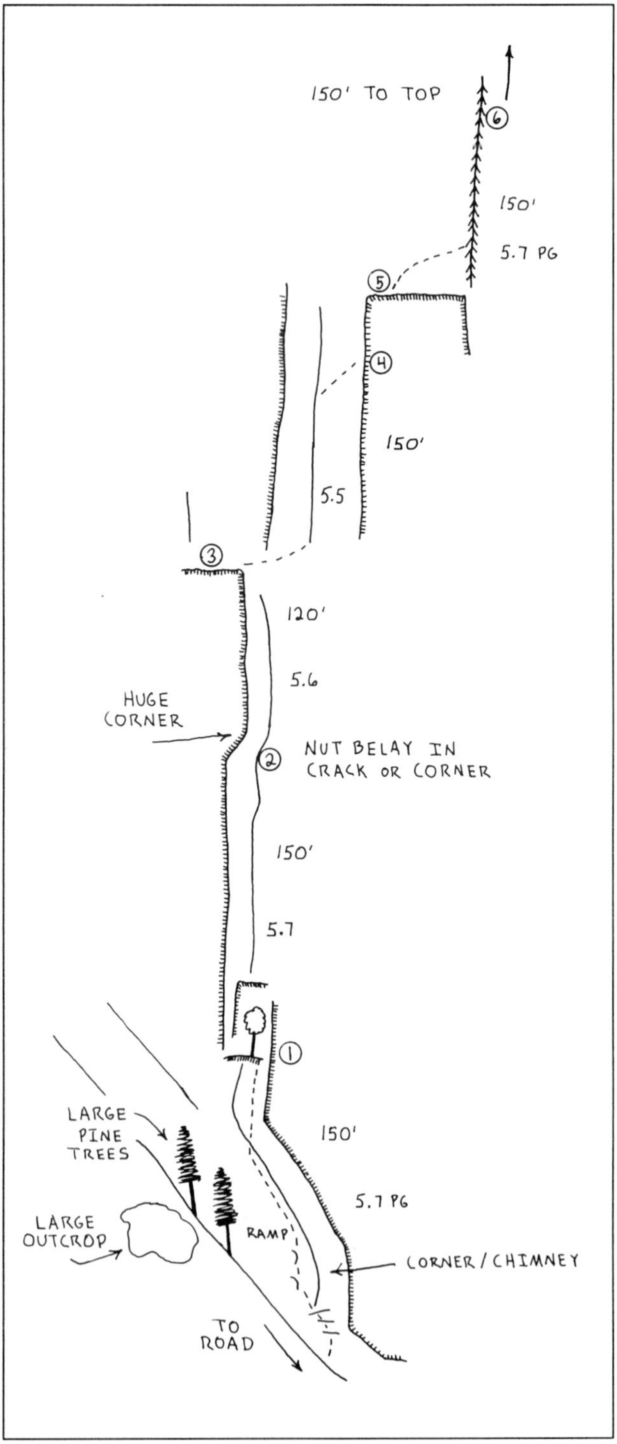

Olive Oil, 5.7
(topo opposite)

Oak Creek Canyon Overview

1 Resolution Arête 5.11 or 5.10 A1
4 Catwalk 5.6+ PG
8 The Black Orpheus 5.9+
11 Solar Slab 5.6 PG 👍

OAK CREEK CANYON

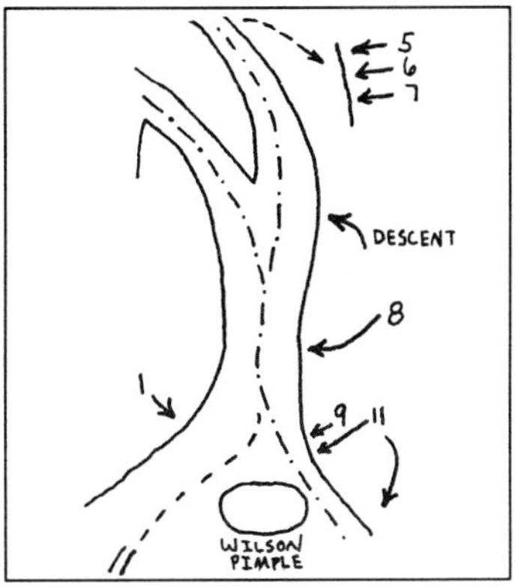

This canyon is on a par with the Black Velvet, harboring some of the best routes at Red Rocks. The approaches are generally much longer than those in the Black Velvet Canyon, however. Routes are described from left to right, starting on Mount Wilson, and ending at **Solar Slab** near the right (north) edge of the canyon. As of press time, the spur road leading from the scenic loop road to Oak Creek Canyon wasn't complete. When it's done, it will be faster to approach from the end of the spur road than via Oak Creek Road. For now, drive 1.4 miles south (toward Blue Diamond) along Route 159 from the exit of the scenic loop road to Oak Creek Campground. Walk or drove along the rough and rocky Oak Creek Road to its end (about 1.5 miles), then follow the old roadbed around the left side of the huge dirt mound blocking the canyon (the hill is called the Wilson Pimple – the large cliff above on the left is Mount Wilson). The road leads to a trail, which drops into the main Oak Creek drainage.

MOUNT WILSON

The east face of Mount Wilson is probably the largest cliff in Red Rocks, although most of it is broken by buttresses and towers. Only one long route is described on this massive wall, and I haven't done it (yet).

1 **Resolution Arête 5.11 or 5.10 A1**
FA: Phil Broscovak, Geoffrey Conley – January, 1981 FFA: Paul Van Betten, Richard Harrison – 1984

Due to the wandering and featured nature of the route, it's nearly impossible to haul gear. Plan to go fast and light, with the second carrying the pack. Bring a double set of Friends and TCUs, a set of wires, and LOTS of slings to cut down on rope drag. There are almost no fixed anchors on the route. The route has been done in six hours by a very fast party.

The climb ascends cracks in the right center of a huge, pyramid-shaped buttress, then climbs an obvious pillared buttress that starts just right of a huge, tree-covered ledge (Sherwood Forest).

Walk or drive along the rough and rocky Oak Creek Road to its end (about 1.5 miles), then follow the old roadbed around the left side of the huge dirt mound blocking the canyon (the Wilson Pimple). Angle up and left (southwest) toward Mount Wilson, aiming for a gully to the right of a hanging gully/waterfall. Scramble up the gully (fourth class) to a ledge with a big tree (possible bivi here). Go left about 50 feet to a chimney formed by a huge block and the main wall.

P1 Worm up the chimney, then climb a crack through a ceiling to a dubious bolt. 5.9.

P2 Climb a crack to the top of a red pillar. 5.8.

P3 Climb a very thin corner on the right side of the pillar. Belay in a chimney. 160 ft., 5.9+.

P4 Continue up and left to the top of the next pillar. 80 ft., 5.8.

P5 Climb the white face above, aiming for a point just right of the top of the triangular buttress. 5.7+, R.

P6 Head down and left through a notch behind the buttress, passing a couple of cracks to a steep, loose corner. 300 ft., third class.

P7 Climb up to a ceiling, trying to avoid the loose rock in the corner. Pull the ceiling, and belay in a corner. 5.9.

P8 Climb a right-facing corner to a belay under a large roof. 5.9 PG.

P9 Fire the roof (either free [5.11] or aid), and belay above after some 5.9 face climbing.

P10 Conquer the corner above, then move left to a huge ledge on the left side of a prow. One belay bolt, possible bivi here. 5.10.

Note: Historically, people have rappelled 100 feet down to the Sherwood Forest ledge from here to bivi. Supposedly, there's a shelter there to protect you from the elements. But if it's wet, you shouldn't be climbing on sandstone!

P11 Head up a left-leaning ramp around a corner, then move up right to a ledge at the base of a steep face. 5.8.

Note: If you go right (west) through a notch, there's reportedly an excellent bivi ledge.

P12 Dance up the steep face and belay on a ledge with a block that's at the base of a left-leaning crack. 5.8.

P13 Hand traverse up the left-leaning crack on friable rock (but good pro) to a belay in a chimney. 5.9.

P14 Slither up the chimney (5.7), then angle and up right on a face (5.5) to the right side of a blocky pillar. Belay at the base of the pillar. Watch for rope drag on this pitch. 5.7.

P15 Climb the chimney (V1), eventually stepping over onto the main wall. Belay up and left on a good ledge with a tree. 5.6.

P16 Shuffle left across a ledge to a chimney on the left (120 ft., third class, V2). Climb the chimney, then belay at a crack on the left.

P17 Jam up a crack, passing a ceiling, to a large, sloping ledge with a big tree. 5.7.

P18-20 Move around left, then climb three easy pitches up to the notch in the summit. 5.2

V1 An offwidth that leads to the same ledge is on the left side of the blocky pillar. 5.8.

V2 The first chimney you encounter (by a dead tree) is 5.8.

Descent: A number of possibilities exist, of which this is one: Walk west to the limestone (about one-half mile), then go down a gully to a tree-filled notch (a large, red pillar with a van-shaped block on top marks this particular gully). Descend either gully from here (the right one will require four rappels; nothing is known about the lefthand gully). Total descent time is about four hours.

To the right of the **Resolution Arête** and much closer to the canyon floor is a steep wall with two striking cracks. This 160-foot-high wall is on a satellite peak to the north of Mount Wilson, and about 150 yards uphill from an abandoned pickup truck. The cliff is black on the upper section, and lighter-colored near the bottom. Two routes are described, but no more is known about this area.

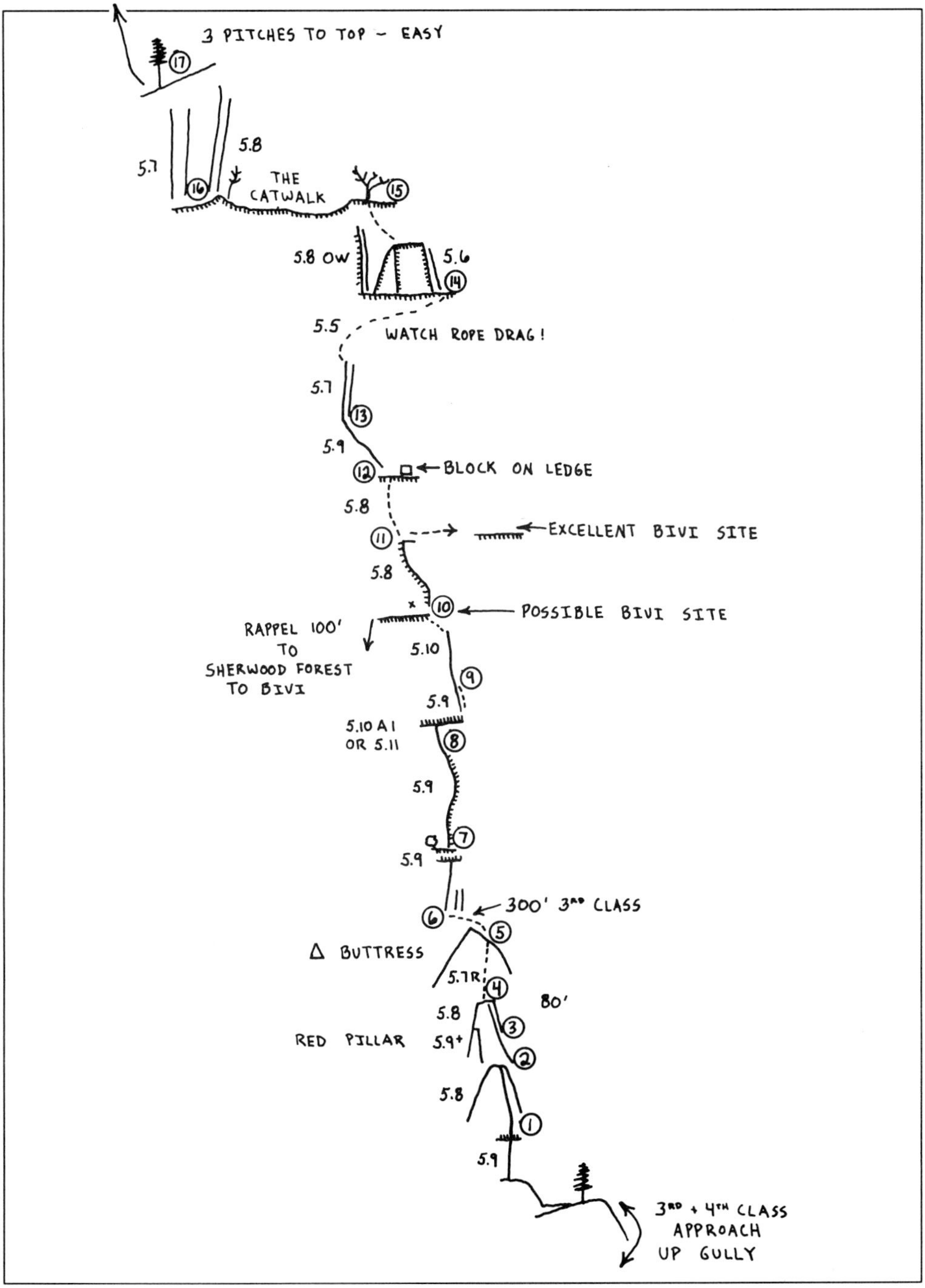

Resolution Arête, 5.11 or 5.10 A1

2 **Afterburner 5.12–**

FA: Paul Van Betten, Sal Mamusia – 1984

A thin finger crack with a fixed pin near the bottom.

3 **Eliminator Crack 5.11**

FA: Paul Van Betten, Sal Mamusia – 1984

According to the first-ascent party, this is an area classic. Begin 30 feet right of **Afterburner** and climb a straight-in finger crack. Near the top, angle right for 40 feet to a belay anchor with fixed wires. Rappel with two ropes.

4 ***Catwalk 5.6+ PG***

FA: Margo Young, Joe Frani – February, 1975

A good introduction to Red Rock's longer routes. Walk or drive along the rough and rocky Oak Creek Road to its end (about 1.5 miles), then follow the old roadbed around the left side of the huge dirt mound blocking the canyon (the Wilson Pimple). The road leads to a trail, which drops into the main Oak Creek drainage. Hike up Oak Creek for about an hour until you reach the point where the canyon splits. Take the right (north) fork, and follow this to the rear of the canyon. The route climbs an obvious, left-leaning crack system that passes through two very prominent black water streaks. Total approach time is about two hours. The route is in the sun most of the day.

Start at the base of the water streaks, above several large pine trees in the northern Oak Creek drainage. Scramble up slabs as far as you dare, angling to the right of the rightmost water streak.

P1 Continue up right via roped climbing (if needed) to a belay on a ledge about 400 feet above the pine trees, at the base of the left-leaning crack system. A huge roof is about 80 feet above.

P2 The first of the technical pitches. Follow the left-leaning crack past numerous huecos to a belay ledge just below the roof. 80 ft., 5.4 R.

P3 Continue up the crack past the left side of the roof. Follow the crack to a belay in a pothole, just left of the rightmost black streak. 130 ft., 5.6.

P4 Climb the crack to a right-facing corner packed with scrub oak. Stretch the rope, if you can, to a belay on a spacious ledge just above the bushes. 165 ft., 5.6.

P5 Continue up the crack into a huge, right-facing corner. Follow this past numerous ledges to a belay below a right-facing chimney/corner on the left. 150 ft., 5.5.

P6 Climb the chimney, exiting left at its top. Belay on the highest of three ledges on the left. 80 ft., 5.6.

P7 The best pitch on the route. Pussyfoot up the steep, black, finger-and-hand crack above. As the angle eases, move right to a belay ledge. 150 ft., 5.6+.

P8 Scamper up an easy face to pine trees and the summit. 60 ft., 5.3.

Descent: Head down left (west) into the obvious drainage, and follow the upper part of Oak Creek downstream. The descent is very easy – you'll be back at your pack in less than 15 minutes!

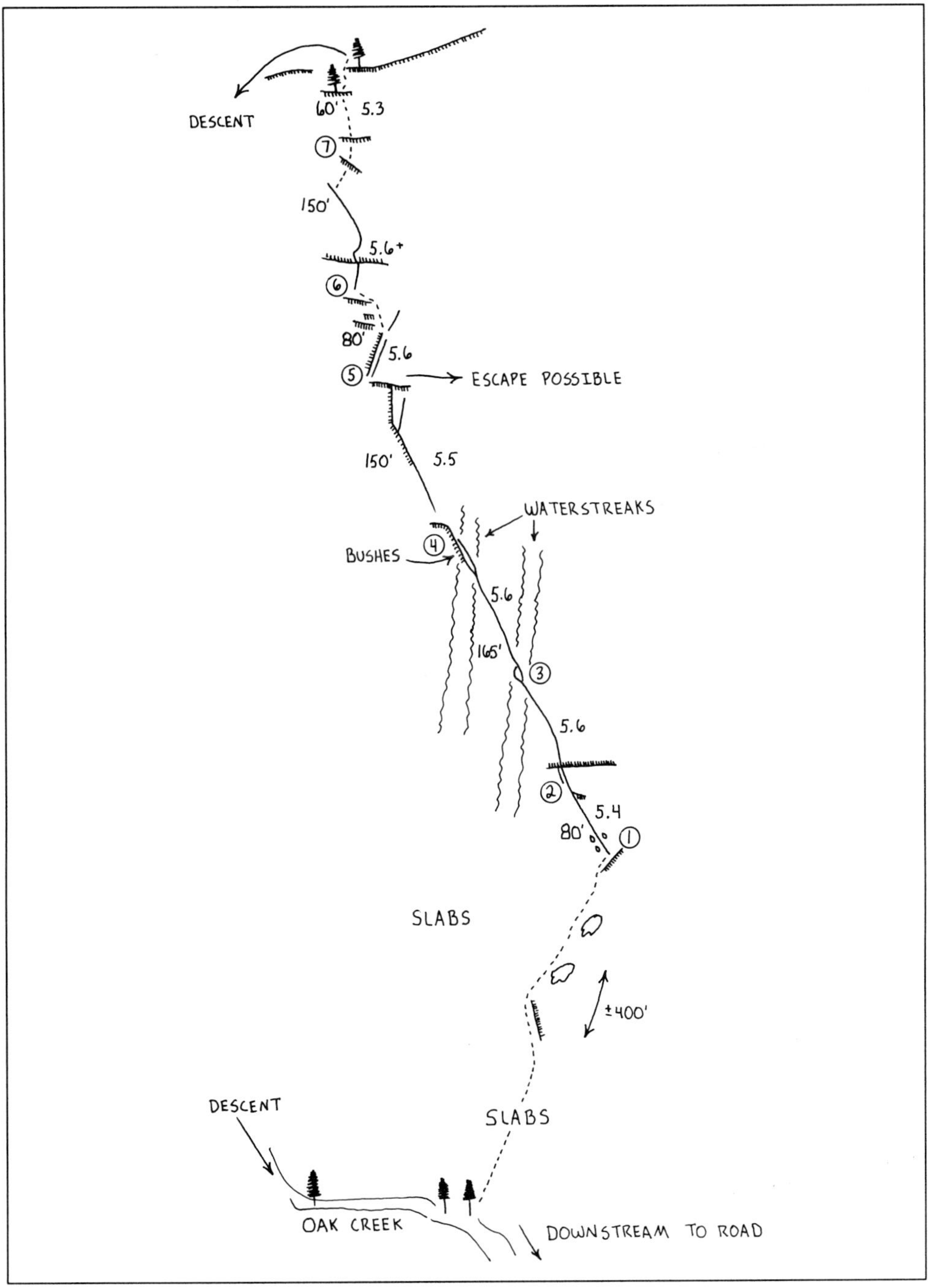

Catwalk, 5.6+ PG

Catwalk, 5.6+ PG

5 **Eagle Dance 5.10– A1**

FA: Jorge & Joanne Urioste – March, 1980

This route is named for the likeness of a huge eagle (flying west) formed by desert varnish in the center of the wall. This climb goes through the eagle's neck; **Levitation 29** goes through the tail. The climb is on a section of cliff that gets sun all day, and is visible from the road. Bring lots of quickdraws, lightweight aiders (or long slings), and the usual assortment of wires, TCUs and Friends up to #2.5.

Walk or drive along the rough and rocky Oak Creek Road to its end (about 1.5 miles), then follow the old roadbed around the left side of the huge dirt mound blocking the canyon (the Wilson Pimple). The road leads to a trail, which then drops into the main

Oak Creek Canyon, north wall

5 Eagle Dance 5.10– A1

6 Levitation 29 5.11 PG

7 Rainbow Buttress 5.8 PG

Oak Creek drainage. Hike up Oak Creek Canyon for about an hour, until it splits. Continue up the right (north) fork to large pine trees and a huge, slabby ramp that leads back up right toward the canyon wall on the right. Follow the ramp (some cairns) to the base of the route. This approach takes about two hours.

Start about 50 feet right of a huge, black pillar that rests against the cliff, at a shallow dihedral.

P1 Climb the dihedral and crack above to a belay ledge with bolts. This ledge is about 30 feet above the top of the black pillar. 180 ft., 5.8.

P2 Move right and climb past two bolts (use long slings), then follow a seam up left past eight more bolts (and a possible belay) to a belay stance atop a block at bolts. 150 ft., 5.10–.

P3 Fly straight up the white face, passing through the eagle's neck and by 13 bolts. Belay at a stance with a bolted anchor. 90 ft., 5.10–.

P4 Nine more bolts lead up to a bolt belay on a sloping ledge. 110 ft., 59+.

P5 Move up right past one bolt to a ledge at the base of a short, left-facing corner. Climb up loose flakes, then a right-facing corner (bolt), to a stance with bolts. 60 ft., 5.10–.

P6 Follow a thin crack up to a bulge, then thrash and dangle out the bulge (eight bolts) to a crack and belay anchor. 60 ft., 5.8 A1.

P7 Follow the corner/groove and seven bolts to the next anchor, which is on a ledge. 100 ft., 5.10–.

P8 Go up and left in a corner past four bolts to a ledge. 130 ft., 5.9.

P9 Scamper up a corner to the top.

Descent: Either rappel the route from the top of P7, or walk left (west) along the top of the wall, curving around left (south) onto white rock, and follow the ridge and slabs down left to the top of the Oak Creek drainage. It takes 30 minutes from the summit to the top of Oak Creek Canyon. Follow the drainage down and east (toward the road) past numerous water holes. You'll eventually exit the drainage on its right (south) bank, and follow a trail and the old road back to your vehicle. Once the spur road is complete, you'll probably exit left (north) out of the drainage to return to your car.

6 Levitation 29 5.11 PG 👍

FA: Jorge & Joanne Urioste, Bill Bradley – April, 1981 FFA: Lynn Hill, John Long, Joanne Urioste – May, 1981

Considered by many to be the best route at Red Rocks. The climb is on a section of cliff that gets sun all day, and is visible from the road. Bring lots of quickdraws, and the usual assortment of wires, TCUs and Friends up to #3.

Walk or drive along the rough and rocky Oak Creek Road to its end (about 1.5 miles), then follow the old roadbed around the left side of the huge dirt mound blocking the canyon (the Wilson Pimple). The road leads to a trail, which will then drop into the main Oak Creek drainage. Hike up Oak Creek Canyon for about an hour, until it splits. Continue up the right (north) fork to a huge, slabby ramp that leads back up right toward the cliff on the right. Follow the ramp (some cairns) to the base of the route. This approach takes about two hours.

Start about 200 feet right of a huge, black pillar and 400 feet down from the top of the approach ramp at some varnished cracks leading to a giant roof about 100 feet up.

P1 Climb thin, varnished cracks past four bolts to an anchor. 80 ft., 5.10–.

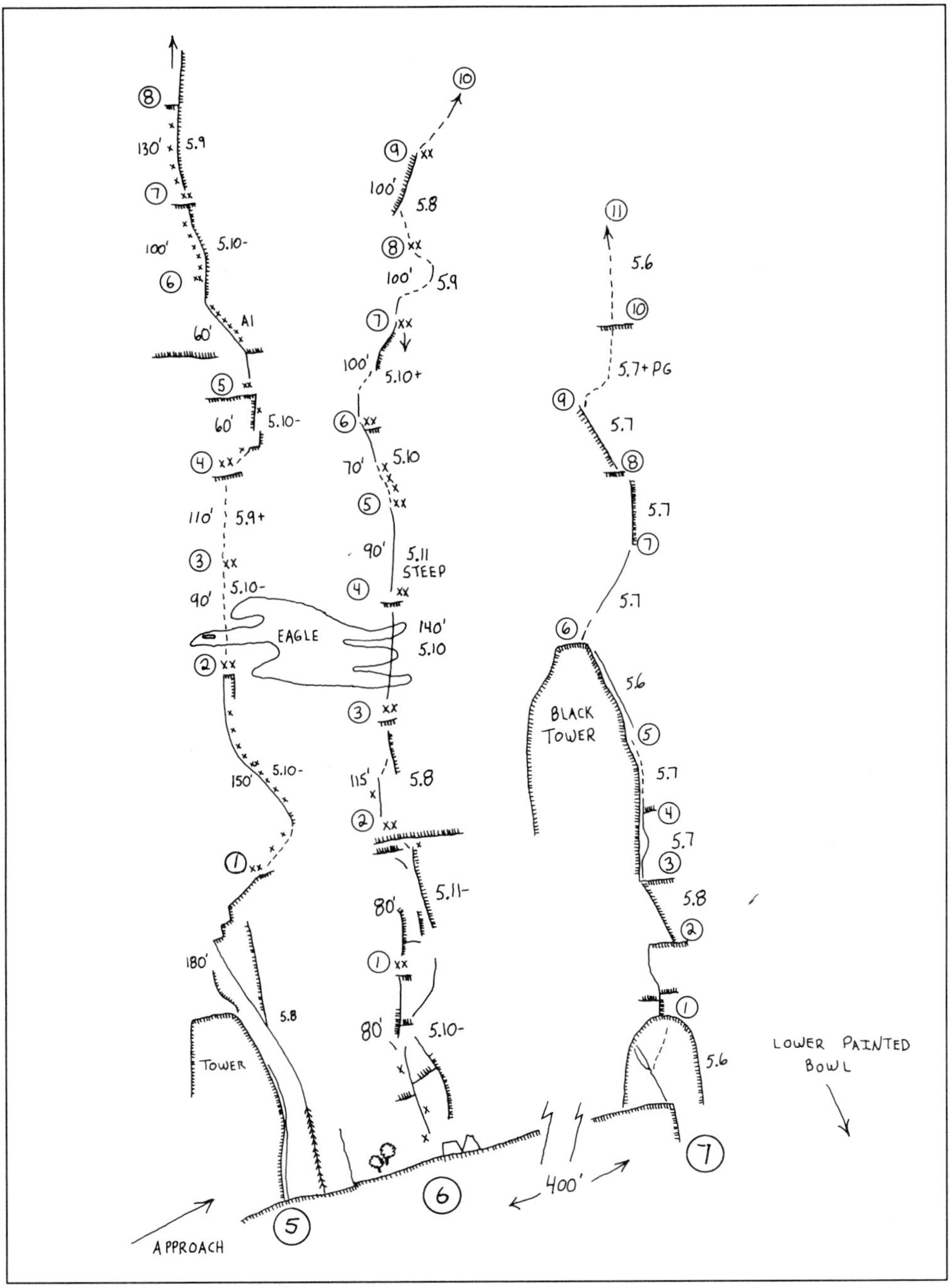

Oak Creek Canyon, north wall

5 **Eagle Dance 5.10– A1**

6 **Levitation 29 5.11 PG**

7 **Rainbow Buttress 5.8 PG**

Oak Creek Canyon, north wall

5 Eagle Dance 5.10– A1

6 Levitation 29 5.11 PG 👍

P2 Move right, then go up to the roof. Fire this (bolts), and belay up and left from bolts. 80 ft., 5.11–.

P3 Climb a crack for 75 feet, then angle up right past bolts to a bolted belay at a stance. 115 ft., 5.8.

P4 Follow a crack up the face past seven bolts to an anchor just below a steeper section of the wall. 140 ft., 5.10.

P5 The pumpfest. Follow the obvious crack and 13 bolts to a bolt anchor. 90 ft., 5.11.

P6 Climb seams up left past five bolts to the fixed belay. 70 ft, 5.10.

P7 Pussyfoot up and left along a white, rounded seam to a depression. A bit of "power liebacking" will get you up the right edge of the depression, and to the safety of the belay anchors. 100 ft., 5.10+.

P8 Wander up and right to a thin crack, and when it ends, go left to a belay on a slab. 100 ft., 5.9.

P9 Climb up and right along corners and cracks to a right slanting, right facing corner. Belay from two bolts, after clipping seven on the pitch. 100 ft., 5.8.

P10 Some fourth-class climbing leads to the top of the wall.

Descent: Many people rappel with two ropes after the seventh pitch. If you elect to hike down, walk left (west) along the top of the wall, curving around left (south) onto white rock, and follow the ridge and slabs down left to the top of the Oak Creek drainage. It should take about 30 minutes to get from the summit to the top of Oak Creek Canyon. Follow the drainage down and east (toward the road) past numerous water holes.

7 Rainbow Buttress 5.8 PG

FA: Joe Herbst – 1970s

A great route, but with the long approach and descent you'll need to move fast! Walk or drive along the rough and rocky Oak Creek Road to its end (about 1.5 miles), then follow the old roadbed around the left side of the huge dirt mound blocking the canyon (the Wilson Pimple). The road leads to a trail, which drops into the main Oak Creek drainage. Hike up Oak Creek Canyon for about an hour, until it splits. Continue up the right (north) fork, to a huge, slabby ramp that leads back up and right toward the huge cliff band on the right. Follow the ramp (some cairns) to the base of the route. This approach takes about two hours. Bring a good selection of gear (including large stuff) for the belays as well as the climbing.

Start at the top of the huge approach ramp, about 400 feet uphill of **Levitation 29,** and left (west) of the Painted Bowl.

P1 Climb a shallow, varnished, left-facing corner that leads to a wider section of crack. Angle right across the white face to a belay ledge. 5.6.

P2 Climb a left-facing corner past a ceiling to easier ground. Belay on the highest ledge, below a clean, left-facing corner.

P3 Climb the obvious left-facing corner to a huge belay ledge. 5.8.

P4 Swim up the offwidth to a belay beneath a ceiling. 5.7.

P5 Chimney up through the ceiling, then climb the face above to a belay beneath double cracks. 5.7.

P6 Follow the double cracks to the top of the black tower, gaining the top from the right side. 5.6.

P7 Step on to the main wall, then follow cracks up and right. 5.7.

P8 Stem up a left-facing corner to its top, then move left to a belay ledge. 5.7.

P9 Follow a left-leaning ramp to another belay. 5.7.

P10 Climb a steep and scary wall on the right to a large and comfy belay ledge. 5.7+ PG.

P11 A loose pitch up the pink face above gets you to the top of the buttress. 5.6.

Descent: Walk left (west) along the top of the wall, curving around left (south) onto white rock, and follow the ridge and slabs down and left to the top of the Oak Creek drainage. It should take about 30 minutes from the summit to the top of Oak Creek Canyon. Follow the drainage down and east (toward the road) past numerous water-holes. Don't leave your gear at the base of the route!

8 **The Black Orpheus 5.9+**

FA: Joanne & Jorge Urioste – April, 1979

A long route with a short crux. This route is in the sun most of the day, with the approach taking about 1.5 hours. From the end of the Oak Creek road, follow the old roadbed and trail up toward the canyon, until the trail drops into the streambed. Walk up the streambed as it weaves back and forth across the canyon, then go 200 yards past a buttress that comes down to wash level on the right (north) side of the drainage. A steeper, brown wall is on the left side of the canyon at this point, and it is another 350 yards to the fork in the Oak Creek drainage (if you reach that, you've gone too far). Scramble up brown slabs on the right side of the canyon, aiming for an obvious, left facing corner system with a prominent "V" notch in it. The corner starts about 600 feet above the streambed. The upper part of the approach is over steeper ground, but it's easy.

Start in the first left-facing corner to the right of a large, white, recessed wall at the bottom of a huge, brown buttress. Above, a giant, brown, right-facing corner marks the top of the route. The brown corner is visible from the road, while the rest of the route is hidden until you're in the canyon.

P1 Climb the left-facing corner past two bolts to a belay in the "V" notch (small Friends for the belay). 165 ft., 5.7.

P2 Continue up the corner (5.8), then climb past two bolts on a ledge to a left-leaning crack. Climb past one more bolt, step right, then up a corner to a large ledge. 165 ft., 5.8.

P3 Diagonal left on a huge ledge for 75 feet, then go up vertical and left-leaning cracks to a stance just above varnished rock, on the edge of lower-angled white rock. 165 ft., 5.5.

P4 Scamper up the easy white face to a platform. 100 ft., 5.0.

P5 Follow a left-leaning crack/ramp to a sloping platform below a steep headwall. 150 ft., fourth class.

P6 Angle left across a smooth, brown slab. Belay at the very left end of the ledges under a small triangular ceiling (Friends for the belay). 200 ft., fourth class.

P7 Make an exposed traverse left 20 feet to a shallow dihedral (bolt). Climb the dihedral and chimney, then exit right to a belay ledge (nuts and large Friends). 160 ft., 5.9.

P8 Scramble up ledges, then climb a short, steep, thin crack (5.9+, two bolts) to a corner. Jam up beautiful cracks to the second ledge above. 120 ft., 5.9+.

P9 Lieback up the huge dihedral past one bolt, then traverse right 35 feet to a belay anchor (bolt and drilled piton). 120 ft., 5.7

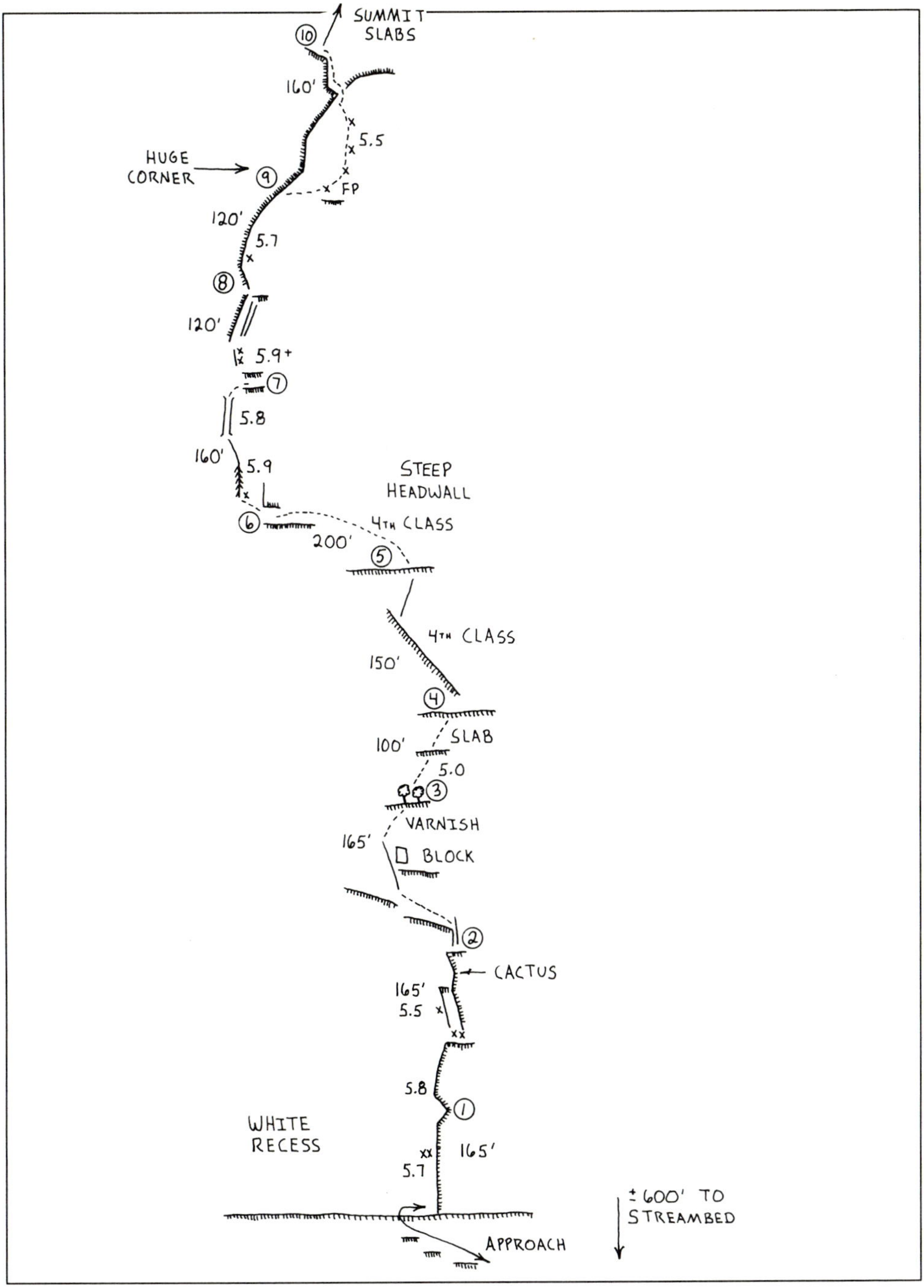

The Black Orpheus, 5.9+

P10 Climb up the loose pink face past bolts to the dihedral, then exit left out of that into another corner. Follow this to easy summit slabs. 160 ft., 5.5+.

Descent: If you have your gear with you, it's probably best to descend down the gully to the right (east) of the buttress as for **Solar Slab.** This can be done without a rope if you are good at downclimbing, or, if you aren't, with a few rappels. In winter, the gully may contain ice and snow, as it is in the shade all day.

If you left your gear at the streambed below the climb, contour left (west) along ledges in the summit slabs, then go down a ramp. Do an 80-foot rappel (bolt and fixed wire) to a ledge, then walk right (west) 150 feet to the end of the ledge. Another 80-foot rappel (thread and fixed nuts) down a chimney leads to a ledge with lots of vegetation, from which yet another 80-foot rappel will put you in the lower section of the Painted Bowl (there are other ways to get here, including a route using two 150 foot rappels directly down from the first anchor). From the base of the

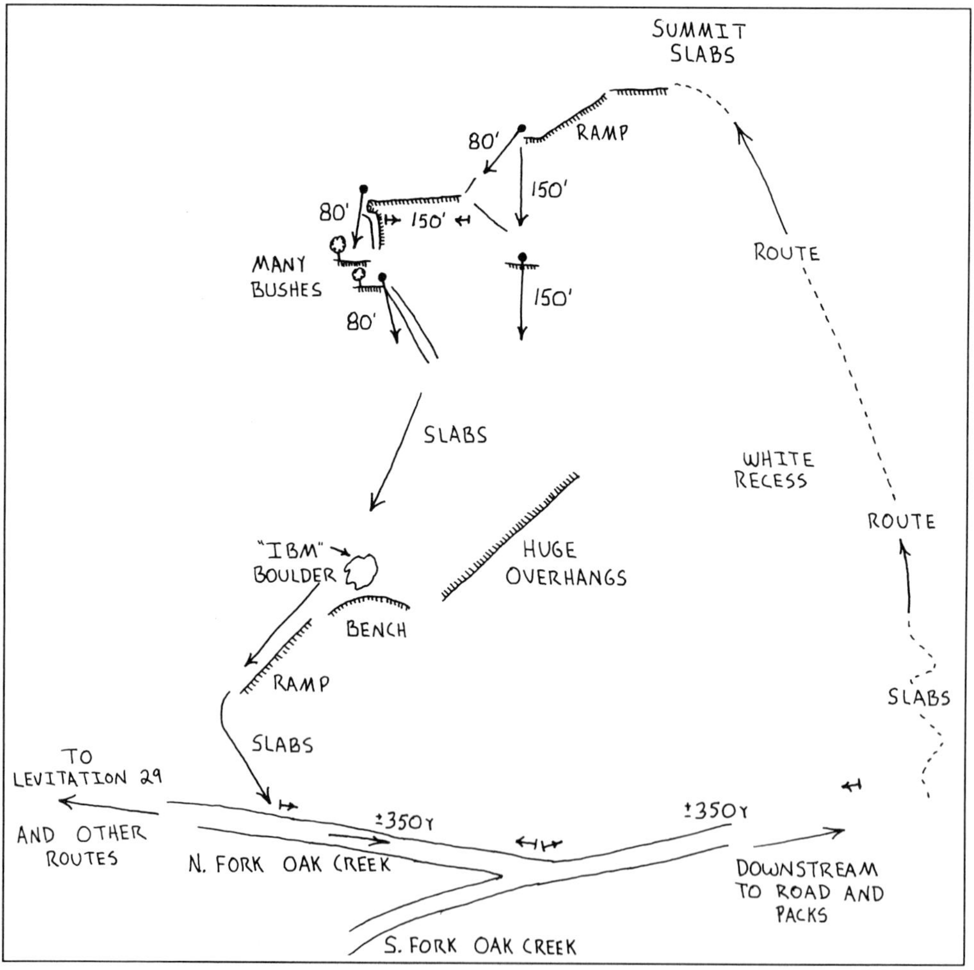

Descent for The Black Orpheus

rappels, head down white slabs toward an obvious bench with a large boulder (that looks like an IBM Selectric typewriter ball). From the boulder, head right (west) down a low-angled ramp to the streambed. You should now be about 700 yards upstream of your gear, and 350 yards above the fork in Oak Creek. Head downstream to your packs, and the road.

9 Beulah's Book 5.9-

FA: Randy Grandstaff, Dave Anderson – 1979

Bring lots of gear, up to a #4 Camalot. The approach takes about an hour, and the climb is in the sun most of the day. For fast parties, it's possible to combine this route with **Solar Slab,** to give nearly 1,500 feet of great climbing. On the far right (north) side of the canyon, there is a huge, obvious gully running about 500 feet up the cliff to the base of a white face. This white face is the **Solar Slab,** and the obvious, right-facing corner system about 100 feet left of the gully is **Beulah's Book.**

From the end of the Oak Creek road, follow the old roadbed and trail up toward the canyon to where the trail drops into the streambed. Walk up the streambed about 150 yards, then follow a faint trail 200 yards up to the base of the routes. The trail ascends the hillside about 75 yards left (west) of the red rock band in the hillside.

Start 100 feet left of the **Solar Slab Gully** at a series of dihedrals. The climb begins at the dihedral distinguished by a large, jammed block about 20 feet up and an oak tree growing out of the corner's base.

P1 Climb the dihedral past the jammed block, then climb the narrow face just left of the chimney past a bolt. Step back right into the chimney, and follow it to a ledge. 165 ft., 5.6.

P2 Continue up the corner/chimney system, passing a flaring, bombay section (bolt, #4 Camalot) to a belay at the base of an obvious lieback corner. Power up the corner (5.8+, V1) to a ceiling, then step left to a belay ledge in white rock (complicated belay with Friends, TCUs and wires). 150 ft., 5.9–.

P3 Wander up the white face, angling slightly right to an eventual belay at some left-leaning cracks. 150 ft., 5.5.

P4 A short, easy pitch leads up to a huge ledge with large boulders on it. 60 ft., 5.3.

P5 Scramble up slabs to the huge terrace that **Solar Slab** starts from. 150 ft., third class.

V1 The face to the right of the corner can be climbed (5.7 X).

Descent: Either continue up **Solar Slab,** or descend the **Solar Slab Gully** by downclimbing and/or rappelling. Only one rope is needed if you decide to rappel the gully rather than downclimb. All the rappel anchors are fixed.

10 Solar Slab Gully 5.3

FA: unknown – 1970s

A great excursion for the novice climber. Most climbers use this as an approach to **Solar Slab,** or as a descent from **Beulah's Book.** The route can be rappelled with one rope, and all of the anchors are fixed. The crux section is a short waterfall (usually dry) near the top.

On the far right (north) side of the canyon is a huge, obvious gully running about 500 feet up the cliff to the base of a white face. The gully is the **Solar Slab Gully,** and the white face above is the **Solar Slab.**

Oak Creek Canyon

9 **Beulah's Book 5.9-**

10 **Solar Slab Gully 5.3**

11 **Solar Slab 5.6 PG** 👍

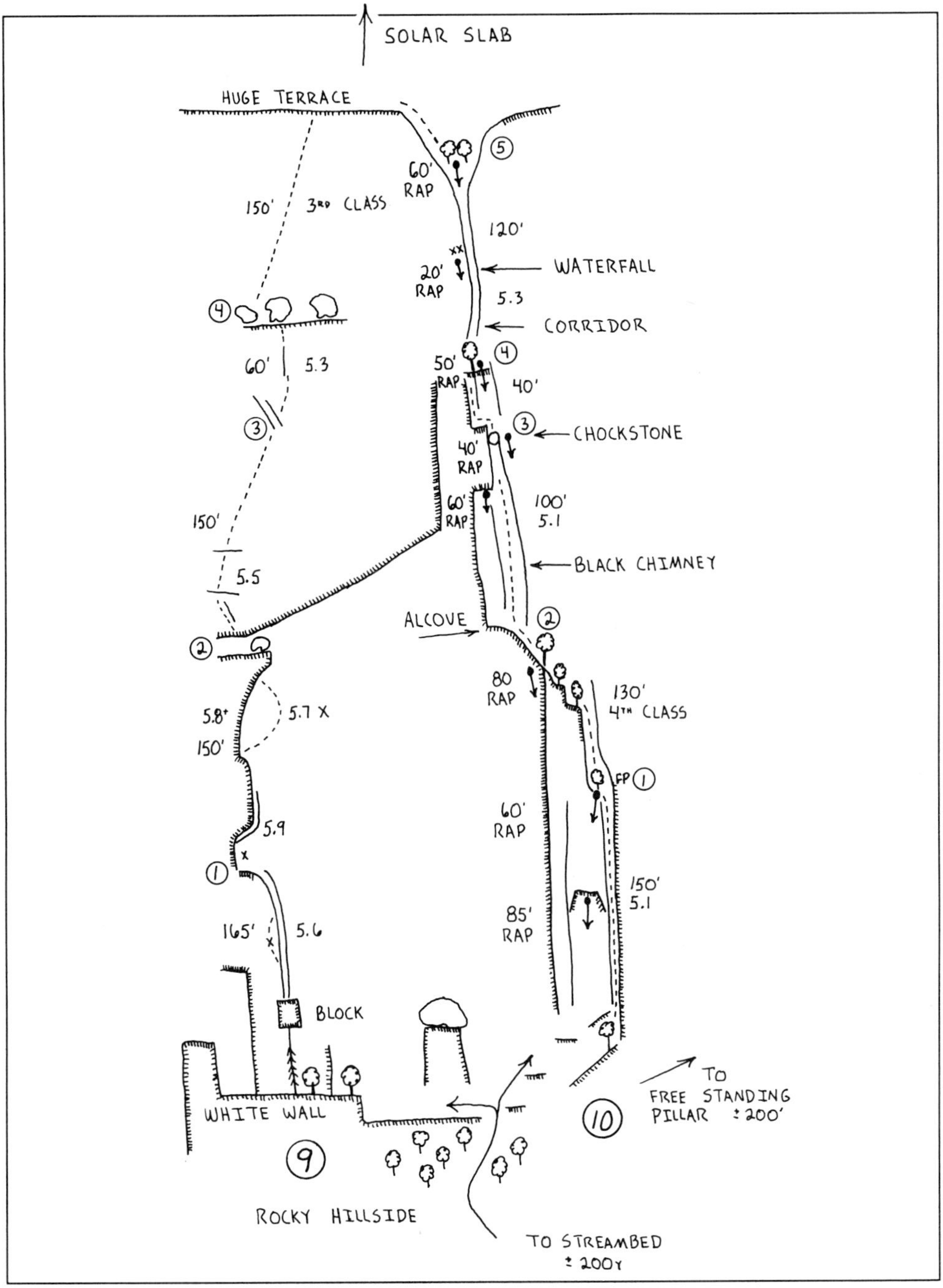

Oak Creek Canyon

9 **Beulah's Book 5.9-**

10 **Solar Slab Gully 5.3**

From the end of the Oak Creek road, follow the old roadbed and trail up toward the canyon, to where the trail drops into the streambed. Walk up the streambed about 150 yards, then follow a faint trail 200 yards up to the base of the route. The trail ascends the hillside about 75 yards left (west) of the red rock band in the hillside. It takes about an hour to reach the base of the gully.

Start at the base of an obvious gully about 100 feet left of a prominent, right-facing corner system (**Beulah's Book**), and 200 feet left of a free-standing pillar (**The Friar,** 5.9).

P1 Start at the righthand chimney, near a thin oak tree. Climb straight up a varnished eight- to 12-inch wide crack, passing ledges at 40 and 80 feet, to yet another ledge with a tree and fixed piton. 150 ft., 5.1.

P2 From the tree and pin, scramble up the bush-filled gully, then angle up left along ledges past a gnarled oak tree with rappel slings (80 ft). Continue up to a huge alcove at the base of a dark, waterworn chimney. 130 ft., fourth class.

P3 Climb straight up the black gully/corner, and belay on a ledge to the left, just above a chockstone with numerous slings around it. About 60 feet up the pitch, you'll pass a rappel anchor made from a natural thread. 100 ft., 5.1.

P4 A short and easy chimney leads to a tree in a corridor. 40 ft., third class.

P5 Walk up the corridor, then ascend a 20-foot waterfall (5.3) to a bolt and piton. Scramble up the gully to the huge terrace. 120 ft., 5.3.

Descent: Rappel the route, or continue up **Solar Slab.**

11 Solar Slab 5.6 PG 👍

FA: Joe Herbst, Tom Kaufman, Larry Hamilton – January, 1975

In the summer, this climb would be best named "Sizzle Slab." A long route, with a long descent. Bring a good assortment of gear, as there are no fixed anchors.

A huge, obvious gully runs about 500 feet up the cliff to the base of a white face on the far right (north) side of the canyon. This white face is the **Solar Slab,** and the obvious, right-facing corner system about 100 feet left of the gully is **Beulah's Book.**

From the end of the Oak Creek road, follow the old roadbed and trail up toward the canyon to where the trail drops into the streambed. Walk up the streambed about 150 yards, then follow a faint trail 200 yards up to the base of the routes. The trail ascends the hillside about 75 yards left (west) of the red rock band in the hillside. It takes about an hour to reach the base of the approach gully.

The **Solar Slab Gully** approach entails climbing up to about 5.3 in difficulty, and is an enjoyable excursion for the novice climber. The gully is about 500 feet long, with the most difficult section near the top. There are fixed anchors up the gully, as this is the descent route for **Beulah's Book.** The gully ends on a large terrace below the white **Solar Slab.**

P1 Begin on the terrace about 100 feet up and left of the top of the approach gully, below a white slab and an obvious hand crack that doesn't reach the terrace. Climb the slabby face to varnished plates left of the crack. Eventually step right into the crack, and follow it to a belay ledge with a prominent bush. 165 ft., 5.5.

P2 Follow the left-leaning ramp/chimney, passing a ledge about 90 feet up (possible belay here). Continue up the corner above to belay on a ledge with a dead tree. 165 ft., 5.5.

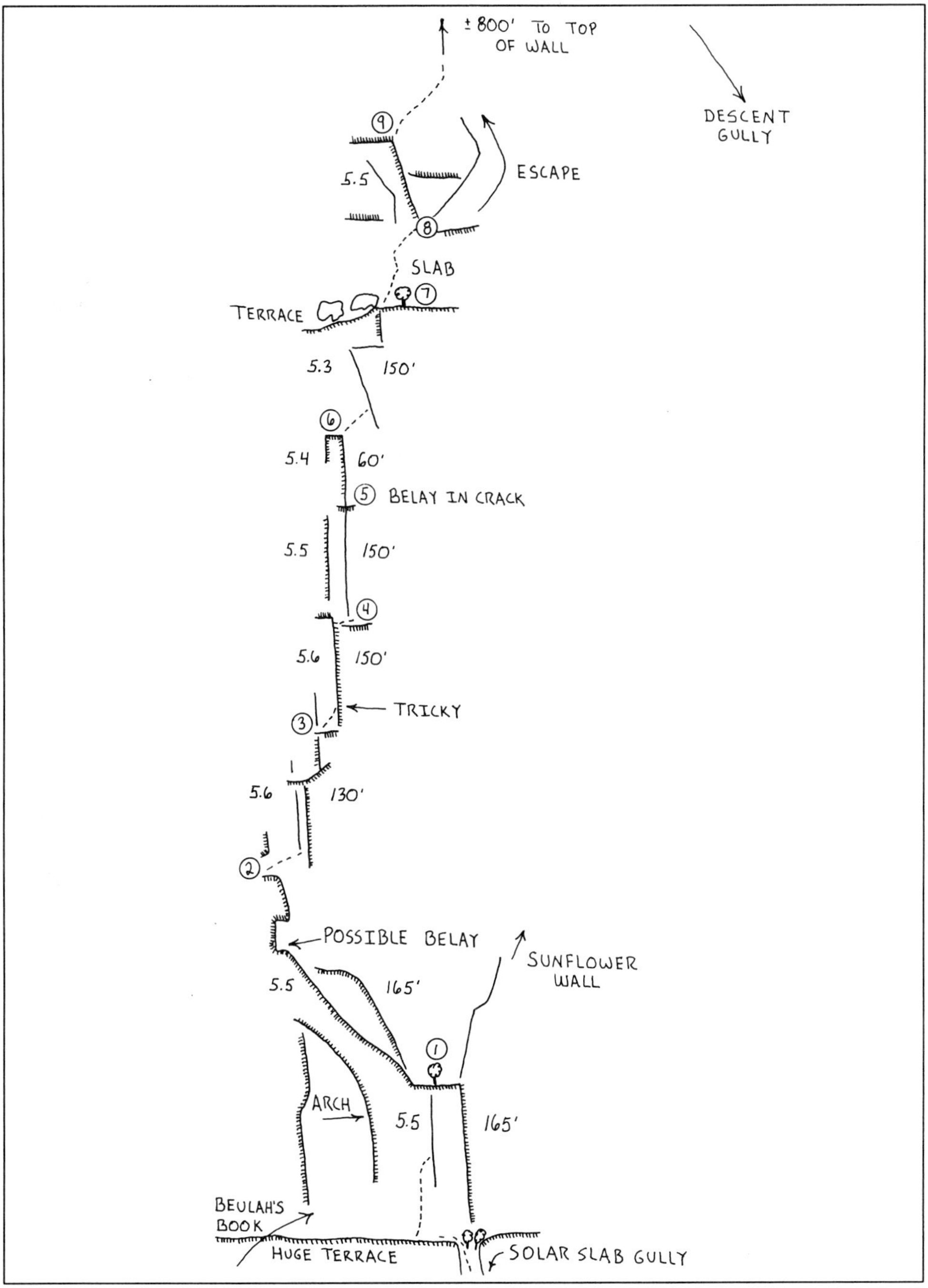

Solar Slab, 5.6

P3 Traverse right 15 feet, then climb a finger-and-hand crack to a ledge. Traverse right 10 feet, and follow a small, right-facing corner to a belay stance (#2.5, 3 Friend and small wires). 130 ft., 5.6.

P4 Traverse 10 feet right and climb a left-facing flake/corner (tricky) to a ceiling. Step down and right to a belay ledge. 150 ft., 5.6.

P5 Climb the obvious hand crack directly above, belaying at a stance in the crack. 150 ft., 5.5.

P6 Continue up the crack, which becomes a right-facing corner. Belay at the top of the pillar. 60 ft., 5.4.

P7 Angle right across a white face to an obvious, low-angled crack. Climb the crack to a ledge, then move right 10 feet and climb a right-facing corner to a huge terrace. 150 ft., 5.3.

P8 Walk and scramble up easy slabs to the base of a varnished, left-leaning dihedral. 150 ft.

Note: If time is short, you can avoid the final pitch by traversing right around the outside corner, then scrambling to the top.

P9 Climb the corner to the top. 100 ft., 5.5.

Descent: Walk about 800 feet up easy slabs to the bright, red rock. Head right (east) and enter a huge gully system. Two or three rappels may be needed, depending on your downclimbing ability. The descent can be done unroped, if you can down-solo 5.6. In winter, the gully may contain ice and snow, as it is in the shade all day. The bottom of the descent gully is about 400 feet right (east) of the base of the approach gully.

An alternative descent heads down left (west) at the red rock, and goes down into the Painted Bowl (as for the **Black Orpheus**). This may be a better option in snowy and icy conditions.

FIRST CREEK CANYON

Lots of rock here, but only a few routes that are noteworthy enough to be included in this guide. Park at the First Creek trailhead 7/10 of a mile south of Oak Creek on Route 159, and follow the old road in toward the canyon (west). When the trail forks, take the Upper Trail (left), then the left fork when this trail splits again. Stay on the left (south) side of the drainage to the mouth of the canyon. All of the routes described here are on the left (south) wall of the canyon as you enter it. Scramble about 150 yards uphill to the base of a varnished buttress with a white top. The approach takes about 45 minutes, and is primarily flat. These routes are in the shade in the afternoon.

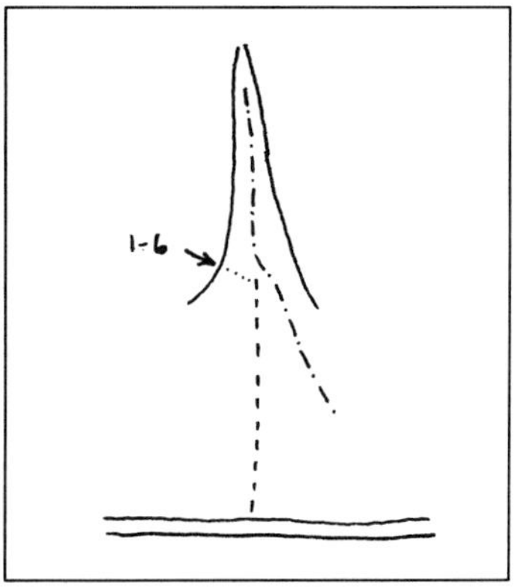

Lotta Balls Wall

1 **Lotta Balls 5.8 PG**

FA: Betsy & Joe Herbst, Randy Grandstaff, Tom Kaufman – March, 1977

Named for the surrealistic rock formations on the second pitch, not for an inordinate amount of courage. Start 50 feet right of a gigantic boulder at the northeast corner of Lotta Balls Wall, and 10 feet right of an oak tree growing out of the cliff.

P1 Climb a series of stacked blocks, then move right to a notch in a ceiling about 20 feet up. Pull through the ceiling into a left-facing corner, then follow a huge white flake up and right to a belay stance with two bolts. 100 ft., 5.6.

P2 Climb 40 feet up the famous marble-studded face, passing two bolts. Continue up an easy right-facing corner to a spacious ledge. 150 ft., 5.8.

P3 Continue up the easy corner to a roof 75 feet above, then step left and follow an obvious crack. Move left at the end of the pitch to a belay ledge with a tree. 165 ft., 5.5.

P4 Scramble to the top of the buttress. 100 ft.

Descent: Go down a gully to the left (east) of the buttress. Two short rappels and scrambling lead back to the base of the route.

2 **Bruja's Brew 5.9 PG**

FA: Todd Swain, Debbie Brenchley – December, 1991

This'll cure a powerful thirst! Start eight feet right of **Lotta Balls** below a left-facing corner capped by a roof.

P1 Climb up the corner and crack to the roof, then traverse right to the nose. Continue straight up the face past one bolt, then angle right to a ledge. Go up the obvious crack above about 10 feet, then swing out right on knobs. Climb up a left facing corner to a belay stance with one bolt and nut placements. 135 ft., 5.9.

P2 Shoot straight up the varnished face to a belay about 35 feet below the center of the roof looming above. 150 ft., 5.6.

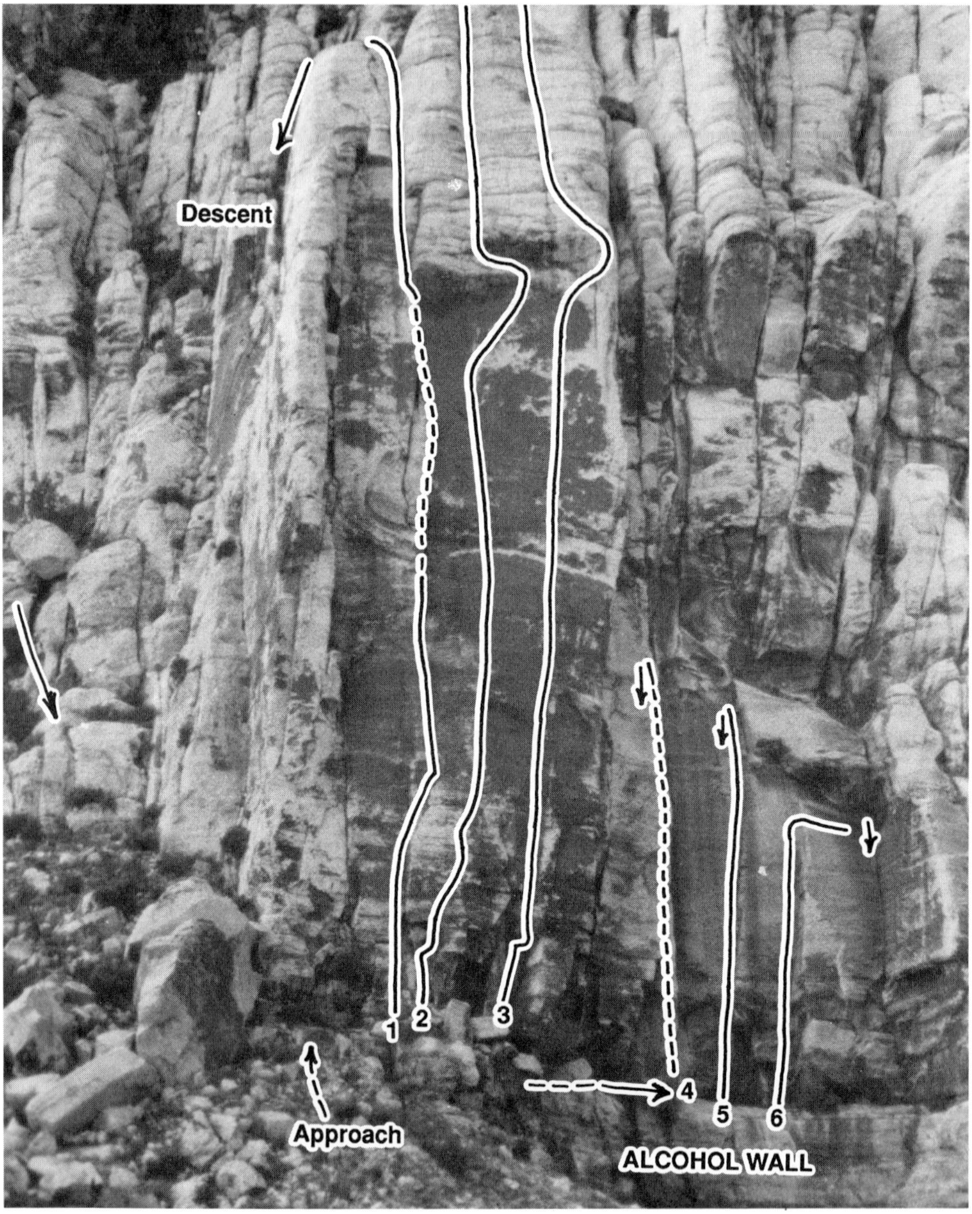

First Creek Canyon

Lotta Balls Wall
1 Lotta Balls 5.8 PG 👍
2 Bruja's Brew 5.9 PG
3 Black Magic 5.8 PG

Alcohol Wall
4 Gin Ricky 5.10
5 Rob Roy 5.10- PG 👍
6 Mai Tai 5.10+ R

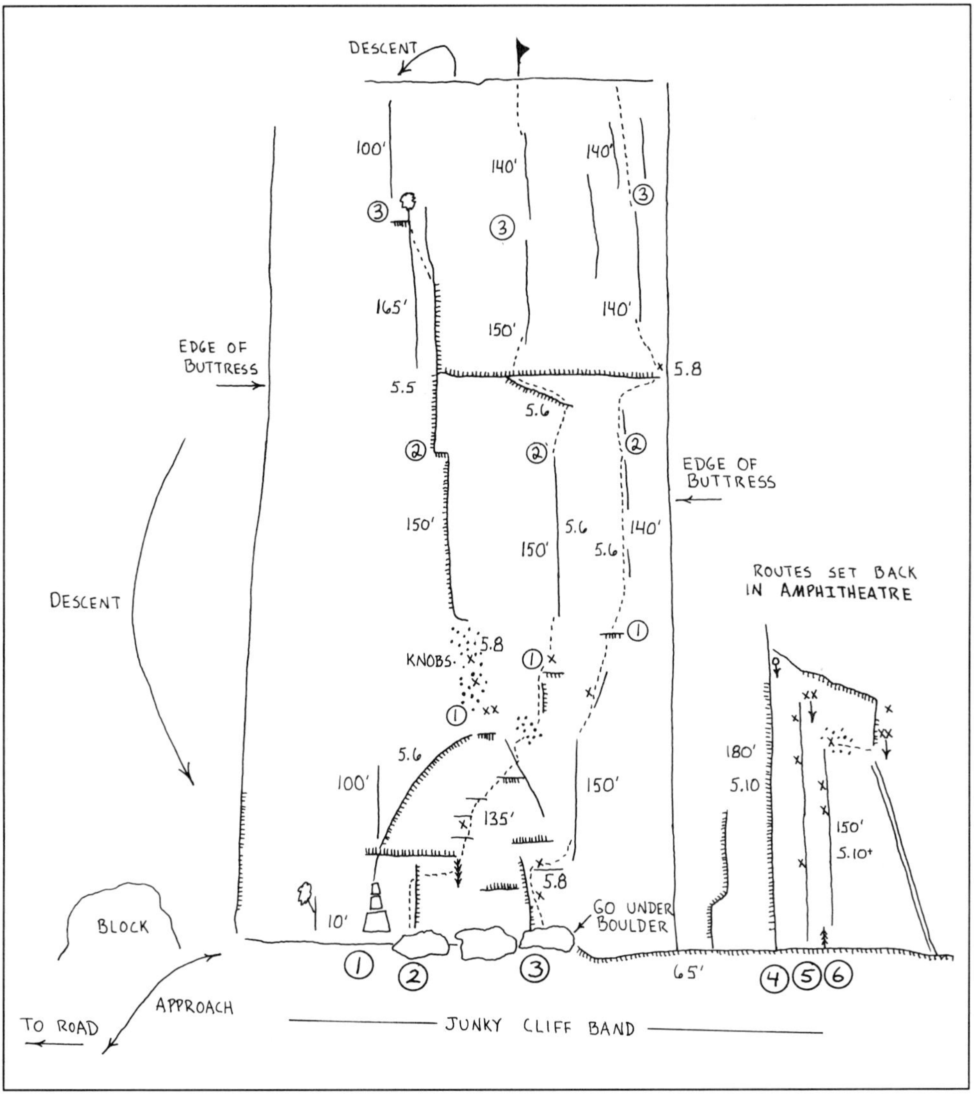

First Creek Canyon

Lotta Balls Wall

1 **Lotta Balls** 5.8 PG
2 **Bruja's Brew** 5.9 PG
3 **Black Magic** 5.8 PG

Alcohol Wall

4 **Gin Ricky** 5.10
5 **Rob Roy** 5.10- PG
6 **Mai Tai** 5.10+ R

P3 Move up to the center of the roof, then angle out left on a ramp system. Belay above in the white rock at a crack. 150 ft., 5.6.

P4 Continue up the easy white rock to the top of the buttress. 140 ft.

Descent: Go down a gully to the left (east) of the buttress. Two short rappels and scrambling lead back to the base of the route.

3 **Black Magic 5.8 PG**
FA: Jorge & Joanne Urioste – April, 1978
Bring your rabbit's foot for the intimidating first pitch. Begin 40 feet right of **Lotta Balls** atop a boulder, and just left of a left-facing corner.

P1 Climb a flake and the varnished face above past two bolts. At the second bolt, traverse right, then up an obvious thin crack. Continue up the crack and varnished face above past one more bolt to a belay stance (natural thread, nuts). 150 ft., 5.8.

P2 Continue straight up the brown face to a belay in a crack about 35 feet below the right center of the roof. 140 ft., 5.6.

P3 Climb up to the roof, and traverse out right to the nose and a bolt. Move straight up easier white rock to a belay stance in a crack with bushes growing out of it. 140 ft., 5.8.

P4 Scamper up easy white rock to the top. 140 ft.

Descent: Go down a gully to the left (east) of the buttress. Two short rappels and scrambling lead back to the base of the route.

Alcohol Wall

This wall hosts a number of excellent one pitch routes, all of which are in the shade all day. Bring two 165-foot ropes to rappel off. From the base of **Lotta Balls,** walk right (west) along a ledge system, and go under the boulder that **Black Magic** starts on. Follow the ledge system for 50 feet to the base of a huge right-facing corner. Just right is the start of **Gin Ricky.**

4 **Gin Ricky 5.10**
FA: Richard Harrison, Paul Crawford, Paul Van Betten, Sal Mamusia, Paul "Obi" Obenheim – 1983
Bring lots of gear for this one - from wires to a #4 Friend. Begin below a long, right-facing corner. Follow the corner to shaky rappel anchors 180 feet up.

5 **Rob Roy 5.10- PG**
FA: Richard Harrison, Paul Crawford, Paul Van Betten, Sal Mamusia, Paul Obenheim – 1983
A bit sporty, but excellent. Bring wires and camming units up to #2.5. Start 10 feet right of **Gin Ricky** below a left-facing corner system. Climb the face past a bolt, then follow the corner past two more bolts to the rappel anchors. 150 ft.

6 **Mai Tai 5.10+ R**
FA: Richard Harrison, Paul Van Betten, Paul Obenheim, Sal Mamusia – 1983
A stiff drink - beware. Begin 12 feet right of **Rob Roy** at a short dihedral capped by a ceiling. Ascend the dihedral to the obvious, left-facing corner. Follow this past three bolts. At the third bolt, traverse right past a plethora of knobs to a two-bolt anchor in the large, left-facing corner (**Friendship,** 5.9). 150 ft.

BLACK VELVET CANYON

Black Velvet is home to the most famous and classic routes at Red Rocks. The approach hike isn't too long (compared to some of the other canyons), and actually is quite enjoyable. To reach the trailhead, drive 4.65 miles west on Route 160 from its intersection with Route 159. Turn right (north) at this point and follow a dirt road 1.95 miles to the second dirt road on the left. Make this left turn, drive ⁵⁄₁₀ of a mile to a "T' intersection, then turn right and drive ³⁄₁₀ of a mile to the parking areas at the end of the road. You'll be driving on rough dirt roads, but there is no need for a special type of vehicle. To continue beyond the normal parking areas (there is no real benefit) you'll need 4WD. As of press time, there are three distinct parking areas at the end of the passable road, and the BLM allows camping here. There is no water, trash pickup or bathroom, so please do your part to keep this area clean and unpolluted. Again, if we don't police ourselves, there could be major repercussions!

The first 15 routes described are on the left (south) side of the canyon, on Whiskey Peak. They are described from left to right, and each has its own approach and descent descriptions.

1 **Frogland 5.8–**

FA: Mike Gilbert, Joanne & Jorge Urioste – May, 1978

The sustained nature of the route may keep you hopping! Bring a good selection of gear, as all of the pitches are long and wander a bit.

Follow the roadbed about 300 yards from the parking area, then take a trail that branches off right where the road makes a hard left turn. Hike this trail about a half mile until it forks. Take the left trail (the right fork drops down a hill into the main drainage) 200 yards to a red dirt ridge. Follow a faint trail steeply uphill, and head for the left (east) edge of an obvious red and pink rock band below the main canyon wall. Once atop the rock band, contour right (west) about 200 yards to the base of the route.

Start at a clearing on a ledge 100 feet right (west) of a huge, white section of cliff. Between the white section of rock and this route are numerous crack systems filled with bushes and trees. The first pitch of this route ascends a left-facing corner system with a large, white flake at its base.

P1 Scramble atop a block, then climb a left-facing dihedral past three bolts to an obvious sapling (V1). Continue up to the highest ledge with oak bushes on it. 140 ft., 5.7.

P2 Climb a beautiful low-angled dihedral above to a ledge (80 ft). Continue straight up the chimney/flake (V2) to another ledge just below a prominent, bushy ledge. 150 ft., 5.6.

P3 Pull a small ceiling, then angle left under the bushy ledge to the main dihedral. Follow this to a bulge, then move right and up to a belay stance in a varnished, left-leaning corner. 150 ft., 5.6.

P4 Angle left across the varnished face to a ledge. Climb the low-angled white dihedral to a bolt, then continue up eight feet to a ceiling. Finger traverse straight left to the arête, then up a thin crack to a stance. Continue up the face and shallow dihedrals above to a stance at a bush. 150 ft., 5.8–.

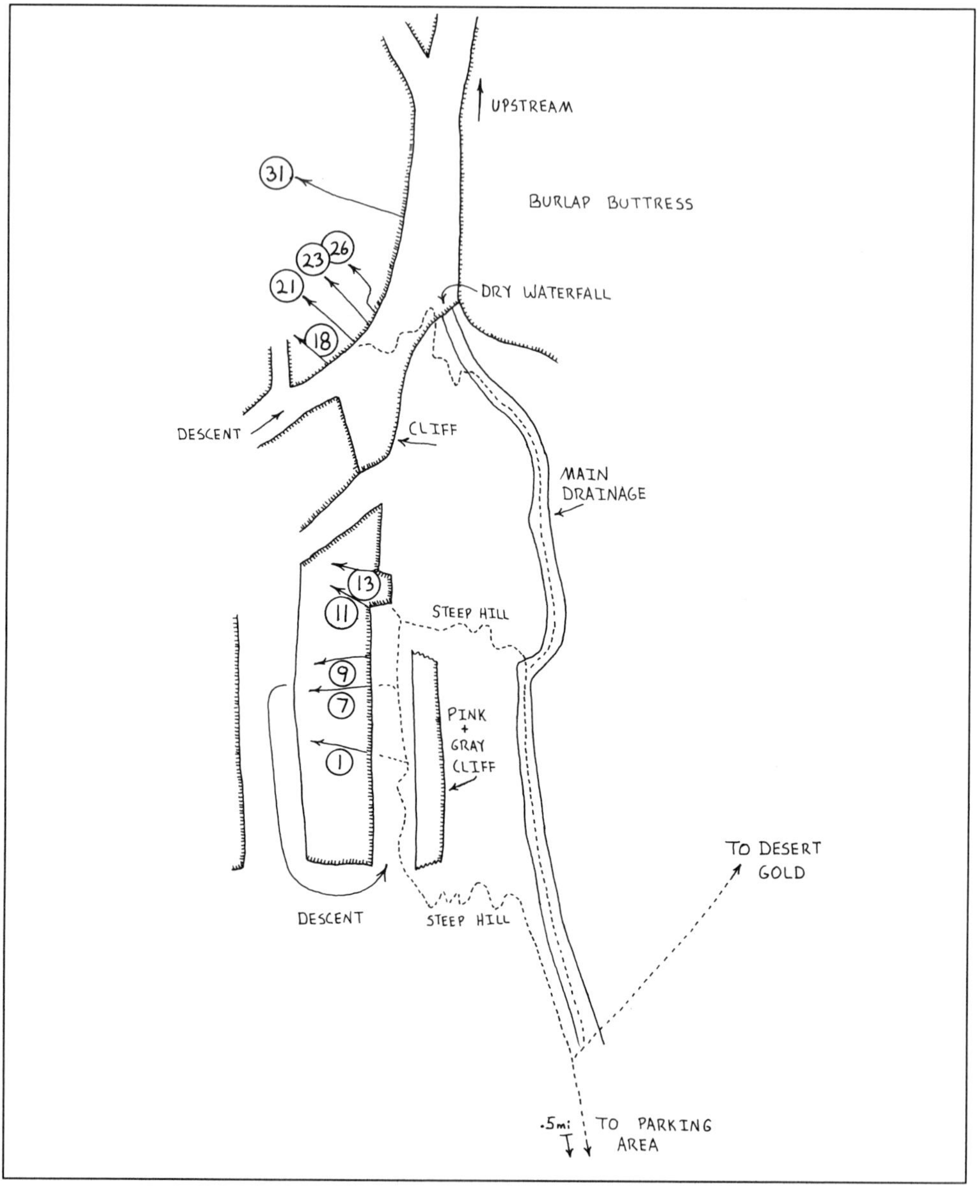

Black Velvet Canyon Overview Map

1	Frogland	5.8–		
7	Ixtalan	5.11		
9	Triassic Sands	5.10		
11	Wholesome Fullback	5.10–		
13	Our Father	5.10+	R	
18	Refried Brains	5.9		
21	Rock Warrior	5.10	R	👍
23	Dream Of Wild Turkeys	5.10-		
26	Fiddler On The Roof	5.10+	PG/R	👍
31	Epinephrine	5.9		👍

Black Velvet Canyon Overview

1	Frogland 5.8–	23	Dream Of Wild Turkeys 5.10-
7	Ixtalan 5.11	26	Fiddler On The Roof 5.10+ PG/R
11	Wholesome Fullback 5.10–	31	Epinephrine 5.9

P5 Face climb up white rock to a bolt, then angle up left into a chimney with a huge chockstone jammed in it. Tunnel easily underneath the chockstone, then step right above it and pull past a white bulge to belay in the easy chimney above. Watch for rope drag. 150 ft., 5.8–.

P6 Scamper up the chimney a bit, then angle right out on the face. Follow thin cracks up to a ceiling and move back left to the corner and a bushy ledge. 120 ft., 5.6, PG.

P7 Scramble up any of the easy routes to the top of the buttress. 100 ft., fourth class.

V1 **Rain Dance** 5.10+ FA: Dave Wonderly, Don Wilson – Spring 1990.

Start just left of the normal route and climb up to a bolt. Angle slightly left and go up features to the sapling.

V2 The original route traversed left to a corner, then went up that corner to rejoin the line.

Descent: From the top of the buttress, head left (east) down a gully toward the road. There are three gullies leading downward – take the rightmost (southernmost) one,

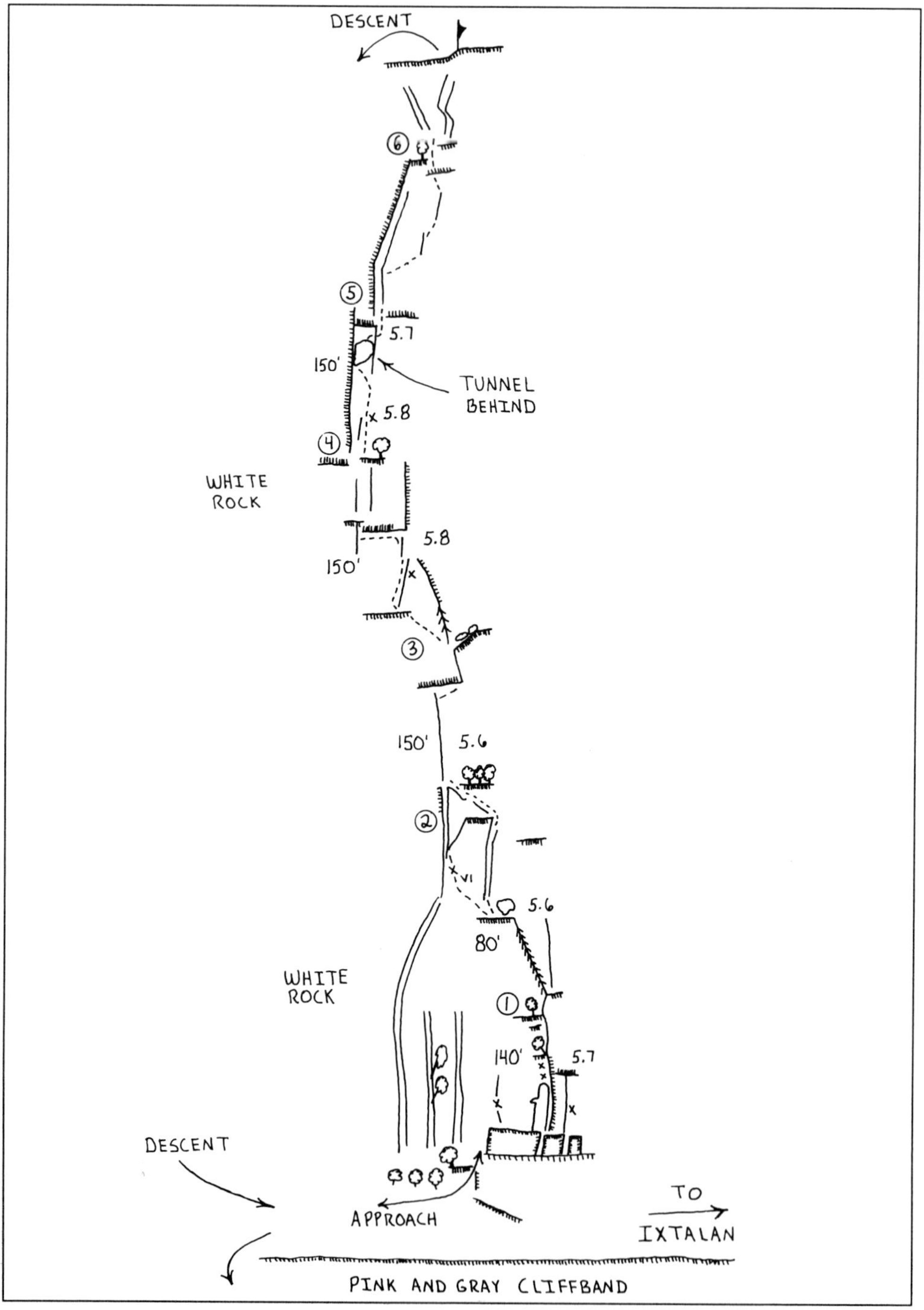
DESCENT
⑥
⑤
5.7
150'
TUNNEL
BEHIND
x 5.8
④
WHITE
ROCK
5.8
150'
③
150'
5.6
②
VI
5.6
80'
WHITE
ROCK
①
140'
5.7
DESCENT
APPROACH
TO
IXTALAN
PINK AND GRAY CLIFFBAND

Frogland, 5.8–

then contour back around to the base of the route. This is very simple, and surprisingly quick.

There are also two excellent routes on the right wall of the descent gully, about 200 yards from the top of **Frogland:**

2 **Back To Basics 5.7**
FA: Wendell Broussard, Ed Prochaska – July, 1992
Start below an obvious, right-facing corner and make difficult moves (using a boulder) into the corner. Rappel with two ropes from a two-bolt anchor.

3 **First Grader 5.6**
FA: Wendell Broussard, Ed Prochaska – July, 1992
Begin 15 feet right of **Back To Basics,** and climb a beautiful finger crack and face to the bolt anchor.

1 **Frogland 5.8–**
6 **Mazatlan 5.10+**
7 **Ixtalan 5.11**
9 **Triassic Sands 5.10**

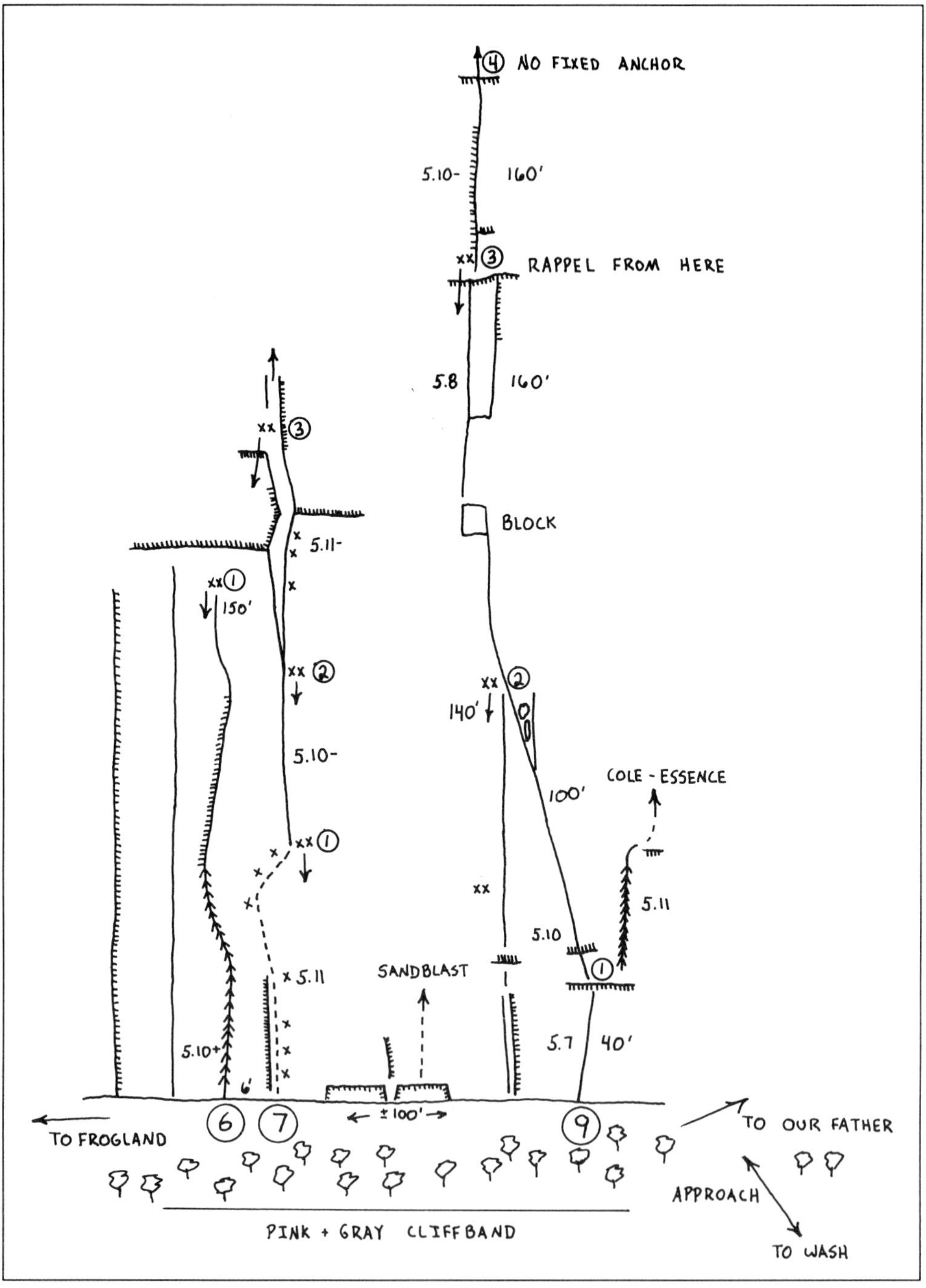

6 Mazatlan 5.10+

7 Ixtalan 5.11

9 Triassic Sands 5.10

4 **Return To Forever 5.10+**
FA Richard Harrison, Paul Crawford, Paul Van Betten, Sal Mamusia, Chick Corea 1983
You'll be jazzed after doing this one. Bring two ropes and some big gear. Not much is known about this route, as you'll gather once you read the route description.

Start about 275 feet right of **Frogland** on a ledge system under a large roof.

P1 Climb the prominent offwidth through the roof, and belay above. 5.10+.

P2 Continue upward. 5.10.

P3 Continue upward. 5.8.

Descent: Rappel the route.

5 **Kenny Laguna 5.10+**
FA Richard Harrison, Paul Crawford, Paul Van Betten, Sal Mamusia 1983
Begin under the same roof system as **Return To Forever.** Again, not much is known about this climb.

P1 Climb a corner through the roof. 5.10+.

P2 Follow a crack system to a corner. 5.10.

Descent: Rappel the route with two ropes.

6 **Mazatlan 5.10+** 👍
FA: Dave Anderson, Randy Grandstaff – 1978
A classic pitch to a shaky belay anchor. Bring a good selection of gear, as well as two ropes for the rappel.

From the parking area, follow the roadbed toward the canyon about 300 yards, then take a trail that branches off right when the road makes a hard left turn. Hike this trail about a half mile, until it forks. Take the right fork, and drop down into the drainage. Follow the rocky creekbed up about 300 yards to a trail leading steeply up and left (south). Take this trail up, skirting the right (west) edge of a pink rock band below the main canyon wall. You should now be roughly below **Wholesome Fullback**, and must contour left (east; toward the road) about 100 yards to the base of this route.

Start 300 feet right of **Frogland** at a clean, varnished dihedral six feet left of **Ixtalan** (the obvious offwidth splitting a roof about 100 feet above the ground). Climb the corner/dihedral to a belay station under a ceiling. The crux is right at the start.

7 **Ixtalan 5.11**
FA: Jorge & Joanne Urioste, Dan "Spiderman" Goodwin – June, 1981
Sharpen your offwidth skills before trying this one! The bolts next to the offwidth on pitch three were placed on aid, using a giant wooden Friend!

To approach this route, follow the roadbed about 300 yards from the parking area, then take a trail that branches off right where the road makes a hard left turn. Hike this trail toward the cliffs for about a half mile, until it forks. Take the right fork, and drop down into the drainage. Follow the rocky creekbed upstream about 300 yards to a trail leading steeply up and left (south). Take this trail up, skirting the right (west) edge of a pink rock band below the main canyon wall. You should now be roughly below **Wholesome Fullback**, and must contour left (east; toward the road) about 100 yards to the base of this route.

Rope up directly below the obvious offwidth crack that splits a roof about 100 feet above, and six feet right of a beautiful varnished dihedral.

P1 Power up a shallow right facing corner past four bolts with red hangers, then angle right past three more bolts to a hanging belay at the base of the **Ixtalan** crack. 70 ft., 5.11c.

P2 Lieback and jam up the widening crack to another hanging belay. 60 ft, 5.10-

P3 The longest 60-foot pitch you'll ever do! Struggle up the offwidth, then lieback through the roof to a belay stance with bolts. 60 ft., 5.11–.

Descent: Either continue up the easy chimney above (not too interesting), or rappel the route.

8 Sandblast 5.9+ R

FA: Joe Herbst, Larry Hamilton – May, 1972 FFA: Paul Van Betten, Nick Nordblom Fall – 1987

The first pitch of this route climbs the original aid line of **Triassic Sands.** It then trends left and continues up for two pitches of new climbing.

Approach this somewhat loose climb by following the roadbed about 300 yards from the parking area, then take a trail that branches off right where the road makes a hard left turn. Hike this trail toward the canyon about a half mile, until it forks. Take the right fork, and drop down into the drainage. Follow the rocky creekbed up about 300 yards to a trail leading steeply up and left (south). Take this trail up, skirting the right (west) edge of a pink rock band below the main canyon wall. You should now be roughly below **Wholesome Fullback,** and must contour left (east; toward the road) about 200 feet until you are below a striking finger-and-hand crack (**Triassic Sands**).

Begin at an obvious left-facing facing flake/corner with a wide crack in its back.

P1 Climb the left-facing flake/corner to its top, then follow the thin crack up to a belay anchor. 100 ft., 5.9.

P2 Go left, then climb a thin seam and loose flakes to a belay. 120 ft., 5.9+.

P3 A short, easy pitch up a wide crack leads to a ledge. 50 ft., 5.7.

Descent: Rappel with two ropes.

9 Triassic Sands 5.10

FA: Joe Herbst, Larry Hamilton – May, 1972 FFA: Augie Klien, Tom Kaufman, Randy Grandstaff, Chris Robbins, Joe Herbst – Spring 1979

An old route, on even older rock! Bring numerous pieces in the three-inch range for the second pitch. Many people rappel with two ropes from the top of the third pitch. If you continue above, there are no fixed anchors.

Approach this route by following the roadbed about 300 yards from the parking area, then take a trail that branches off right where the road makes a hard left turn. Hike this trail toward the canyon about a half mile until it forks. Take the right fork, and drop down into the drainage. Follow the rocky creekbed up for about 300 yards to a trail leading steeply up and left (south). Take this trail up, skirting the right (west) edge of a pink rock band below the main canyon wall. You should now be roughly below **Wholesome Fullback,** and must contour left (east; toward the road) about 200 feet until you stand below a striking finger-and-hand crack.

Start 100 feet right of the prominent **Ixtalan** crack system and 20 feet right of a left-facing flake/corner. The climb begins at a left-facing corner with a three-inch crack in it.

P1 Climb the left-facing corner to a ledge at the base of a striped dihedral. 40 ft., 5.7.

6 Mazatlan 5.10+ 👍
7 Ixtalan 5.11

9 Triassic Sands 5.10

P2 Step left (V1) and jam the slightly left-leaning finger crack past a ceiling, then continue up the hand-and-fist crack to a belay at funky bolts just left of the crack. 100 ft., 5.10.

P3 Continue up the crack past a block, then go up one of two cracks to a good ledge with bolts. 160 ft., 5.8.

P4 Climb the right facing corner to another ledge (no fixed anchors). 160 ft., 5.10–.

P5 & 6 Two easy pitches up a series of broken corners lead to the top of the buttress.

V1 *Cole Essence* 5.11

FA: Charles Cole (of Five Ten fame), Randy Grandstaff – circa 1990.
Climb the striped dihedral, exiting right to a belay station on the arête. Either rappel, or continue up **Archeopteryx.**

Descent: Either rappel from the top of the third pitch (two 150 foot rappels), or head left (east) down a gully toward the road from the top of the buttress. There are three gullies leading downward – take the rightmost (southernmost) one, then contour back around to the base of the route. This is very simple, and surprisingly quick.

10 Archeoptryx 5.11 R

FA: Nick Nordblom, Lynn Robison – Fall 1988

Named for a fossilized bird-type thing of the Jurassic period (the age of dinosaurs).

To approach this route, follow the roadbed about 300 yards from the parking area, then take a trail that branches off right where the road makes a hard left turn. Hike this trail toward the cliffs about a half mile until it forks. Take the right fork, and drop down into the drainage. Follow the rocky creekbed upstream about 300 yards to a trail leading steeply up and left (south). Take this trail up, skirting the right (west) edge of a pink rock band below the main canyon wall. You should now be roughly below **Wholesome Fullback,** and must contour left (east; toward the road) to the base of this route.

Start either atop **Cole Essence** (a variation to **Triassic Sands**), or in the gully to the right of the prominent **Triassic Sands** crack. The route basically follows the arête above the **Cole Essence** dihedral for three pitches.

P1 Angle out left from the gully and climb past bolts to a belay. 5.10–, R.

P2 Continue up the arête past more bolts to another belay. 5.10–.

P3 Scary and difficult climbing up the arête leads to another belay. 5.11, R.

Descent: Rappel the route with two ropes.

11 Wholesome Fullback 5.10–

FA: Cal Folsom, Lars Holbeck – May, 1975

An excellent route to round out a climbing day. Bring gear up to a #4 Friend, with emphasis on the 1- to 3-inch sizes.

This route is reached by following the roadbed about 300 yards from the parking area, then taking a trail that branches off right where the road makes a hard left turn. Hike this trail toward the canyon about a half mile, until it forks. Take the right fork, and drop down into the drainage. Follow the rocky creekbed upstream about 300 yards to a trail leading steeply up and left (south). Take this trail up, skirting the right (west) edge of a pink rock band below the main canyon wall. You should now be roughly below **Wholesome Fullback,** which climbs the left side of a prominent pillar that only goes part-way up the cliff.

Begin 200 feet right of the **Triassic Sands** finger-and-hand crack, and about 10 feet right of a right-facing corner, below an obvious finger crack in a brown varnished slab.

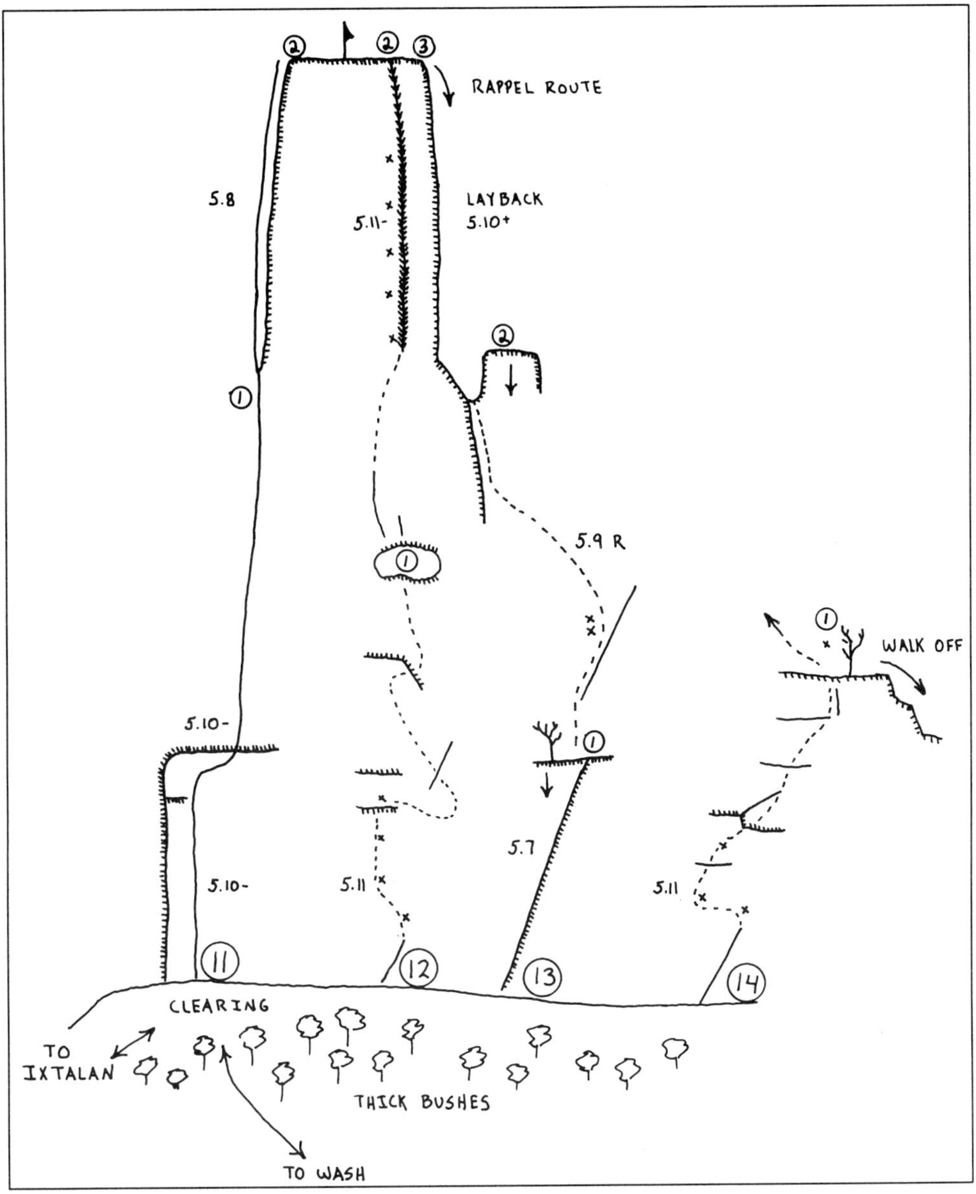

11 **Wholesome Fullback 5.10–**
12 **The Delicate Sound Of Thunder 5.11 PG/R** 👍
13 **Our Father 5.10+ R**
14 **Tales From The Gripped 5.11**

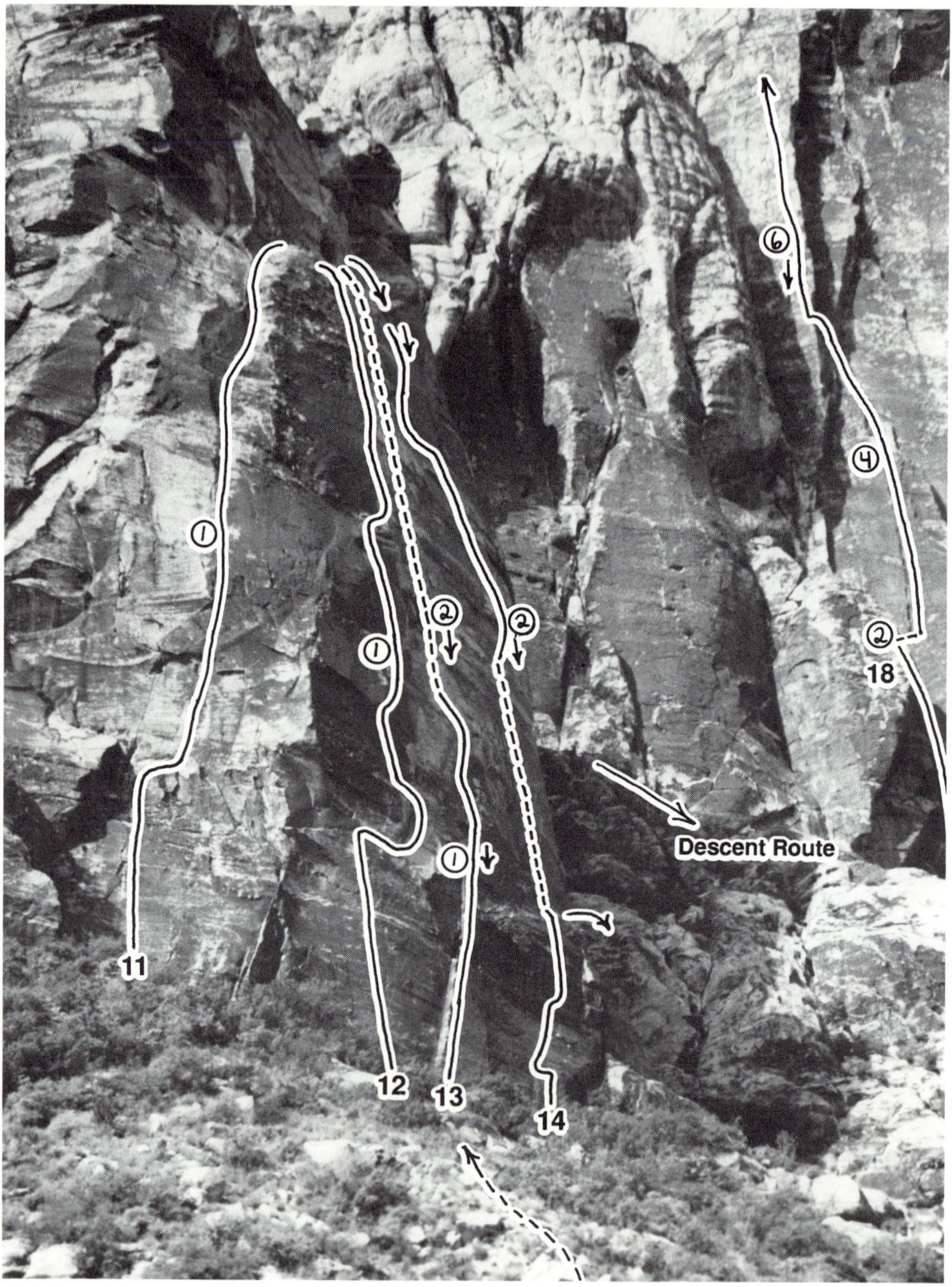

11 Wholesome Fullback 5.10–
12 The Delicate Sound Of Thunder 5.11 PG/R
13 Our Father 5.10+ R
14 Tales From The Gripped 5.11
18 Refried Brains 5.9

P1 Climb the slabby face to the crack, then follow the crack past a ledge to an overhang. Jog right, then continue up the crack to a belay at the base of a chimney. Watch for rope drag at the overhang. 150 ft, 5.10–.

P2 Follow the chimney to the top of the pillar. 100 ft., 5.8.

Descent: Rappel down **Our Father,** on the right (west) side of the pillar, in three short rappels.

12 The Delicate Sound Of Thunder 5.11 PG/R

FA: Dave Wonderly, Marge Floyd, Dave Evans – November, 1988

As awesome as it sounds! Not for the faint of heart. Your rack should include gear up to a #2 Friend.

This route is best approached by following the road from the parking area about 300 yards, then taking a trail that branches off right where the road makes a hard left turn. Hike this trail toward the canyon for about a half mile until it forks. Take the right fork, and drop down into the drainage. Follow the rocky creekbed up about 300 yards to a trail leading steeply up and left (south). Take this trail upward, skirting the right (west) edge of a pink rock band below the main canyon wall. You should now be roughly below **Wholesome Fullback,** which climbs the left side of a prominent pillar that only goes partway up the cliff.

Start about 50 feet right of **Wholesome Fullback** at a short, small, right-leaning corner. **The Delicate Sound Of Thunder** is the left-facing corner about 10 feet left of **Our Father.**

P1 Wander up the face past four bolts, making difficult moves past the second bolt. Traverse right from the fourth bolt, making 5.10 moves way out. Climb up to a ceiling, then swing around right and up the face to an alcove (funky anchors, nothing good fixed). 140 ft., 5.11, PG/R.

P2 Climb a short crack above the alcove, then continue up the obvious arête past five bolts to the top of the pillar. Excellent positions! 100 ft., 5.11–.

Descent: Rappel down **Our Father,** on the right (west) side of the pillar, in three short rappels (only one rope needed).

13 Our Father 5.10+ R

FA: Rick Wheeler, Joe Herbst, Randy Grandstaff, Vern Clevenger (of Tuolumne fame) – Spring 1977

Say your prayers before leading the second pitch! Bring extra 2- to 3.5-inch gear.

This route is best approached by following the road from the parking area about 300 yards, then taking a trail that branches off right when the road makes a hard left turn. Hike this trail toward the canyon about a half mile, until it forks. Take the right fork, and drop down into the drainage. Follow the rocky creekbed up about 300 yards, until you reach a trail leading steeply up and left (south). Take this trail up, skirting the right (west) edge of a pink rock band below the main canyon wall. You should now be roughly below the route, which climbs the right side of a prominent pillar that only goes partway up the canyon wall.

Begin 60 feet right of **Wholesome Fullback** at a right-leaning crack/corner, and below a prominent white right-facing corner marking the right side of a pillar leaning against the main canyon wall.

P1 A fun pitch in itself. Climb the right-leaning crack/corner to a belay ledge with a tree. 60 ft., 5.7.

P2 Climb up the face to doubled bolts, then angle left into the obvious, right-facing corner. Belay above, atop a block (fixed anchor). 100 ft., 5.9, R.

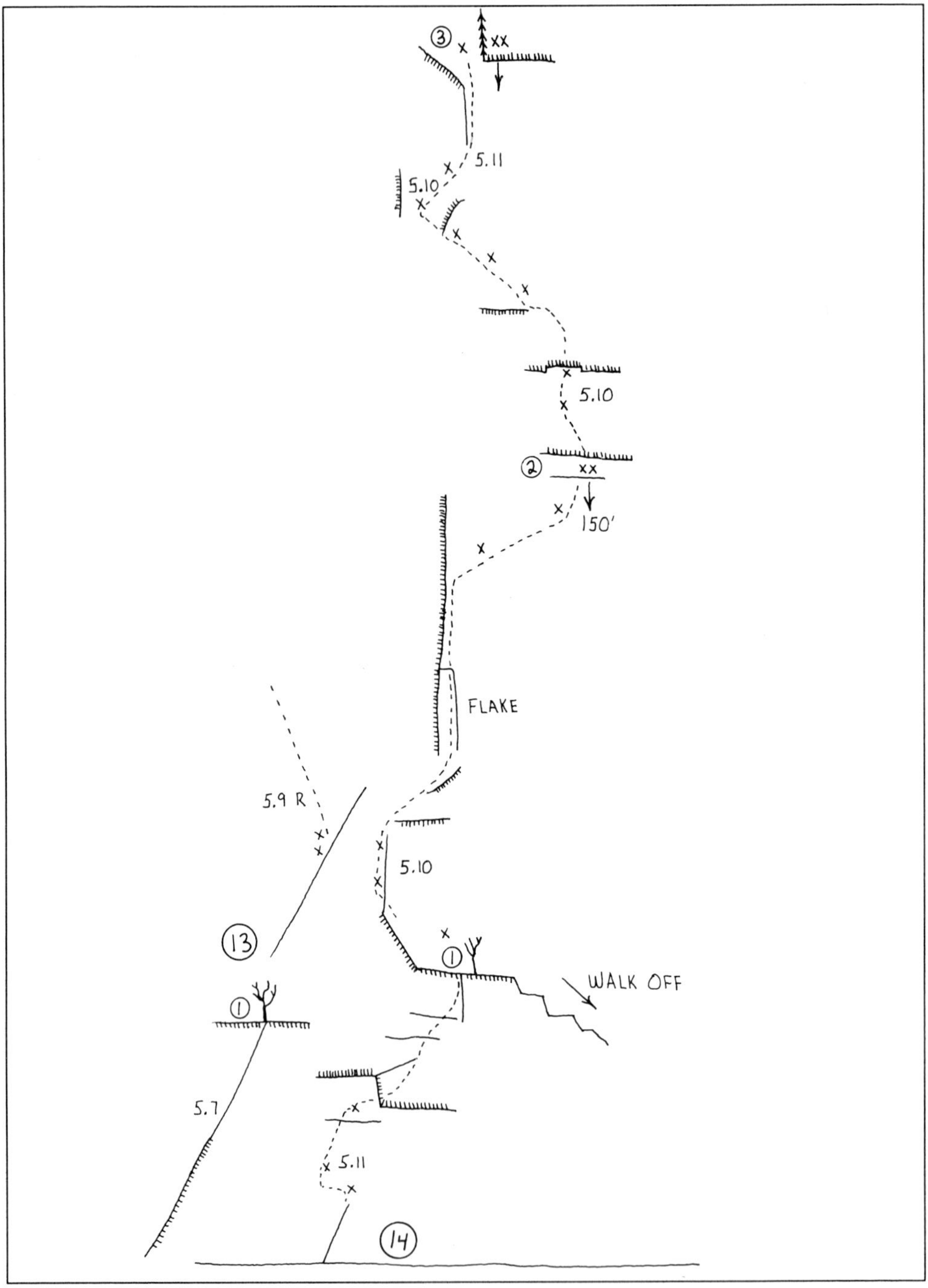

Tales from the Gripped, 5.11

P3 Jam and lieback up the perfect right-facing corner above. 50 ft., 5.10+.

Descent: Rappel the route in three short rappels (only one rope needed).

14 **Tales From The Gripped 5.11**

FA: Todd Swain, Elaine Mathews (of Gunks fame) – November, 1990

Don't worry, it's not that scary! Bring gear up to a #2.5 Friend, and two ropes to rappel with.

Approach this route by following the roadbed about 300 yards from the parking area, then take a trail that branches off right where the road makes a hard left turn. Hike this trail about a half mile until it forks. Take the right fork, and drop down into the drainage. Follow the rocky creekbed upstream about 300 yards to a trail leading steeply up and left (south). Take this trail up, skirting the right (west) edge of a pink rock band below the main canyon wall. You should now be roughly below **Our Father**, which climbs the right side of a prominent pillar that only goes partway up the canyon wall.

Start 20 feet right of **Our Father** at the next set of parallel, right slanting cracks.

P1 Climb the crack to its end (bolt), then move straight left to another bolt. Make difficult face moves up to a ceiling, passing a third bolt. Swing right around the ceiling, and go up to a belay ledge with a bolt and small tree. 60 ft., 5.11.

P2 Go left up a ramp, then climb the arête past two bolts (5.10). Move back right to a flake and a long, right-facing corner. Higher up the corner, follow bolts out right to a hanging belay. 130 ft., 5.10.

P3 Climb past two bolts to an overlap. Pull this (5.10), then angle left to a stance (bolt). Follow two more bolts up left toward a right-facing corner, then angle back right on sloping holds to a vertical seam. Climb up along this to a belay station. 90 ft., 5.11.

Descent: Rappel the two upper pitches with two ropes, then walk off west from the top of the first pitch.

15 *Only The Good Die Young* 5.11

FA: The Uriostes – 1984. FFA: Jimmy Dunn – 1985

This route climbs dihedral systems on the buttress to the right of the **Wholesome Fullback** buttress, and across the gully from **Cutting Edge.** Jay Smith was pictured on the route in an old issue of *Rock & Ice* Magazine, but unfortunately, I don't have a lot of info on the route. It has four pitches; they are reportedly rated 5.10+, 5.10, 5.11 and 5.7+. Apparently, the descent is down the gully to the right, between Whiskey Peak and the Black Velvet Wall.

The next routes are on the Black Velvet Wall itself. This wall is separated from Whiskey Peak by a series of large gullies. The next 15 routes are described from left to right, and are in the shade most of the day (all day in the winter).

16 **Cutting Edge 5.11**

FA: Danny Meyers – 1987

An excellent one-pitch route. The initial 5.10 corner can be climbed up to some fixed nuts to round out a day. Start about 100 yards left of **Refried Brains,** and 100 feet uphill from **Smooth As Silk.** Climb a very thin crack up a shallow corner (5.10, V1), step right and do a hand traverse up and right past bolts to a bolted belay (120 ft). Rap off.

V1 Spark Plug 5.10

FA: Paul Van Betten, Sal Mamusia – 1983

Continue straight up the corner to belay slings (150 ft). This actually was done before **Cutting Edge,** and the crux of the route is the initial corner.

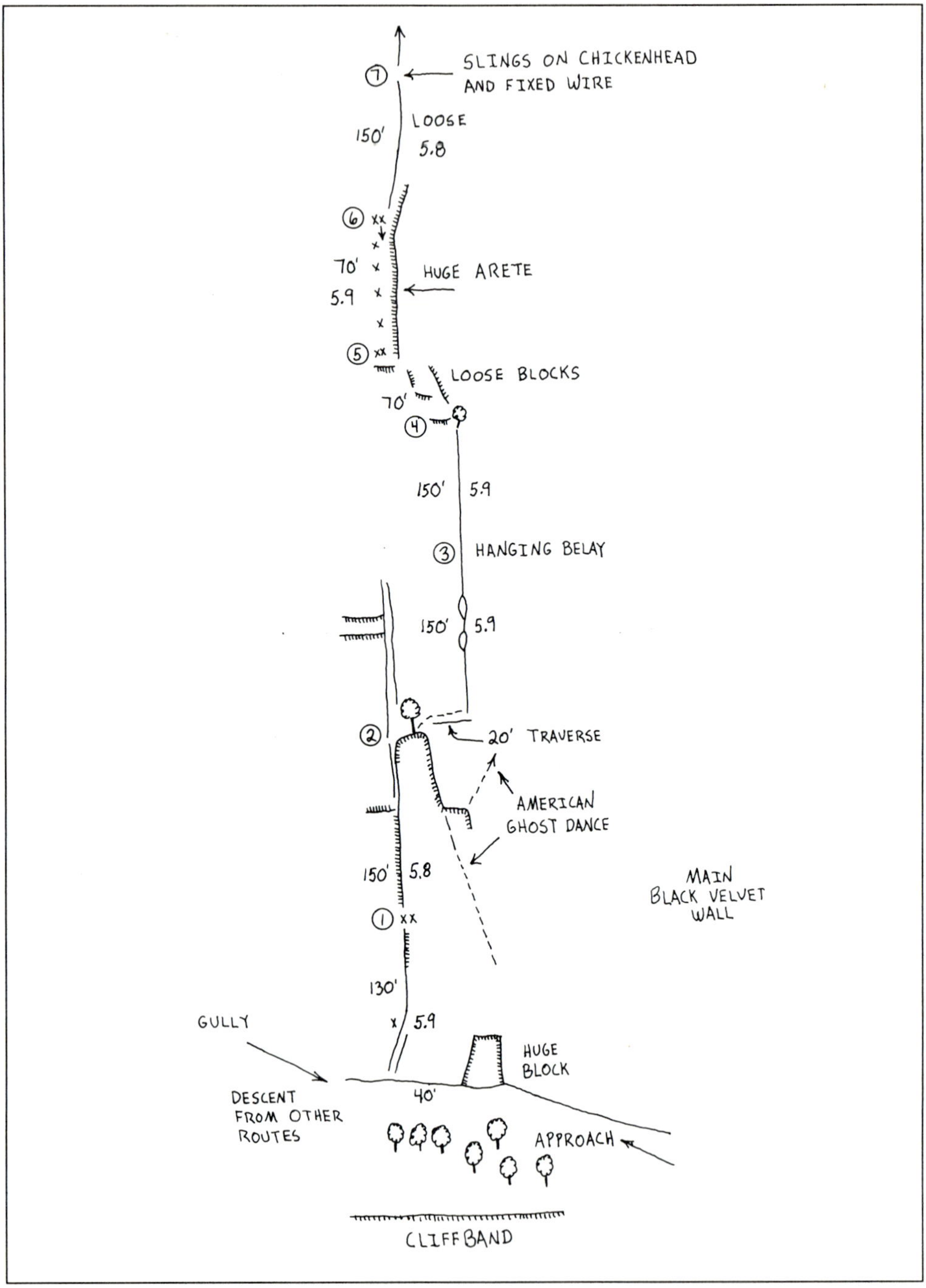

Refried Brains, 5.9

17 **Smooth As Silk 5.10+ PG/R**

FA: Jay Smith, Paul Crawford, Randy Grandstaff, Dave Diegleman – 1981

Bring small TCUs and wires. Approach this route by following the roadbed about 300 yards from the parking area, then take a trail that branches off right where the road makes a hard left turn. Hike this trail toward the canyon about a half mile until it forks. Take the right fork, and drop down into the drainage. Follow the rocky creekbed upstream about 600 yards until the drainage is blocked by a cliff. Go left (southeast) into the bushes on a path, then scramble up the cliff on big ledges. Follow trails up left about 100 yards to the base of the large, smooth wall. Continue up along the base of the wall about 200 yards, the last of which are in a large gully.

Start just right of an obelisk leaning against the wall, at a pair of right-leaning cracks.

P1 Climb a corner/crack that goes right, then up leaning cracks on a smooth face to a belay anchor in an alcove. 140 ft., 5.10.

P2 Go up an obvious, big, flaring corner to anchors. 150 ft., 5.10.

Descent: Rappel with two ropes.

18 **Refried Brains 5.9**

FA: Joanne & Jorge Urioste, Stephanie Petrilak – November, 1979

A good pun – the route is OK too. Bring two ropes to rappel the route, and large gear for the wide cracks.

Approach by following the road about 300 yards from the parking area, then take a trail that branches off right where the road makes a hard left turn. Hike this trail toward the canyon about a half mile until it forks. Take the right fork, and drop down into the drainage. Follow the rocky creekbed upstream about 600 yards until the drainage is blocked by a cliff. Go left (southeast) into the bushes on a path, then scramble up the cliff on big ledges. Follow trails up and left about 100 yards to the base of the large, smooth wall. This section of cliff has some of the best routes in all of Red Rocks. **Refried Brains** is at the left margin of this wall, and starts near the base of an obvious tree-filled gully leading up left (southeast).

Start about 160 feet right of **Smooth As Silk** and 40 feet left of a huge block leaning against the base of the crag.

P1 Climb past a bolt to reach an obvious crack. Follow this to a belay below a prominent right-facing corner. 130 ft., 5.9.

P2 Continue straight up, following the obvious crack-and-corner system. Stretch the rope to belay atop a pillar at the "tree-of-a-thousand-slings." 150 ft., 5.8.

P3 Traverse 20 feet straight right on a shelf to a crack. Follow this up past a couple of offwidth sections to a hanging belay in the crack. 150 ft, 5.9

P4 Continue up the crack system to a bush. Belay above on a series of ledges. 150 ft., 5.9.

P5 Wander up and left past loose blocks to an obvious bolt belay on the arête. 70 ft., 5.7.

P6 Climb the varnished face to the left of the arête past four bolts to another bolted belay. 70 ft., 5.9.

P7 & 8 These are best avoided, as the rock deteriorates, and there are poor fixed anchors atop pitch seven. If you want to continue, follow cracks to the top of the pillar. 5.8.

Descent: Rappel the route with two ropes.

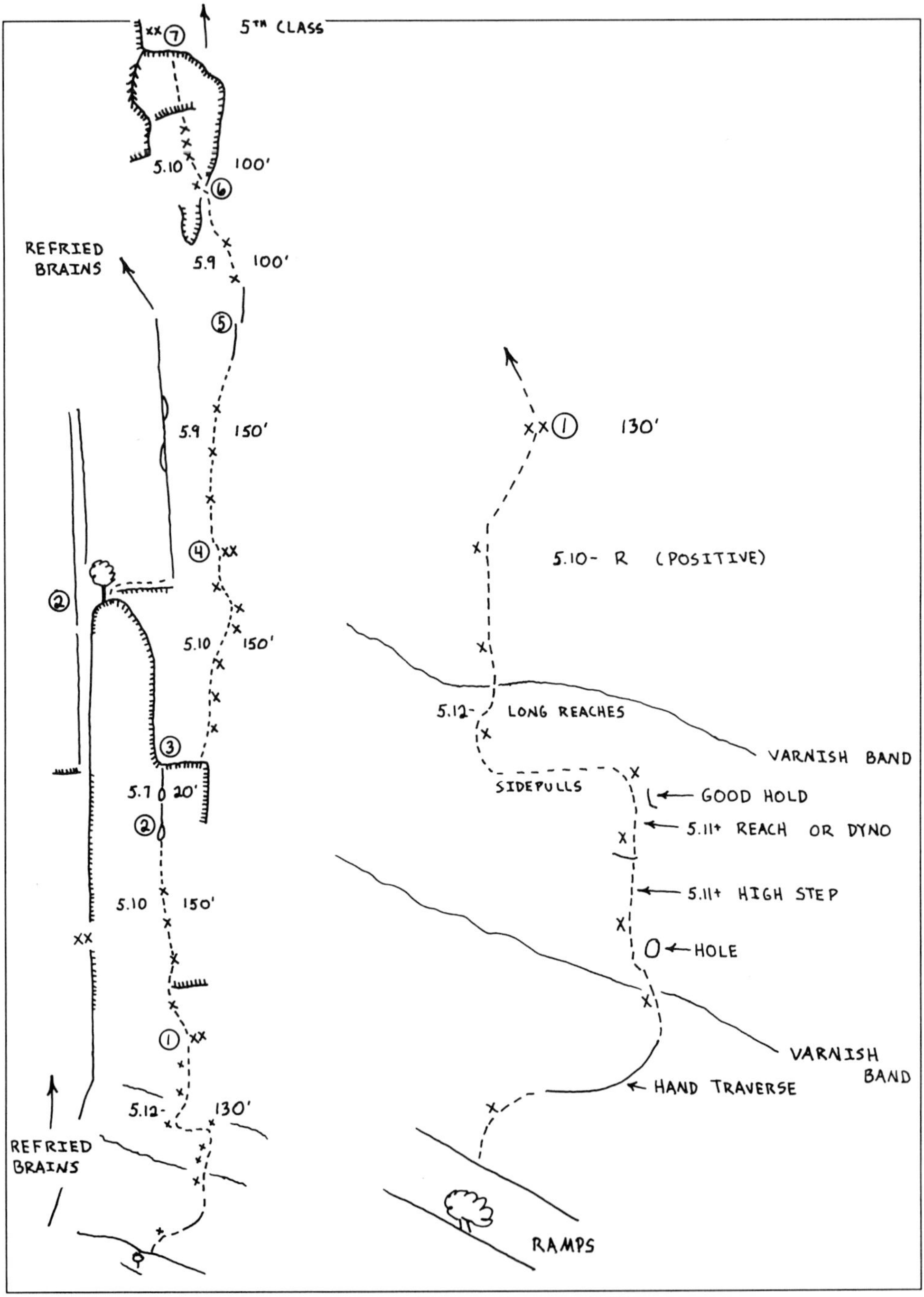

American Ghost Dance, 5.12–

Detail of pitch one to right

19 American Ghostdance 5.12-

FA: Jordy Morgan, Kevin Fosburg – November, 1988

The technical test piece of the wall. Many people rappel after the first pitch. If you decide to do the whole route, bring wires, TCUs and up to a # 2.5 Friend. Approach by following the road about 300 yards from the parking area, then take a trail that branches off right where the road makes a hard left turn. Hike this trail toward the canyon about a half mile until it forks. Take the right fork, and drop down into the drainage. Follow the rocky creekbed upstream about 600 yards, until the drainage is blocked by a cliff. Go left (southeast) into the bushes on a path, then scramble up the cliff on big ledges. Follow the trails up and left about 100 yards to the base of the large, smooth wall.

Begin at a bush just uphill from **Sandstone Samurai,** and below a bolt that leads to an obvious right-leaning finger traverse below the varnished band.

P1 Climb to a bolt, finger traverse up and right, then continue up past four bolts (many difficult moves). Move left (sidepulls) to a bolt, then make more hard moves to escape the varnished band. Continue up past two more bolts (sporty 5.10–) to the anchor. 130 ft., 5.12–.

P2 Climb past four bolts to a belay in a crack. 150 ft., 5.10.

P3 A short pitch up a crack leads to a belay ledge at a right-facing corner. 20 ft., 5.7.

P4 Clip six bolts (moving slightly left after the fifth bolt) to a bolted belay. 150 ft., 5.10.

P5 Three bolts lead to a belay in a crack. 150 ft., 5.9.

P6 Continue up the crack, then move out left and climb past two bolts to a right-facing corner/flake. Belay at a bolt at a corner. 100 ft., 5.9.

P7 Climb up and slightly left past two bolts and a ceiling to a bolted belay on a ledge. 100 ft., 5.10.

P8 Fifth-class climbing and scrambling lead to the top.

Descent: Go left (east; toward the road) until you can walk down to the notch between Whiskey Peak and the Black Velvet Wall. Head down the gully between the two formations to the base of the climb, and your gear.

20 Sandstone Samurai 5.11- R/X

FA: Paul Van Betten, Nick Nordblom – Spring 1988

Leading this is akin to hari kari (or so you'll think if you're on the "sharp end"). The route is so runout that a fall long enough to rip out the quarter-inch bolts is possible. Access this horror show by following the roadbed about 300 yards from the parking area, then take a trail that branches off right where the road makes a hard left turn. Hike toward the canyon about a half mile until the trail forks. Take the right fork, and drop down into the drainage. Follow the rocky creekbed upstream about 600 yards until the drainage is blocked by a cliff. Go left (southeast) into the bushes on a path, then scramble up the cliff on big ledges. Follow the trails up and left about 100 yards to the base of the large, smooth wall.

Rope up at a smooth varnished face to the right of a low ceiling, and left of a short pillar forming a left-facing corner. This is the same starting point as **Rock Warrior,** and 30 feet left of **The Prince Of Darkness.**

P1 Climb 40 feet up white rock to a left-leaning white ramp (bolt). Traverse right on the white slab (V1), then diagonal up and left past two bolts to a smooth, varnished section. Make hard and scary moves straight up to another bolt, and then the belay (two bolts and wires). 140 ft, 5.11–, R/X.

P2 Climb up to a short seam (TCU and wire), then continue up and slightly left (a couple of poor RPs may go in) to a bolt 50 feet above the belay. Head up and slightly right to the next belay anchor. 140 ft., 5.10–, X.

P3 Wander straight up the face to a bolt anchor, placing some RPs for pro along the way. 150 ft., 5.10–, R.

P4 Continue straight up, then angle right to a crack over a small roof. There are no bolts on the pitch, but a bolt and pin make up the anchor. 150 ft., 5.10–, R.

P5 Climb a small right-facing corner, then traverse up and left to the anchor. Five bolts on the pitch. 150 ft., 5.11–, R.

V1 There are some newer bolts with SMC hangers just left of this route. I've been unable to determine if this is a totally separate route, or merely a variation.

Descent: Rappel the route.

21 Rock Warrior 5.10 R ☝

FA: Richard Harrison, Jay Smith, Nick Nordblom – Fall 1983

A classic route, but LOTS scarier than **The Prince Of Darkness.** Bring a selection of small-sized gear, two ropes and a cool head. Approach by following the roadbed about 300 yards from the parking area, then take a trail that branches off right where the road makes a hard left turn. Hike this trail toward the canyon about a half mile until it forks. Take the right fork, and drop down into the drainage. Follow the rocky creekbed upstream about 600 yards until the drainage is blocked by a cliff. Go left (southeast) into the bushes on a path, then scramble up the cliff on big ledges. Follow the trails up left about 100 yards to the base of the large, smooth wall. This section of cliff probably has the best long routes in all of Red Rocks, including this one.

Rope up at a smooth, varnished face to the right of a low ceiling, and left of a short pillar forming a left-facing corner. This is the same start as **Sandstone Samurai**, and is 30 feet left of **Dream of Wild Turkeys** and **The Prince Of Darkness.**

P1 Climb 40 feet up and right on white rock (easy, but dangerous) to a slab. Clip a bolt, climb up, then traverse right until beneath the anchor. Climb up past one more bolt, and make sporty moves to the belay. 150 ft., 5.10–, R .

P2 Angle slightly left from the belay to a bolt, then wander straight up to another bolt by a shallow, left-facing corner. Make difficult moves up the arête of the corner to a seam, which is followed up and slightly right past a bit more fixed gear to the anchor. 150 ft., 5.10.

P3 Go slightly left from the belay, then up the face past a little bit of fixed gear to a ceiling. Pull this, and move up to a belay station. 150 ft., 5.10–, R.

P4 Wander up the face to a three-bolt belay at a corner (the first-ascent party bivied here in hammocks). 150 ft., 5.9, R.

P5 Climb the corner, then up the face past a few bolts to another belay station. 150 ft., 5.9, R.

P6 Climb over a ceiling, then up along cracks and seams to a belay. 150 ft., 5.10–, R.

Descent: Either continue up (5.8/9, then third class), or rappel the route with two ropes.

22 The Prince Of Darkness 5.10 ☝

FA: Jorge & Joanne Urioste, Bill Bradley, Mike Ward – Fall 1984

This route is impressive – not only for the positions you'll be in, but for the amount of effort needed to drill all the bolts you'll encounter (some say it's over-bolted). Bring lots

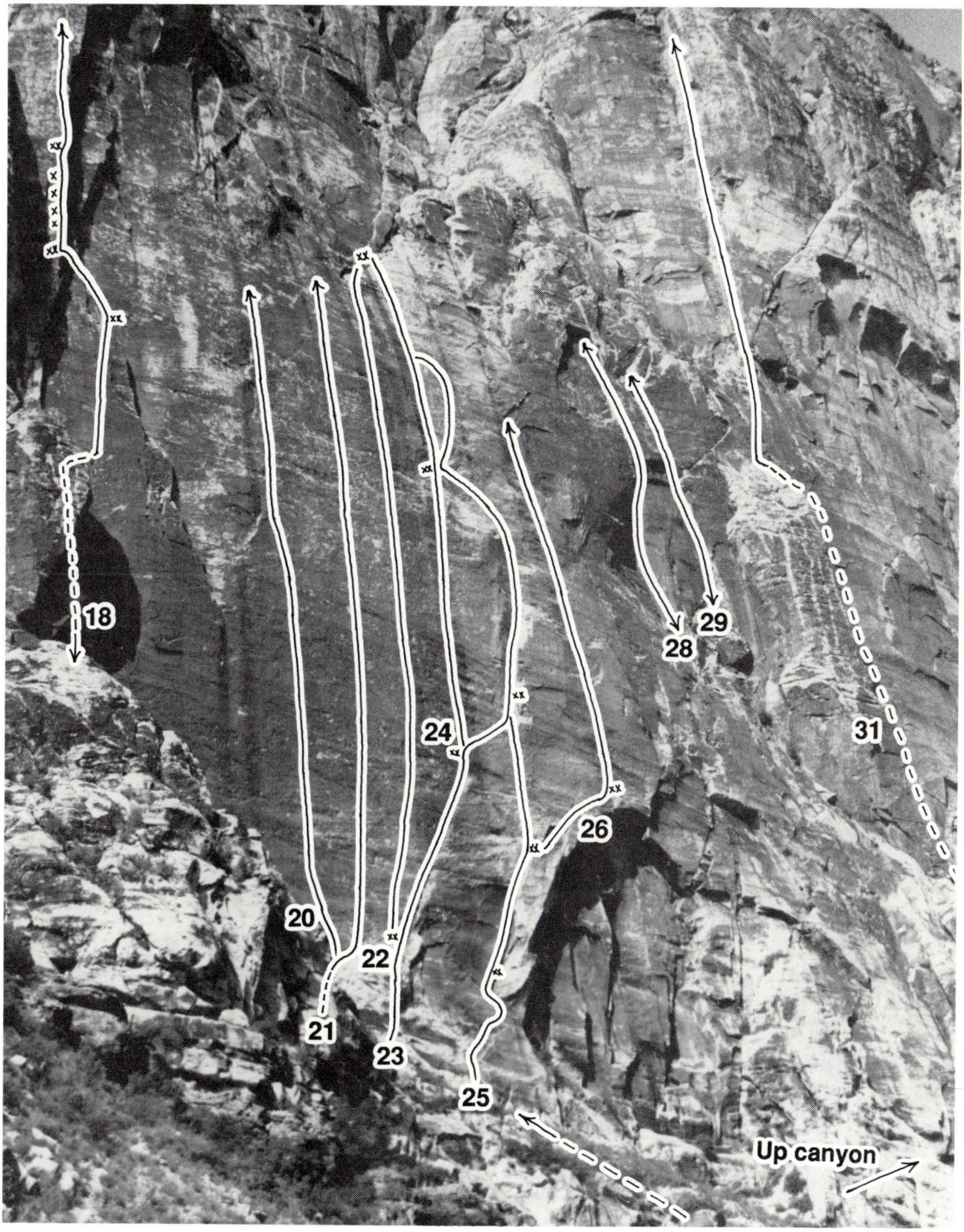

18 Refried Brains 5.9
20 Sandstone Samurai 5.11- R/X
21 Rock Warrior 5.10 R
22 The Prince Of Darkness 5.10
23 Dream Of Wild Turkeys 5.10-
24 Yellow Brick Road 5.10
25 The Gobbler 5.10-
26 Fiddler On The Roof 5.10+ PG/R
28 My Little Pony 5.11+
29 Velveeta 5.10+
31 Epinephrine 5.9

of quickdraws, a few medium-sized stoppers, a butt bag (all the belays are hanging belays), and two ropes for the descent. The bolt hangers are painted black, as the route name might imply (ominous, eh?).

To approach, follow the roadbed about 300 yards from the parking area, then take a trail that branches off right where the road makes a hard left turn. Hike this trail toward the canyon about a half mile, until it forks. Take the right fork, and drop down into the drainage. Follow the rocky creekbed upstream about 600 yards until the drainage is blocked by a cliff. Go left (southeast) into the bushes on a path, then scramble up the cliff on big ledges. Follow trails up and left about 100 yards to the base of the large, smooth wall. This section of cliff has some of the best routes in all of Red Rocks. **The Prince Of Darkness** follows the left edge of a prominent black water streak in the center of the smooth wall.

Begin as for **Dream Of Wild Turkeys,** below the left end of an obvious, right-leaning crack 100 feet up, and directly below a right-facing crack/corner about 40 feet up.

P1 Scamper up easy rock to the base of a short, right-leaning crack/corner with a vertical crack leading straight up. Follow either feature up to a slab, and a belay station with three bolts. 75 ft., 5.6.

P2 Follow a crack/seam system up, then slightly right, passing 14 bolts to a three-bolt belay station. 110 ft., 5.10b/c.

P3 Continue straight up the seam past 15 bolts to a three-bolt belay. 130 ft., 5.10a.

P4 Zip up along the crack past 13 bolts (at least two are missing hangers) to a three-bolt belay. 125 ft., 5.9.

P5 Step left, then follow a crack past eight bolts to a three-bolt belay. 125 ft., 5.9.

P6 Power up the smooth, varnished slab (crux) past 13 bolts to a large ledge and a two-bolt belay (same belay as for **Dream of Wild Turkeys**). 100 ft., 5.10c.

Descent: Rappel this route, **Yellow Brick Road,** or **Dream of Wild Turkeys** with two ropes.

23 Dream Of Wild Turkeys 5.10-

FA: The Uriostes – early 1980s

One of the earliest routes up this section of cliff. The name is a spoof of a famous climb located on a sea cliff in Wales. Bring an assortment of gear up to a #3 Friend, and two ropes to rap with.

Approach this climb by following the roadbed from the parking area about 300 yards, then taking a trail that branches off right when the road makes a hard left turn. Hike this trail toward the canyon about a half mile until it forks. Take the right fork, and drop down into the drainage. Follow the rocky creekbed upstream about 600 yards until the drainage is blocked by a cliff. Go left (southeast) into the bushes on a path, then scramble up the cliff on big ledges. Follow trails up and left about 100 yards to the base of the large, smooth wall.

Begin the climb as for **The Prince Of Darkness,** below the left end of an obvious, right-leaning crack 100 feet up, and directly below a right-facing crack/corner about 40 feet up.

P1 Scamper up easy rock to the base of a short, right-leaning crack/corner with a vertical crack that leads straight up. Follow either feature up to a slab and a belay station with three bolts. 75 ft., 5.6.

P2 Angle right past a bolt into the prominent right leaning crack, and follow this to a belay anchor. 110 ft., 5.8+.

P3 Go up the crack a bit, then traverse right past six bolts to the base of a prominent white flake/corner system and the belay anchors. 80 ft., 5.9.

P4 Climb the flake/corner system to its end (5.8, possible belay here), then face climb left past bolts to a bolt anchor. 165 ft., 5.10–.

P5 Angle up left across a slabby face (six bolts) to a ledge at the base of a left-facing corner. 50 ft., 5.9+.

P6 Follow the left-facing corner/ramp up right to a crack. Go up the crack and face above (bolts), then traverse back left (more bolts) to a vertical crack in a water streak. Belay from two bolts on a scooped ledge. 140 ft., 5.9.

P7 Climb the left-slanting crack/seam past five bolts to a spacious ledge with two bolts. 75 ft., 5.9.

P8-12 It's possible to continue up, but most folks rappel from here.

Descent: Rappel with two ropes, using anchors on **Yellow Brick Road,** and/or this route.

24 Yellow Brick Road 5.10

FA: The Uriostes, Mike Ward, Bill Bradley – Fall 1985

You don't need to be a wiz to know that the bolt hangers are painted yellow on this one. Really a three-pitch variation to **Dream Of Wild Turkeys;** the climbing is safe and enjoyable.

Approach this climb by following the road from the parking area toward the canyon about 300 yards, then taking a trail that branches off right when the road makes a hard left turn. Hike this trail toward the canyon (west) about a half mile until it forks. Take the right fork, and drop down into the drainage. Follow the rocky creekbed upstream about 600 yards until the drainage is blocked by a cliff. Go left (southeast) into the bushes on a path, then scramble up the cliff on big ledges. Follow trails up left about 100 yards to the base of the large, smooth wall.

Start at the base of **Dream of Wild Turkeys** and **The Prince Of Darkness,** below the left end of an obvious, right-leaning crack 100 feet above, and directly below a right-facing crack/corner about 40 feet up.

P1 Scamper up easy rock to the base of a short, right leaning crack/corner with a vertical crack that leads straight up. Follow either feature up to a slab, and a belay station with three bolts. 75 ft., 5.6.

P2 Angle right past a bolt into the prominent right-leaning crack, and follow this to a belay anchor. 110 ft., 5.8+.

P3 Continue straight up the crack and face above to a hanging belay from bolts. 120 ft., 5.10b/c.

P4 Follow 10 bolts up the face to rejoin **Dream of Wild Turkeys** at a belay station. 125 ft., 5.10a/b.

P5 Ascend the left-facing flake to a bolt, then move left and up a crack/corner (two more bolts) to a two-bolt belay on a scooped ledge.

Descent: Either continue up **Dream of Wild Turkeys,** or rappel the route with two ropes.

25 The Gobbler 5.10-

FA: The Uriostes, Bill Bradley, Mike Ward – July, 1980

A good way to round out the day, or to start **Dream Of Wild Turkeys.** Make sure you have some long slings and gear up to 3 inches.

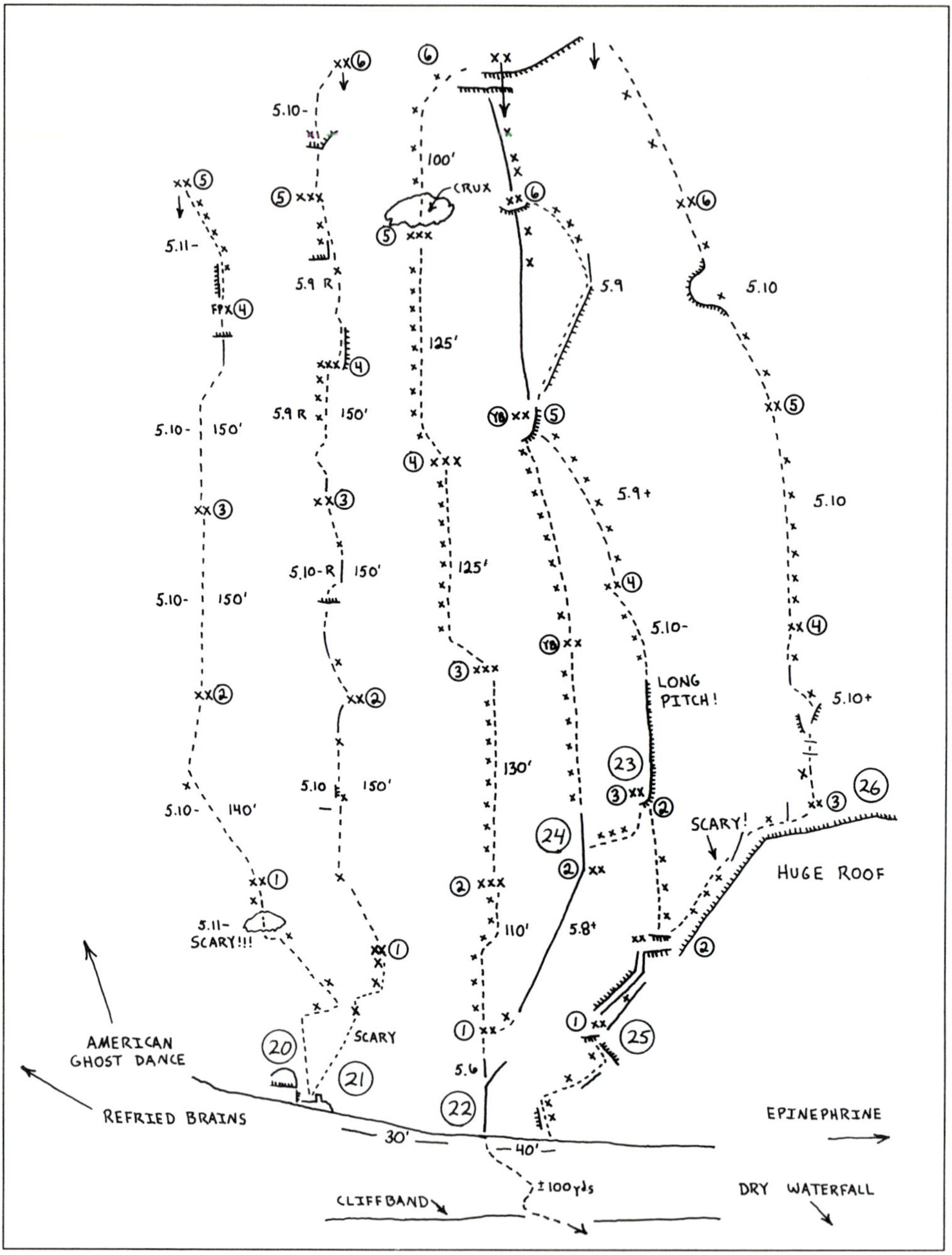

20 **Sandstone Samurai 5.11- R/X**
21 **Rock Warrior 5.10 R**
22 **The Prince Of Darkness 5.10**
24 **Yellow Brick Road 5.10**
23 **Dream Of Wild Turkeys 5.10-**
25 **The Gobbler 5.10-**
26 **Fiddler On The Roof 5.10+ PG/R**

This route is best approached by following the road from the parking area about 300 yards, then taking a trail that branches off right when the road makes a hard left turn. Hike this trail toward the canyon about a half mile, until it forks. Take the right fork, and drop down into the drainage. Follow the rocky creekbed upstream about 600 yards until the drainage is blocked by a cliff. Go left (southeast) into the bushes on a path, then scramble up the cliff on big ledges. Follow trails up and left about 100 yards to the base of the large, smooth wall.

Start below a right-leaning gash about 60 feet up (rappel anchors are clearly visible) and 40 feet right of **Dream of Wild Turkeys.** This climb is at the left (east) end of a huge arch/ceiling at the base of the Black Velvet Wall.

P1 Climb easy white rock for 30 feet to a bolt in a depression. Go up and left 10 feet to another bolt, then up to a horizontal break. Move up right past two bolts, then finger traverse up and right to a left-leaning crack/corner. Follow this past a bolt to a ledge and belay station (watch for rope drag). 110 ft., 5.9.

P2 Jam cracks just right of the right-leaning gash/chimney past one bolt to another anchor (5.9, possible belay here). Power up the steep face past more bolts to a belay on **Dream of Wild Turkeys.** This belay is at the base of a white, left-facing flake/corner system. 130 ft., 5.10–.

Descent: Either continue up **Dream of Wild Turkeys**, or rap the route. Watch that your ropes don't get stuck in the cracks!

26 Fiddler On The Roof 5.10+ PG/R

FA: Dave Wonderly, Warren Egbert, Jenny Richards – November, 1990

Bring your prusiks! This exciting route starts at the second anchor on **The Gobbler,** and traverses out right above the lip of the huge arch/ceiling. Mike Ward says it's the best route in the canyon - quite a statement!

Start below a right-leaning gash about 60 feet up (rappel anchors are clearly visible) and 40 feet right of **Dream of Wild Turkeys.** This climb is at the left (east) end of a huge arch/ceiling at the base of the Black Velvet Wall.

P1 Climb easy white rock for 30 feet to a bolt in a depression. Go up and left 10 feet to another bolt, then up to a horizontal break. Move up right past two bolts, then finger traverse up and right to a left-leaning crack/corner. Follow this past a bolt to a ledge and belay station (watch for rope drag). 110 ft., 5.9.

P2 Jam cracks just right of the right-leaning gash/chimney past one bolt to another belay anchor (**The Gobbler** continues up from here). 60 ft., 5.9.

P3 Trend out right along the lip of the huge roof (don't fall!), passing four bolts and a few gear placements, to a belay station. 165 ft.

P4 Climb pretty much straight up the face past three bolts to a bolted belay. 150 ft., 5.10+.

P5 Continue up the magnificent varnished face past six bolts and some traditional gear placements. Fixed anchor. 150 ft., 5.10.

P6 Follow two bolts up the face to a ledge (5.10), then continue up past one more bolt to the belay. 150 ft., 5.10.

P7 Two more bolts lead to Turkey Ledge.

Descent: Rappel **Dream of Wild Turkeys** with two ropes.

27 **Sour Mash 5.10**

FA: The Uriostes – July, 1980

A primarily natural line up the wall just right of the huge arch mentioned in **Fiddler On The Roof** and **The Gobbler.** Carry a good selection of pro, and two ropes. Access this climb by following the roadbed from the parking area about 300 yards, then taking a trail that branches off right when the road makes a hard left turn. Hike this trail toward the canyon about a half mile until it forks. Take the right fork, and drop down into the drainage. Follow the rocky creekbed upstream about 600 yards until the drainage is blocked by a cliff. Go left (southeast) into the bushes on a path, scramble up the cliffband as for the other routes, then follow one of the trails up to the base of the wall.

Begin below a pyramid-shaped face that is just right of the huge arch at the base of the Black Velvet Wall.

P1 Climb a slabby face to a large ledge that is at the base of the pyramid-shaped section. 100 ft., 5.7.

P2 Jam up a crack on the right side of the face, going up and left past four bolts to an easy crack. Follow this to a ledge with saplings. 90 ft., 5.10.

P3 Go up an arête to a ceiling, then up and right to a right-leaning crack. Follow the crack to a belay anchor. 75 ft., 5.8.

P4 Climb to the left edge of a light-colored ceiling, then angle left to a belay ledge (bolt). 75 ft., 5.8.

P5 Go up the obvious crack to a belay. 100 ft, 5.7.

P6 Continue up the crack to a belay anchor. 110 ft., 5.9.

P7 Follow nine bolts and a seam to a belay at the right end of a light-colored ceiling. 100 ft., 5.10.

P8 Pull the ceiling, then follow a thin crack and six bolts up to an anchor on the obvious, right-leaning ramp. 100 ft., 5.9+.

Descent: Rappel the route with two ropes.

28 **My Little Pony 5.11+**

FA: Paul Van Betten, Richard Harrison, Shelby Shelton – Summer, 1990

Not much is known about this route. It starts just left of the left side of the **Epinephrine** tower (aka the Black Tower), and goes out the left side of a giant scoop above. The route is seven pitches long, and you can rappel with two ropes.

29 ***Velveeta* 5.10+**

FA: Richard Harrison, Wendell Broussard – Summer, 1990

This route climbs out the right side of the scoop that is just left of the **Epinephrine** tower (aka the Black Tower). It is six or seven pitches long.

Note: The left side of the **Epinephrine** tower (aka the Black Tower) holds an offwidth route called **Malicious Mischief.** It's 5.10 and was first climbed by Joe Herbst, Stephanie Petrilak and Mike Gilbert in May, 1978.

30 **Chalk Is Cheap 5.10+**

FA: Mike Ward, Mike Clifford, Eric Sutton – Fall 1989

This is supposed to be quite good, but as of press time, I hadn't done it. Bring two ropes, and the typical selection of gear.

Start 50 feet left of **Epinephrine.**

P1 Climb a smooth face to a corner, and belay on a small ledge. 115 ft., 5.8.

P2 Jam up a crack to a belay in a broken area below a bombay chimney. Friends and nuts for the belay. 80 ft., 5.8.

P3 Wiggle up the bombay chimney to a steep black face. Climb the face to a fixed peg, then continue up the face 30 feet to a small crack in an overhang. Belay 15 feet above the roof. 140 ft., 5.10+.

P4 Climb a big white crack until you run out of rope. Belay off Friends and nuts. 100 ft., 5.10.

P5 Continue up the crack to top of tower. 110 ft., 5.9.

Descent: Rappel **Epinephrine.**

31 **Epinephrine 5.9** 👍

FA: The Uriostes, Joe Herbst – August, 1978

One of the best climbs I've done, but you'd better be solid on 5.9 chimneys! A long route, with sustained climbing and lots of third- and fourth-class scrambling to get off. As Yvon Chouinard says in *Climbing Ice,* "If you bring bivi gear, you will bivi." (On this route, that may mean twice!) The pitches are described as they were originally done, but it's entirely possible to combine pitches (especially above the top of the tower) to make the climb go faster.

Approach this fine outing by following the roadbed about 300 yards from the parking area, then take a trail that branches off right when the road makes a hard left turn. Hike this trail toward the canyon about a half mile until it forks. Take the right fork, and drop down into the drainage. Follow the rocky creekbed upstream about 600 yards until the drainage is blocked by a cliff. Go left (southeast) into the bushes on a path, scramble up the cliff band as for the other routes, then go right and down to the pebbly streambed.

Epinephrine is 60 yards up canyon from the waterfall and starts below a gray face with three bolts (red hangers) that are 15 feet right of a right slanting crack. If speed is a consideration, you can avoid the first pitch by starting 50 feet further right (30 feet left of a yellow, left-facing corner) and soloing up easy ledges.

P1 Climb the gray face past three bolts to a bushy ledge. 60 ft., 5.8.

P2 From the left side of the ledge, follow the obvious features up and slightly left past three bolts to another vegetated ledge. 100 ft., 5.7.

P3 Climb an easy chimney, and belay above at one of many trees. 150 ft., 5.6.

P4 Scramble up to the base of the chimneys, which are on the right side of the huge pillar (the Black Tower).

P5 Struggle up the beautiful chimney to a belay station. 150 ft., 5.9.

P6 Continue up the chimney to another anchor (awesome positions). 75 ft., 5.9.

P7 Another pitch of wiggling and thrashing leads to the top of the chimney section. 90 ft., 5.9.

P8 Scramble to the top of the tower.

Note: The top of the tower is quite spacious, leans slightly inward, and is really the only place to bivi. Many folks climb to here, then rappel back down the route.

P9 Face climb past two bolts to a belay. 75 ft., 5.7.

P10 Pull a ceiling, then go up to a bushy ledge. 75 ft., 5.7.

P11 Traverse right about 50 feet, then climb up to a belay ledge with one bolt. 75 ft., 5.6.

P12 A bit of tricky face climbing past two bolts leads to another belay ledge. 75 ft., 5.9.

P13 Climb the prominent dihedral past five bolts to a belay in an alcove. 110 ft., 5.9.

P14 Continue up the dihedral to belay on a ledge. 75 ft., 5.6.

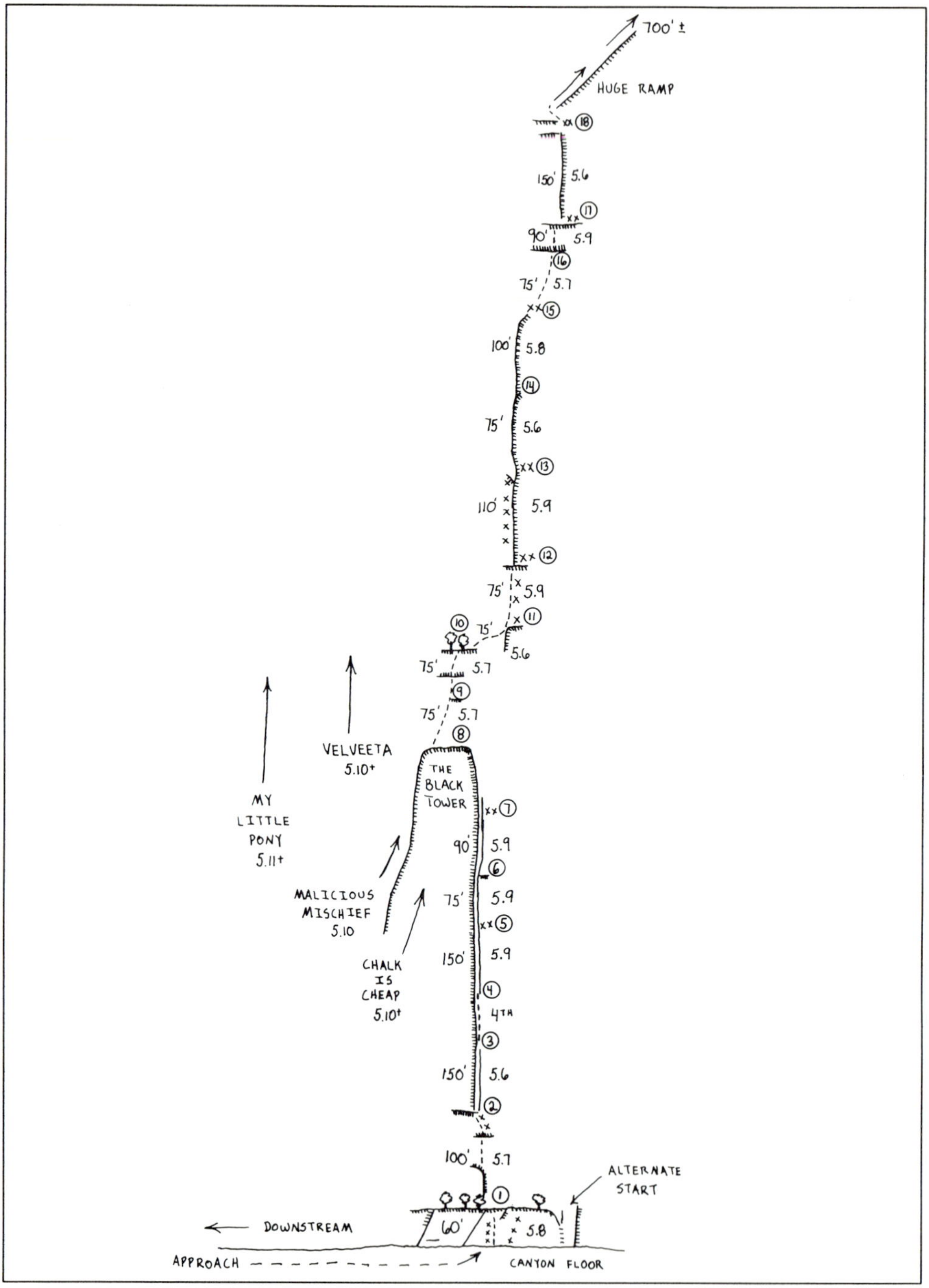

Epinephrine, 5.9

P15 Upward! 100 ft., 5.8.

P16 More of the same. Belay under a roof. 75 ft., 5.7.

P17 Climb the roof on the right (exposed), then up to a belay anchor. 90 ft., 5.9.

P18 Continue up. Belay on a ledge to the left under a ceiling. Bolt anchor. 150 ft., 5.6.

To the top: Move left from the belay onto a huge, right-leaning ramp (many large ledges to organize on). Follow this ramp up and right about 700 feet, passing numerous places where folks have had to bivi (some for the second time). This involves fourth- and easy fifth-class climbing, sometimes with big air below. The last bit of the route follows bushy ledges around an amphitheater to the top of the wall.

Descent: Walk up and left (south) to the highest summit (don't be lured down the first gully you come to), then follow the ridge down to the top of Whiskey Peak. You'll be heading down towards the parking area. From the top of Whiskey Peak, go right (southeast). This is the fastest way to the car – if you have all of your gear with you. If you left your packs at the base of the route, drop down into the left (northwest) gully. Scramble down past **Refried Brains** and the other routes to your pack. The whole descent takes roughly an hour - if you have something other than your tight climbing shoes with you!

The Monument

The next routes are just outside the mouth of the canyon, to the right (north), on a formation named the Monument. The light-colored roof of **Desert Reality** is visible from the parking area, and sits low down on the mountainside. Many other climbs have been done in the area, but only these ultra-classic routes are described here.

From the parking area, walk straight across the desert toward a steep drainage that leads up to the climbs. The approach takes about 45 minutes, and the routes are sunny.

32 **Desert Crack 5.12+**
FA: Paul Van Betten, Sal Mamusia – April, 1987
This short, but very difficult finger crack leads up to the huge roof of **Desert Reality.**

33 **Desert Reality 5.11**
FA: Paul Van Betten, Richard Harrison – February, 1984

The obvious crack out the huge, light-colored roof. This was originally approached from the left via aid (two bolts).

34 **Desert Gold 5.13–**
FA: Stefan Glowacz – May, 1987
The link-up of the two routes listed above.

Photo: Kurt Mauer

Paul Van Betten and Mike Ward challenge Desert Reality, 5.11.

OTHER AREAS

If you tire of Red Rocks, or the weather is uncooperative, there are other climbing areas fairly close to Las Vegas. This section is not meant to be a guide to these areas, but simply to give you options.

CHRISTMAS TREE PASS

This surreal area is within Lake Mead National Recreation Area, a unit of the National Park Service. The rock is monzogranite (like Joshua Tree), but of a fairly coarse and poor quality. Numerous routes have been done at all grades, with the majority being bolt-protected slabs. The large, domed formations are close to the road and face in a variety of directions. See *Summit* magazine (October, 1976) and *Climbing* #94.

JOSHUA TREE

This renowned area is about four hours drive south of Las Vegas. There are more routes in Joshua Tree National Monument than in any other climbing area in the country (and perhaps the world). The weather tends to be a little drier than Las Vegas, but the temperatures are about the same.

KEYHOLE CANYON

This small area has a wealth of Native American rock art (petroglyphs), and a few good climbs. The rock is a fine-grained monzogranite (like the better rock of Joshua Tree), with the longest routes being about half a rope length high. While the climbing is limited, the rock art and canyon formation itself make a trip worthwhile.

MOUNT CHARLESTON

If overhanging limestone in a mountainous setting interests you, this is the place. A relatively new area, it was still being developed at press time. See *Sport Climbing*, Volume 2, #4 for details.

OWENS RIVER GORGE

About a three-hour drive from Las Vegas, this popular sport-climbing area has been written up in numerous magazines and has its own guidebook.

SNOW CANYON STATE PARK

This sandstone area is near Saint George, Utah, less than two hours north of Vegas. Numerous routes have been done; some have been described in *Climbing* #96 and #102.

VIRGIN RIVER GORGE

Located just north of Sin City on Interstate 15 in Arizona, this warm, dry limestone area has a bunch of hard climbs to dangle on. The only drawback is the proximity to the interstate. See *Climbing* #127 and *Rock & Ice* #44 for the scoop on this area.

ZION

The spectacular sandstone walls of Zion National Park are less than three hours north of Las Vegas. Summer is hot and crowded, but spring and fall are perfect. There are lots of exciting and challenging canyoneering trips to do here, as well as big wall free and aid routes. The part visitor center has a notebook with information on the climbs here.

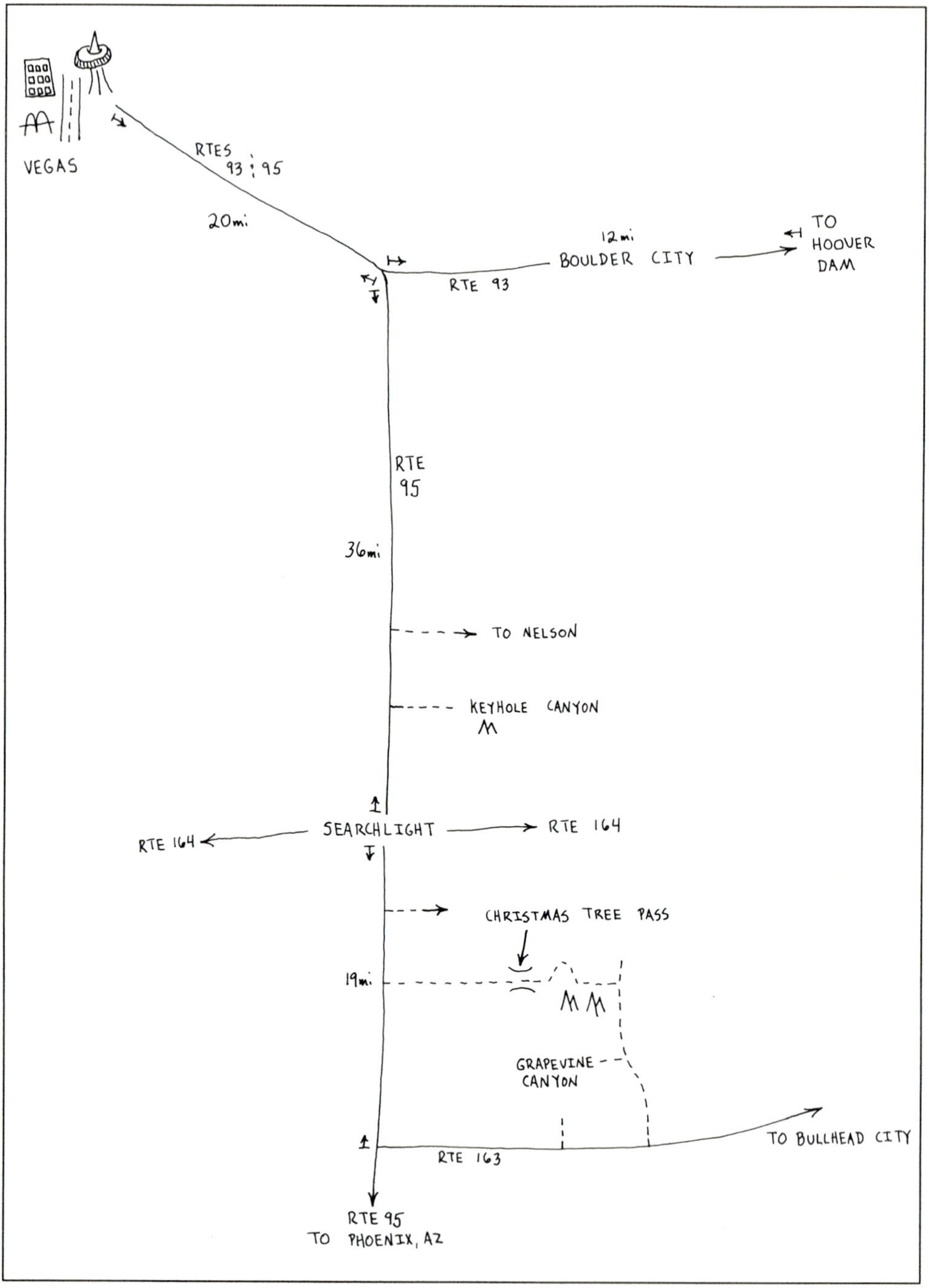

Map to Christmas Tree Pass.

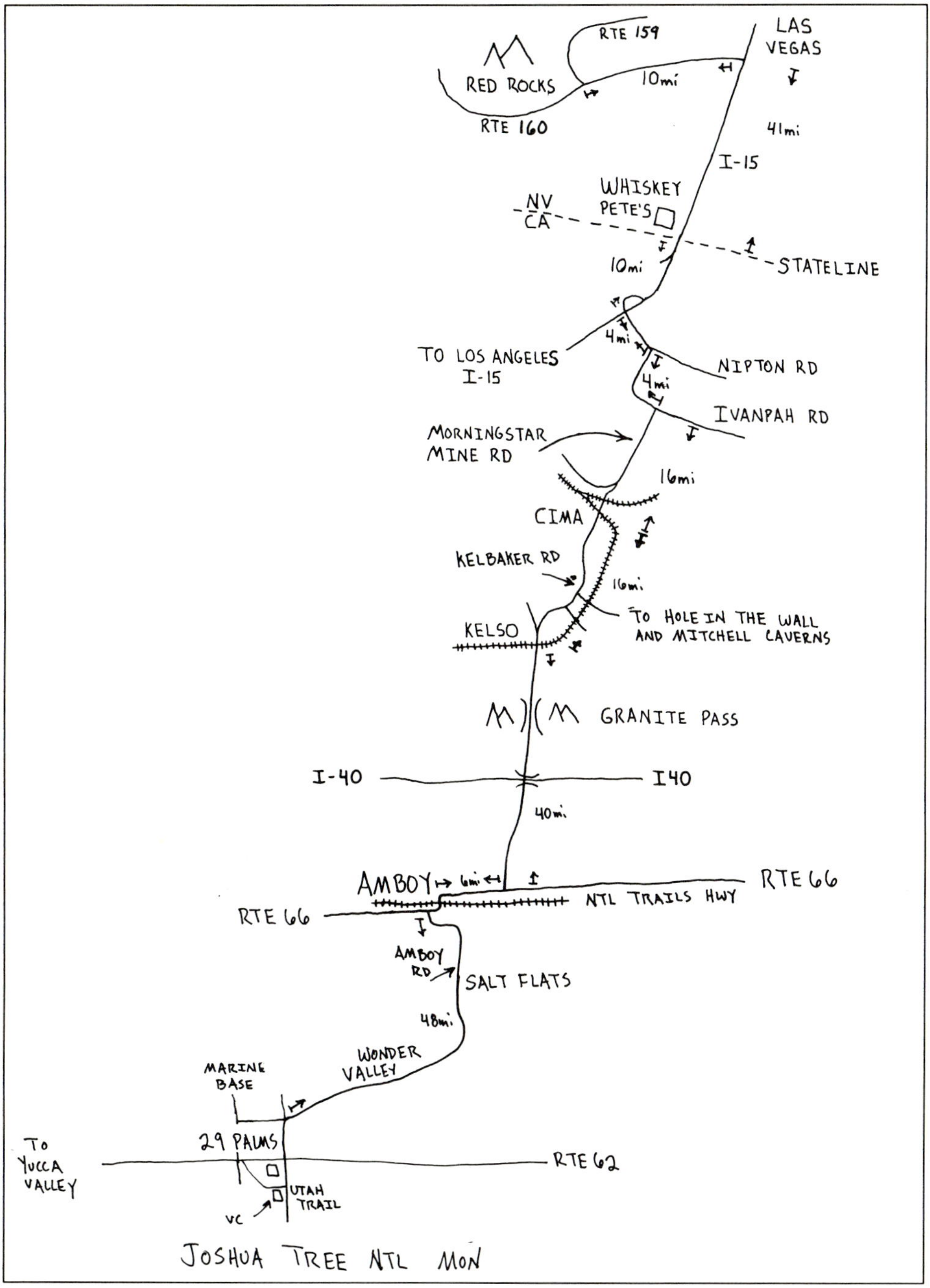

Map to Joshua Tree National Monument.

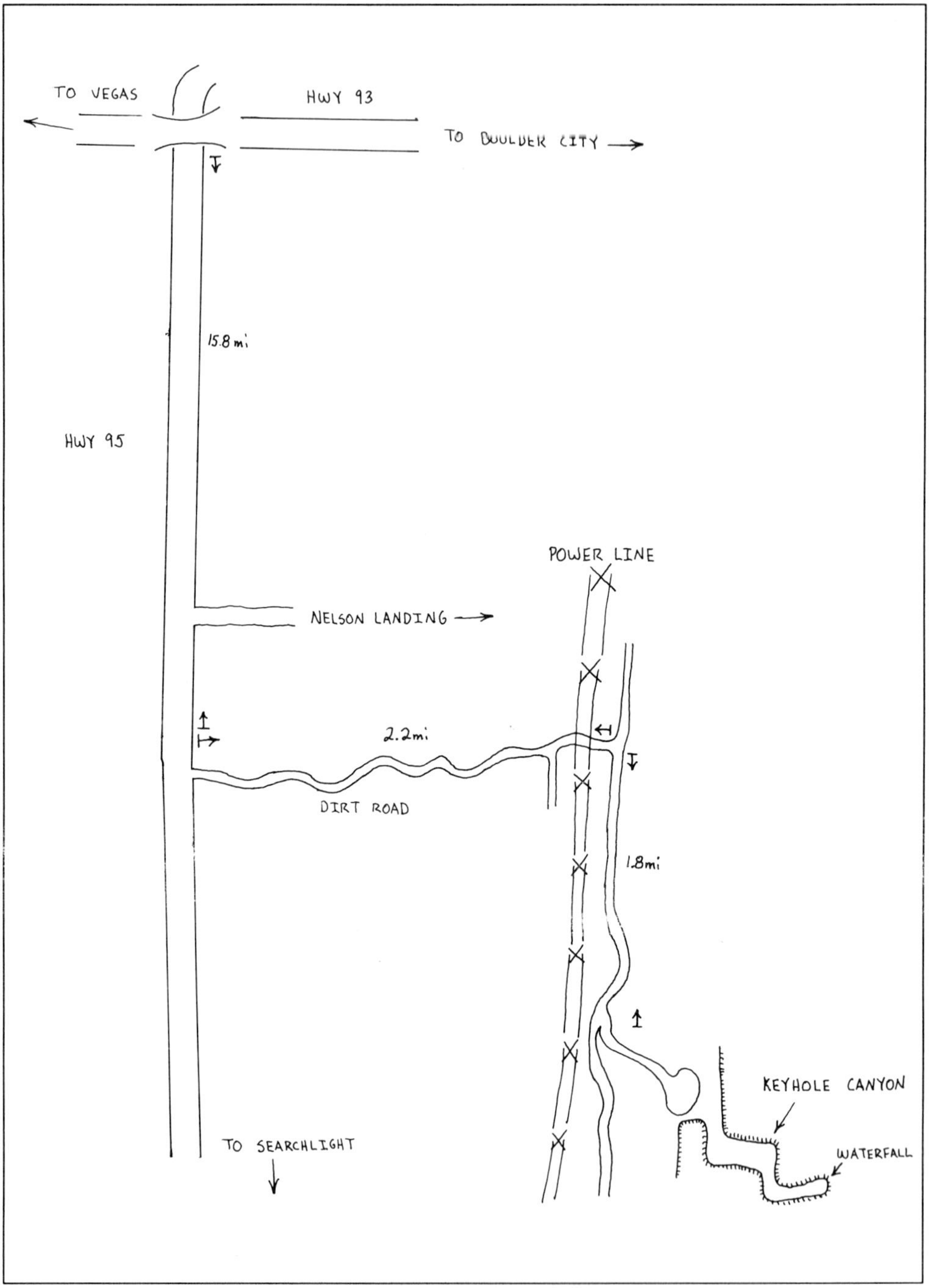

Map to Keyhole Canyon.

INDEX